TROPE
PUBLISHING
Co.

For Tom, true lover of architecture and buildings,
who gave me what's most important in life: love.

And for Aaron, Otto, Bridgett, and the next generation.

THE SALT SHED

THE

TRANSFORMATION OF A CHICAGO LANDMARK

SANDRA STEINBRECHER

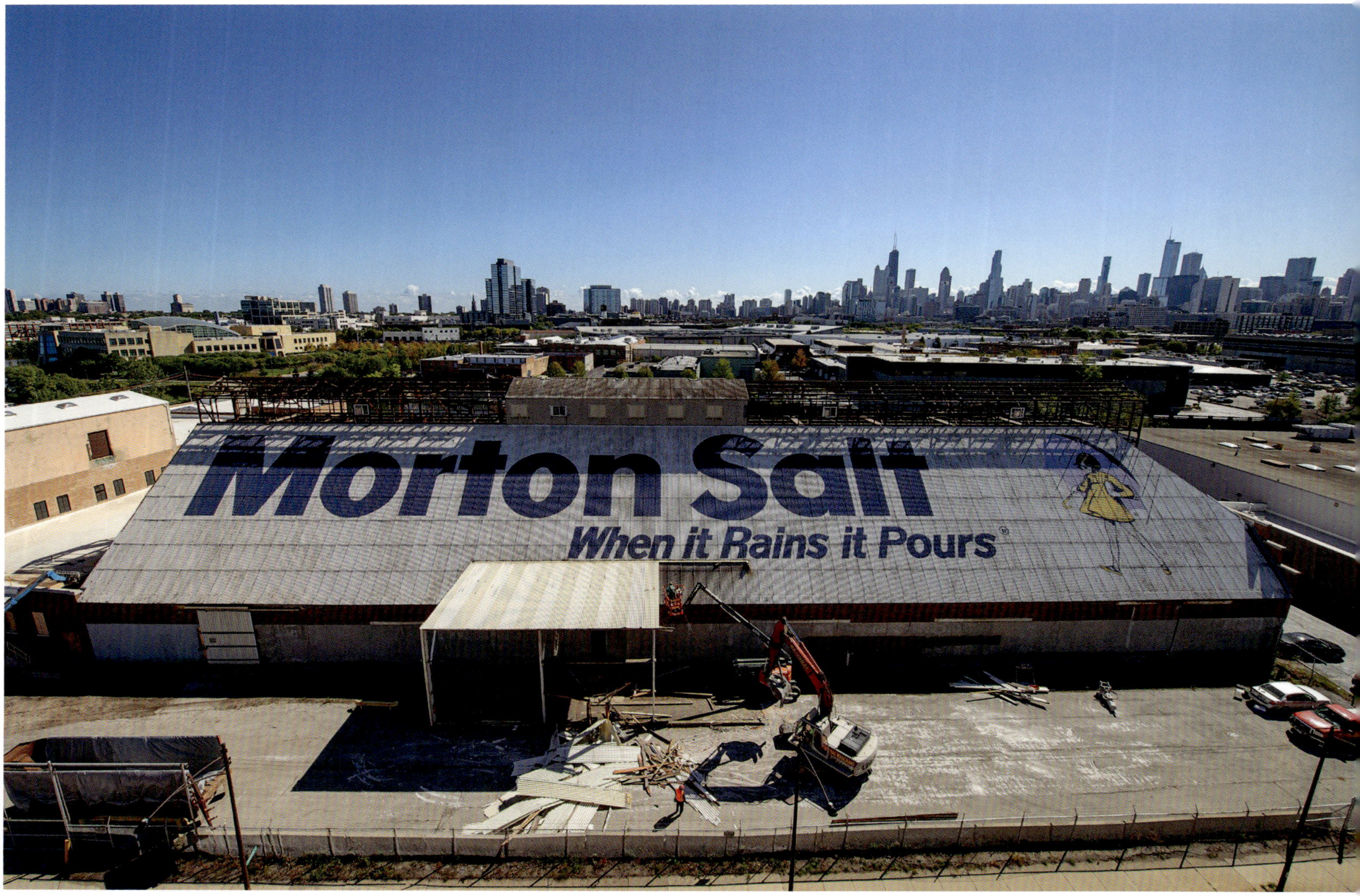
Morton Salt
When it Rains it Pours®

The Morton Salt shed is a survivor from Chicago's river-centric industrial past. Somehow as its neighbors changed and departed, the girl with the umbrella retained her iconic presence and the expansive painted roof became an element of the visual and cultural landscape. I'm happy that the building has received another life and glad for the careful documentation of this new chapter. Saving and repurposing it creates a sense of history, a sense of culture, and a new sense of place for the current and future residents of the city.

~ Carol Ross Barney, FAIA, founder + design principal, Ross Barney Architects + 2023 AIA Gold Medal recipient

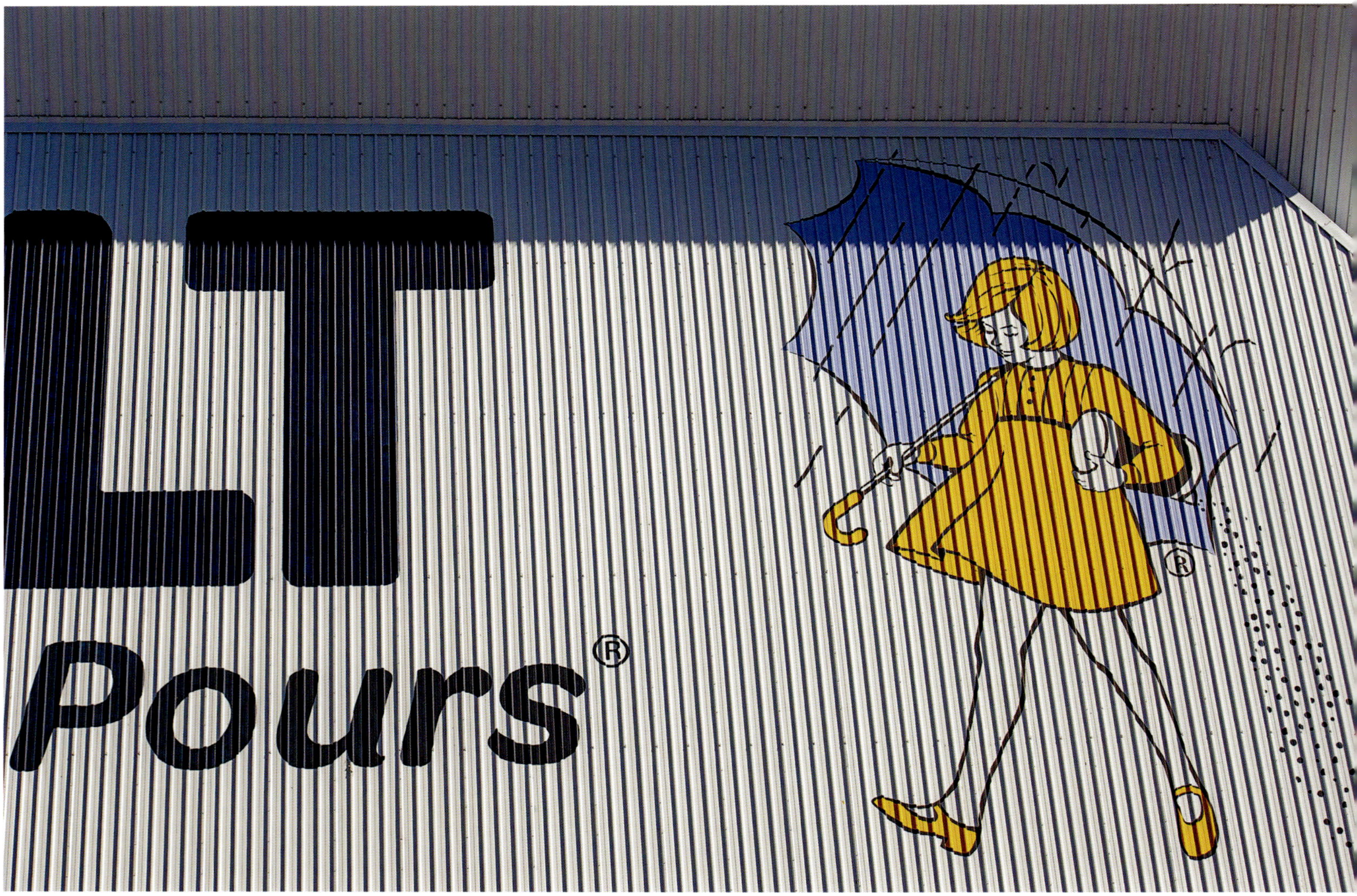
LT
Pours®

Foreword

To love a place fully, to know a place truly, we need to know its past. The hands that built it. The moments that shaped it. The mistakes that marred it. The tragedies that befell it, the triumphs that buoyed it and, importantly, the people who witnessed it.

Whose feet walked here and why? Who broke bread? Who fell in love? Who laughed? Who grieved? Who looked up after a grueling shift and saw the same night sky you or I might glimpse tonight? That's why we preserve. That's why we excavate. That's why we restore. To honor and answer those questions. To pause. To wonder. To cherish.

We protect our past so we're connected to what came before us and so we understand what lies in front of us—today and tomorrow.

But for the past to be more than a ghost, an ephemeral, translucent thing, we need to be able to touch it. Smell it. Hold it in our hands. Our connection needs to be tangible, tactile. This is especially true of old buildings, whose footprints and architecture and long list of purposes and inhabitants narrate our story to us.

The Morton Salt Company Warehouse Complex was built for the most prosaic, yet noble, of pursuits: to store, pack, and distribute salt—a primitive preservative, a peerless flavor enhancer, nature's own road deicer. It was a storage shed and packing plant and distribution site, but it was so much more. It was the lives and livelihoods of its inhabitants—the warehouse workers and truck drivers and barge navigators and crane operators. Eventually it was also a billboard, sharing the iconic Umbrella Girl with drivers on the Kennedy Expressway. Chicagoans knew the Morton Salt complex like they knew the Magikist lips. It was a landmark, long before the City of Chicago officially designated it as one.

So when it was spared demolition and granted new life as a music venue, Chicagoans cheered. Our sturdy old friend wouldn't be leaving us, wouldn't be going the way of the Magikist lips or the Chicago Stock Exchange Building or the original Comiskey Park or so many other icons we've loved and lost.

"This is really a great example of how cities can mine their past for identity in the present and the future," says Pulitzer Prize-winning architecture critic Blair Kamin, a former *Chicago Tribune* writer and a contributing editor of *Architectural Record*. "There

Foreword

was an era in the '60s and '70s when Chicago was all too ready to dispatch with extraordinary examples of its architecture. In the intervening years, though, Chicago has realized that the past isn't necessarily an obstacle to progress. It can be part of progress. And it can be profitable."

The Salt Shed, Kamin said, belongs in the same category as urban revival efforts like New York City's High Line and Chicago's Northerly Island, both of which reimagine and reuse transportation infrastructure with an infusion of nature and a commitment to public use. The river that used to bring barges filled with tons of salt now serves as the backdrop for outdoor concerts, makers' markets, and yoga classes.

The Salt Shed's restoration and rebirth tell a tale of perseverance and preservation. One of effort and evolution. One of imagination. It grew from a place that supports industry to a place that gathers community and revels in artistry.

Chicago-based documentary photographer Sandra Steinbrecher captures this tale in searing, magnificent detail. In the pages that follow, you'll see her images of the building's arteries and bones, stripped of the familiar skin most of us saw from a distance. You'll see plumbing. You'll see repair. You'll see a beautiful, messy rebirth. You'll see mud caked on boots. You'll see human hands attending to every tiny detail. You'll see the light change behind those human hands, as the months tick by and the elements change and, still, the workers toil and build and make something new and gorgeous out of something old and precious.

Steinbrecher's photos show us the labor that goes into a project this immense and complex. So that when we walk or drive or bike by the reinvented Salt Shed, when we stand beneath its fifty-foot-high ceilings or marvel at its original brick façade or walk and dance on its four-inch-thick wood floors, we feel connected to what and who once was there. And we feel immensely grateful for, and frankly a little awed by, what and who brought us there now.

That's why we preserve. To remind us that we're part of something bigger than ourselves—a continuum, a narrative. Humanity.

Heidi Stevens

Chicago-based writer, speaker, and nationally syndicated columnist

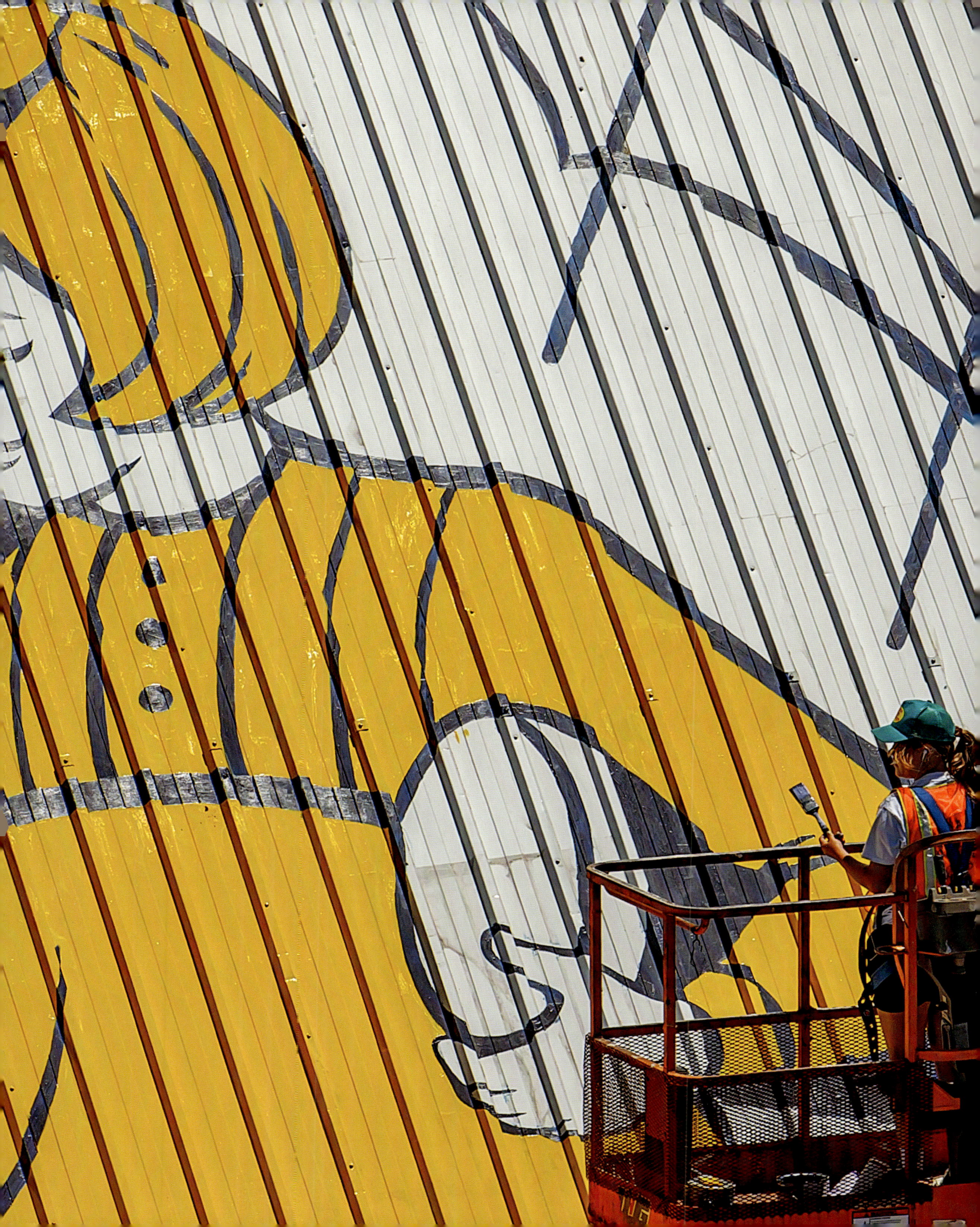

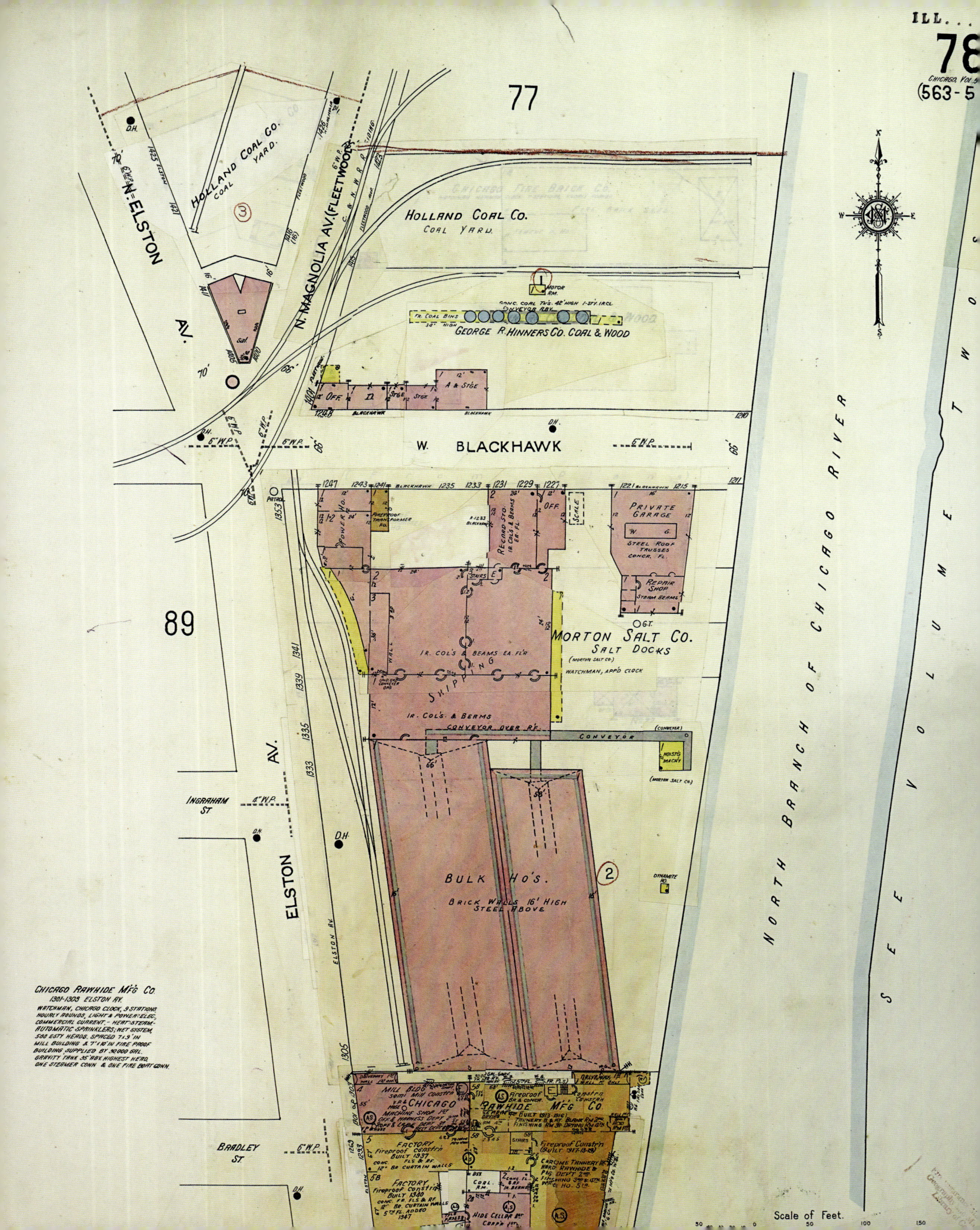
ILL.
78
CHICAGO, VOL. 5
(563-5
77
89
HOLLAND COAL CO.
COAL YARD.
HOLLAND COAL CO.
COAL YARD
N. ELSTON
AV.
N. MAGNOLIA AV. (FLEETWOOD)
GEORGE R. HINNERS CO. COAL & WOOD
CONVEYOR RWY.
W. BLACKHAWK
PRIVATE GARAGE
STEEL ROOF TRUSSES CONCR. FL.
REPAIR SHOP
MORTON SALT CO.
SALT DOCKS
WATCHMAN, APP'D CLOCK
SHIPPING
IR. COL'S & BEAMS EA. FL'R
IR. COL'S & BEAMS
CONVEYOR OVER RF.
CONVEYOR
HOIST'G MACH'Y
BULK HO'S.
BRICK WALLS 16' HIGH STEEL ABOVE
DYNAMITE HO.
NORTH BRANCH OF CHICAGO RIVER
SEE VOLUME TWO
ELSTON AV.
INGRAHAM ST
BRADLEY ST
CHICAGO RAWHIDE MF'G CO.
1301-1303 ELSTON AV.
WATCHMAN, CHICAGO CLOCK, 9 STATIONS HOURLY ROUNDS, LIGHT & POWER: ELEC. COMMERCIAL CURRENT - HEAT: STEAM - AUTOMATIC SPRINKLERS: WET SYSTEM, 500 EST'Y HEADS, SPACED 7'1.9" IN MILL BUILDING & 7'1.6" IN FIRE PROOF BUILDING SUPPLIED BY 30000 GAL. GRAVITY TANK 35' ABV. HIGHEST HEAD, ONE STEAMER CONN. & ONE FIRE BOAT CONN.
CHICAGO RAWHIDE MF'G CO.
MILL BLDG.
FACTORY
Fireproof Constr'n
BUILT 1937
FACTORY
Fireproof Constr'n
BUILT 1940
HIDE CELLAR
Scale of Feet.
50 0 50 100 150

The Salt Shed: A History

In late March 1951, the heavily laden freighter *Jupiter* made its way from Lake Michigan west along the Main Stem of the Chicago River, a journey captured in a photograph in the *Chicago Daily Tribune* with the caption "Largest Craft of Season Enters Chicago River." The *Jupiter* had departed from Manistee, Michigan, heading south with a five-thousand-ton cargo of rock salt, bound for a warehouse along the river at 1357 North Elston Avenue belonging to the largest seller of salt in the country, the Morton Salt Company.

Prior to Morton Salt building on this site in the late 1920s, a tannery had stood upon the property. Industry lined the river, particularly the North and South Branches after the 1909 Plan of Chicago advocated removing it from the Main Stem that fed into the lake. The river provided needed water for much of this industrial work as well as an outlet for the waste produced by it. As the *Jupiter*'s journey demonstrates, the river also served as a route by which goods could be transported. This last use, as a route for travel and commerce, had existed since the time of the Potawatomi, the region's Indigenous inhabitants, who also made use of a nearby trail that became today's Elston Avenue.

The Morton Salt Company Warehouse Complex resembled many industrial sites found along the river. The production shed that received the *Jupiter*'s cargo was a solidly built, ordinary-looking repository for rock salt. Despite its humble appearance, the shed along with the surrounding buildings had been designed by one of the most distinguished architectural firms in Chicago: Graham, Anderson, Probst & White. As the *Jupiter* traveled along the river's Main Stem, it passed the Wrigley Building and the Merchandise Mart, two among the many architectural icons of the city designed by this firm, which could trace its origins to D.H. Burnham & Company, started by the primary author of the 1909 Plan, Daniel Burnham.

The 1909 Plan of Chicago had as one of its chief supporters, Joy Morton, after whom the salt company is named. Civic-minded, Morton contributed to the collection of the Chicago Historical Society, and his estate in suburban Lisle is now the Morton Arboretum. Like many successful Chicagoans, Joy Morton was born elsewhere and

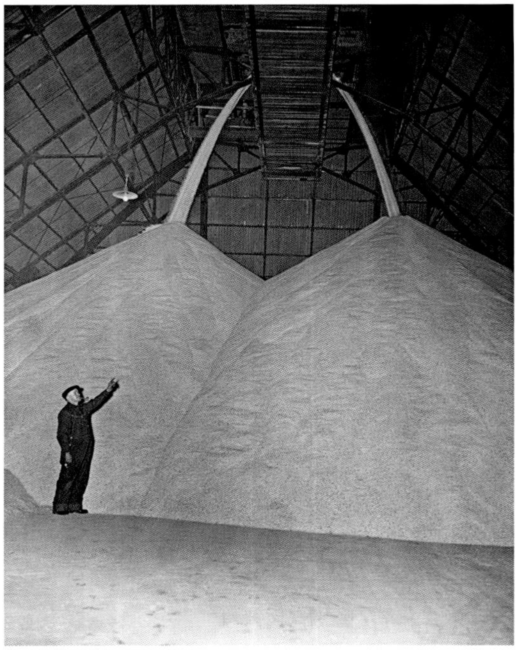

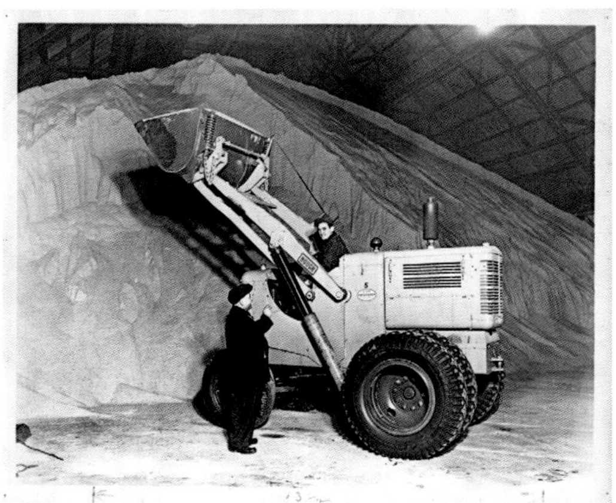

arrived in the city at a moment that fit his ambitions. He joined a firm that had been selling salt out of the city since 1848. Chicago's access to the Great Lakes and other waterways and its centrality to the nation's network of railroads made it the ideal distribution hub for such staples as lumber, grain, pork, and salt. By the end of the nineteenth century, the salt industry had begun to consolidate; smaller companies combined into larger ones and assumed control of the mining, refining, and shipping of the commodity. Morton used existing relationships with the railroads to get favorable transportation rates that allowed him to outpace his competitors. Having built a receiving plant and office near where the river met the lake, he didn't hesitate to move west to Elston Avenue when plans for a bridge across the river, today part of Lake Shore Drive, moved forward.

By the late 1950s, Morton Salt had grown to a company with salt mines, distribution centers, and sales offices in over a dozen states. The production shed on Elston Avenue was a small part of a large enterprise. That didn't mean it wasn't significant to Chicagoans. Each winter the rock salt brought from Michigan by freighters like the *Jupiter* met with a high local demand:

> During the winter months, Morton drivers, loaders, and packers are on 24-hour call. Nevertheless, loading ramps and driveways at the Elston Warehouse are usually jammed with trucks endeavoring to pick up urgently needed salt. Phones jangle in City Sales and are answered long after the rest of the people of Morton's General Office have punched the clock and gone home to supper.

The article in the February 1946 issue of *Morton's Spout* in which the above appears goes on to laud the work of manager John R. Cooper, his assistant Bob Nieman, and foreman John Fralc at the warehouse. Many of the shed's employees had been with the company far longer than it had stood at Elston. They were the individuals who got the salt out of the large lake freighters, using an enormous crane and "clamshell," as well as the long internal conveyor belt that stretched the length of the shed, to deposit tall towers of salt that filled the space from one end to the other. The work

The Salt Shed: A History

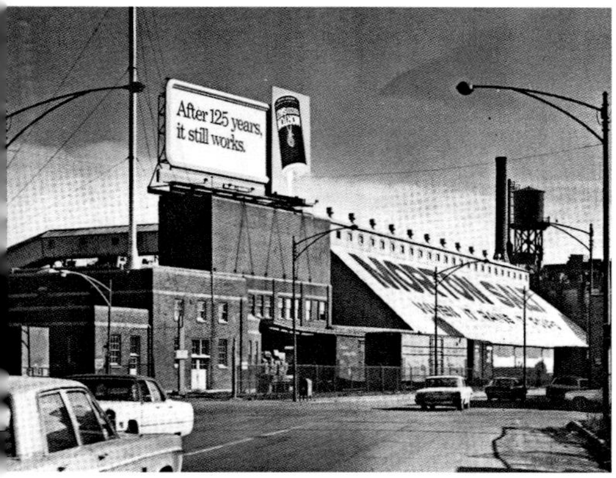

was demanding and occasionally dangerous–an individual tower of salt could stretch forty feet high and weigh ten thousand tons–but highly valued by cities like Chicago that depended upon Morton rock salt to keep their roadways safe in winter year after year until the plant's closure in 2015.

The production shed stands as a sturdy monument to this work and to this industry. Its preservation and transformation, the subject of this book, ensures that a significant part of the city's past survives into the present. The production shed may not be as imposing or ornate as the Wrigley Building, the Merchandise Mart, and other structures designed by Graham, Anderson, Probst & White, but like them, it is a Chicago icon. Recognizing the complex as a whole as an "excellent example of utilitarian twentieth-century industrial architecture," the City of Chicago granted it landmark designation in 2021. In its public notice, the city acknowledged that the production shed had "long been one of the community's most visible structures." Over the years, the company's name and the Morton Salt Umbrella Girl, one of the world's most recognized corporate logos, were painted on the exterior of the shed's roof, ideally positioned to be viewed by the hundreds of thousands of motorists who passed daily on the Kennedy Expressway. Today, the shed is as much a part of the city's landscape as the Sears Tower. And like the tower, it's difficult to imagine Chicago without the Morton Salt shed.

Paul Durica

Historian and Director of Exhibitions at Chicago History Museum

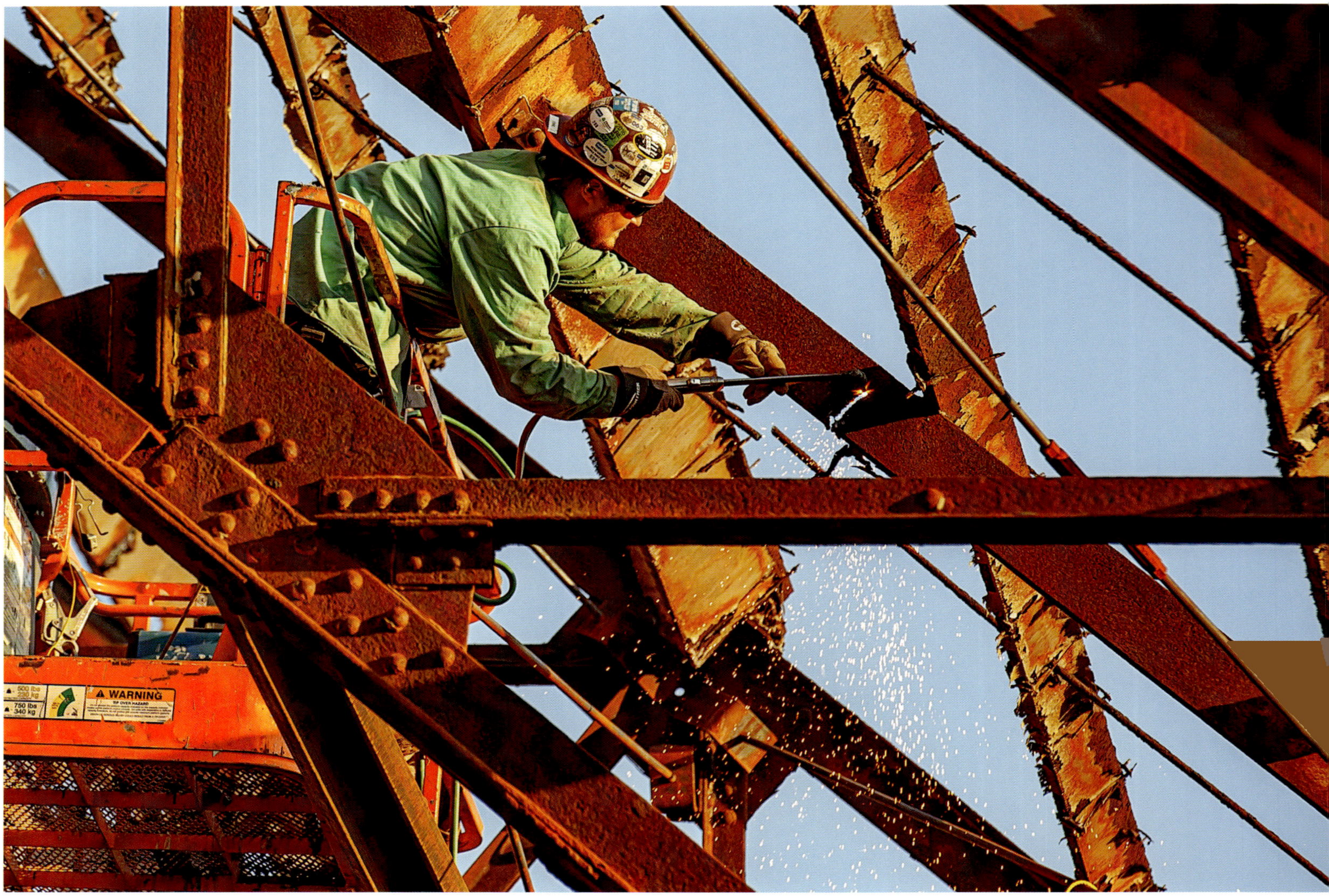
WARNING

Introduction

Seven a.m. on a sunny September morning. I'm standing on the ground, camera pointed up fifty or so feet to where the dawn has lent the rusted steel beams above me a warm glow. I hear a crack and a fizzle as a welding torch is lit. I turn away from a flash of blinding white light, then look back to see a pointed flame eat into the horizontal beam, one of hundreds of steel purlins, bracings and trusses forming an intricate framework that supports the roof above this vast shed. The sharp, bitter smell of burning steel hits my nose, and a red line of fire appears along a cut in the beam as it begins to separate. Finally, it falls smoking to the shed floor, landing with a heavy thud.

Dust and dirt swirl around me. Under the half open roof and a cloudless blue sky, bright orange aerial lifts ferry the ironworkers dressed in worn green welder jackets, as they labor at the painstaking process of repairing and restoring this steel shell. It's one of the many changes going on. When I leave the site hours later, I have no sense of how much time has passed. I only know I have never felt happier while taking photographs.

If you live in or love Chicago, you have at least a fleeting relationship with the historic Morton Salt complex, with its iconic sign and slogan, "When it rains, it pours," and the beloved Umbrella Girl, painted in blue and yellow. For decades, it has captivated people passing along Elston Avenue or on the Kennedy Expressway.

When I first heard about the plans to transform the old Morton buildings into a music venue, I asked if I could shoot some photos. I was granted access, although at the time I had no plan and no specific narrative in mind. But as a documentary photographer, I understood that this would be something special to witness. Sure enough, each time I returned, dramatic stories of the building were unfolding. I felt a childlike sense of discovery, seeing for the first time, up close, a structure being taken apart and then rebuilt.

One day, as I was observing the shed from a windy rooftop across Elston Avenue, conversations with my late husband—an architect who loved the hands-on nature of construction—came flooding back. On bike rides through old cemeteries and walks in abandoned places, we had shared our thoughts about buildings and their history, recognizing those who came before us and the value of what they made.

Introduction

These and other bittersweet memories resonated as I moved around the Morton site. It was powerful and poignant, seeing something new created out of something old, restored instead of demolished.

As the weeks and months passed at the old Morton Salt site, I felt inspired to create images that would do justice to the work of the original designers and builders, to the passionate restoration team and to the dedication to craft and sturdiness so evident here. In Chicago, outstanding architecture was never reserved for grand civic buildings: it's often found in common industrial complexes like these sheds or in power plants and field houses built a century ago. One of the last of its kind, the Salt Shed is a living landmark, celebrating our city's history and evolving culture, filled with crowds of music lovers.

Before that sunny September morning, I hadn't yet photographed the removal of the sign or become consumed with documenting this story, returning again and again, arriving at sunrise many days to catch the light. I hadn't gone underground into confined spaces with the plumbing crew, climbed up on rooftops to hang my camera over low parapet walls, or faced my fear of scrambling up the chicken ladder before the stairs were built, to the shed's second level. I didn't know that the architects of more famous Chicago buildings had also designed this industrial steel structure. I hadn't learned how close it had come to being leveled—one more small reminder of impermanence in our changing world. And although it was all around me, on the ground and in the air, I wasn't thinking about salt and how essential and valuable this simple compound is to life.

Sandra Steinbrecher

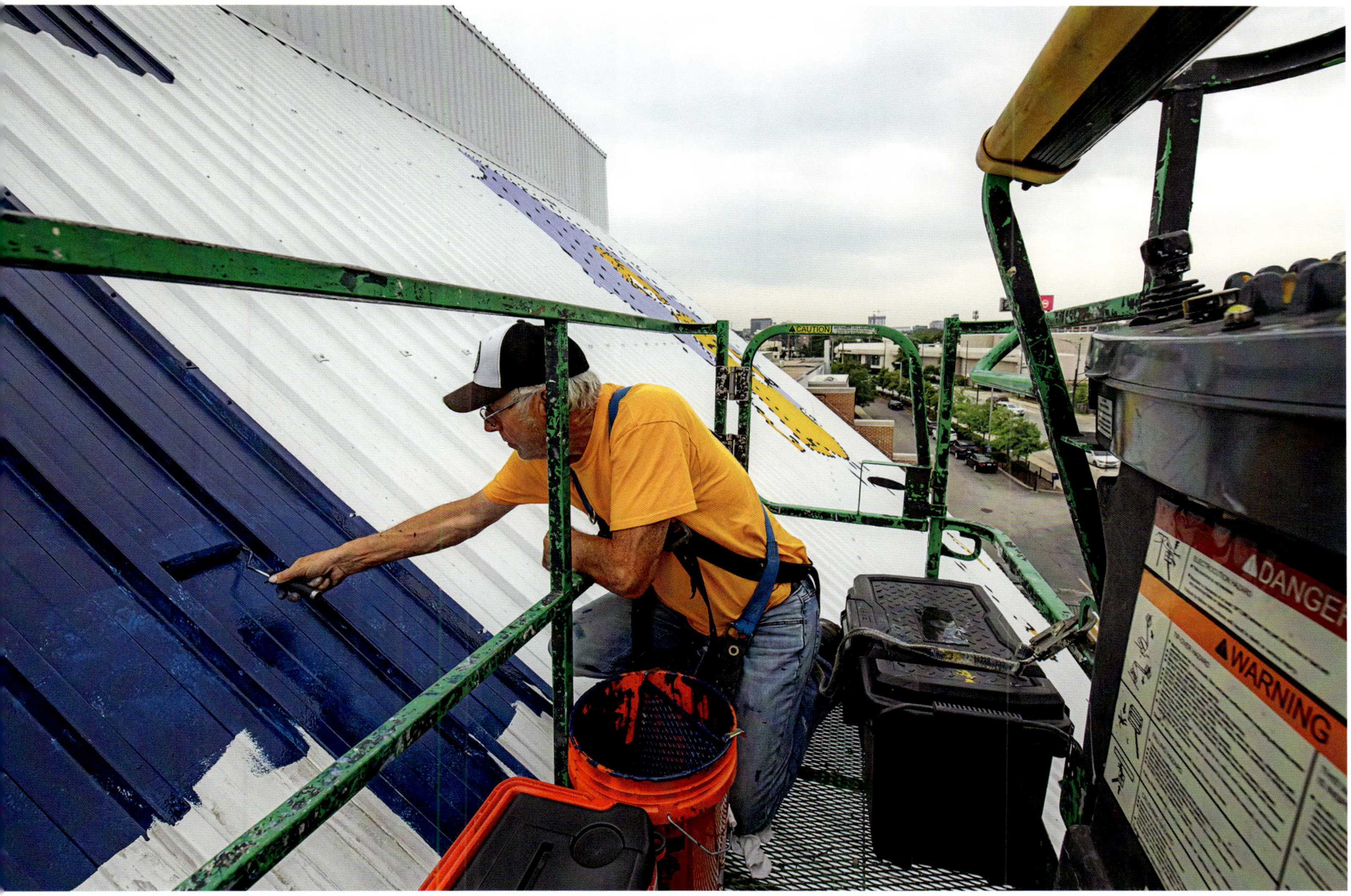
DANGER
WARNING

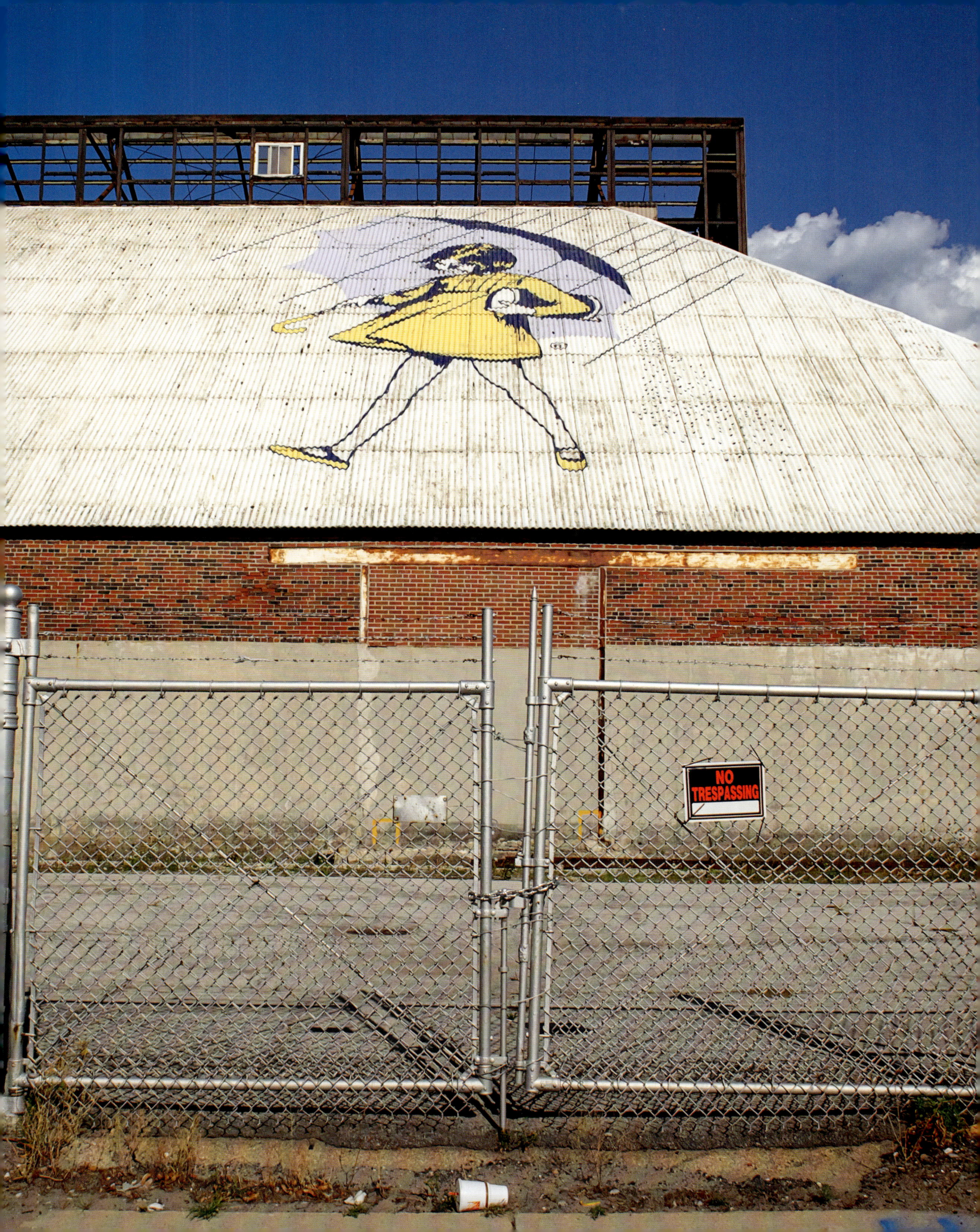
NO
TRESPASSING

Imagine that we've been on this planet for the equivalent of one breath. Look around at how we've shaped it in this time. We build everything—houses, roadways, bridges, skyscrapers, warehouses. What really links us to our past and connects us throughout history is that in some way we're all builders, continuing and honoring the legacy of those who came before us. We haven't been here that long, but for better or worse, the planet is filled with what we've built and with these spaces we've created.

~ Daniel J. Majerowicz, plumbing foreman

№ 1

ICON

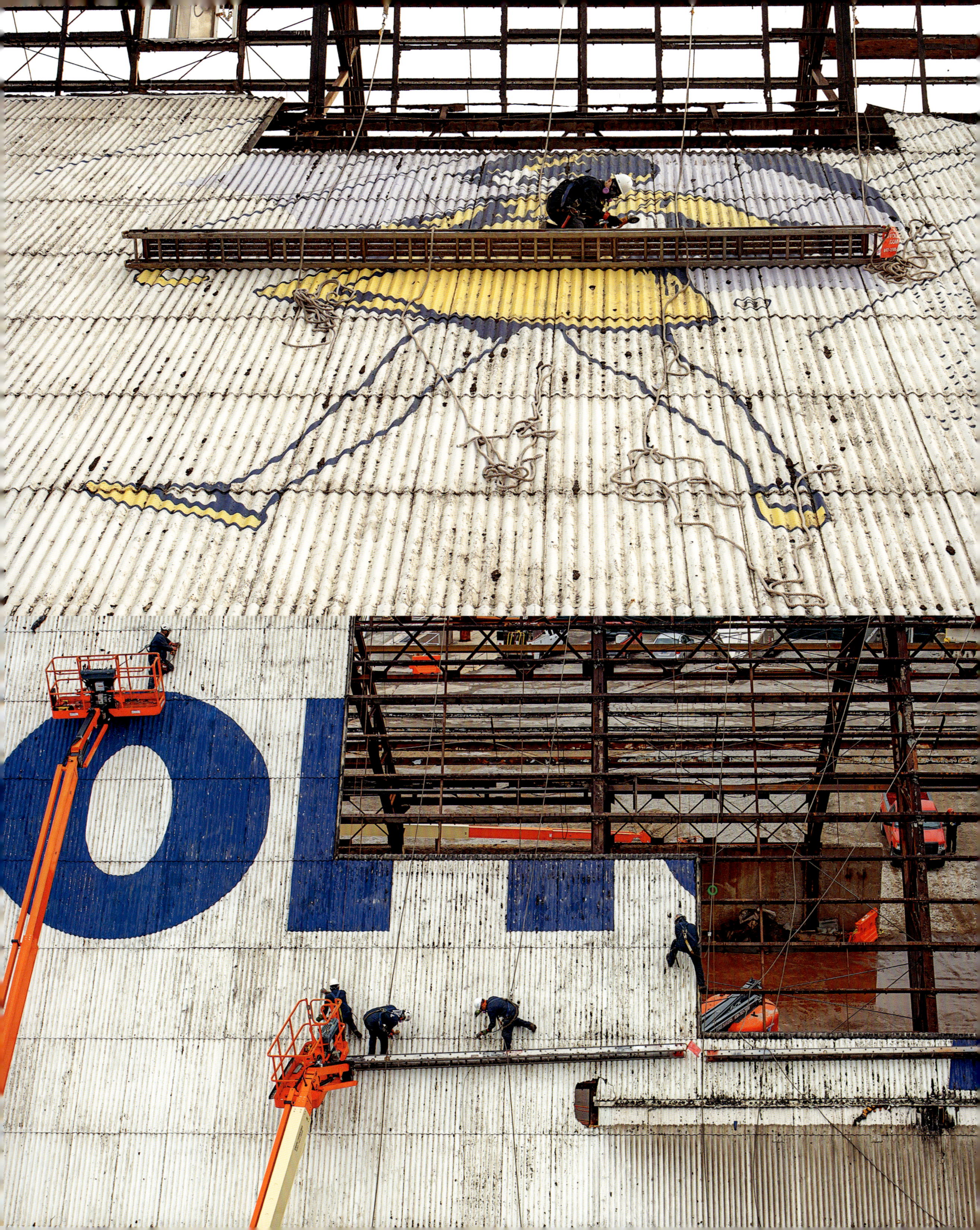

Icon

The 1920s Landmark, Reimagined

Like many Chicagoans, I'd driven or cycled by the old Morton Salt shed for much of my life. Passing through this industrial section of town, part way to my destination, I could imagine that it belonged to a life before mine, a relic from another era. When I got word of plans to restore the building into a modern music venue, I carried my cameras over one morning to take a look.

Entering on Blackhawk Street, I was surprised by the size and breadth of the site–4.2 acres–next to the Chicago River. Standing in the shed's vast space beneath all that steel felt awe-inspiring. Along with a freestanding garage, the complex included a sprawling brick packaging building, with expansive second-floor spaces containing large windows and grand views of the river, the bridges, and the downtown skyline.

Following the building's completion in 1930, the sign with the Morton Salt name and logo was painted on the roof. The Morton Salt Umbrella Girl was added later. Over the years, the block-long billboard was deemed out of city code but was exempted because it predated the construction of the Kennedy Expressway. Recently the sign has been informally recognized as its own cultural landmark.

Hand-painted every five years, the iconic sign covered the original corrugated roof panels made from Transite, a mix of concrete and asbestos that was considered modern and efficient at the time of construction. Underneath the roof, a good portion of the steel components in the framework had corroded and needed repair or replacement to keep the frame structurally sound. Then new, safer, roof panels could be installed.

Those original panels would soon be removed. Given the sign's place in Chicago's collective consciousness, and the fact that commuters had regularly weighed in on its changes, this task seemed momentous. I returned to the site the following week to photograph it. Half a dozen workers, harnessed onto a swing stage or in lifts, worked methodically along the angled roof, removing the heavy panels one at a time with hand tools. Each panel, lowered carefully and loaded onto a forklift, was transferred to a truck for disposal. After a few weeks, the weathered layers had all been peeled away and the spectacular steel shell was fully revealed for the first time since the original architects saw the installation of their design nearly a century before.

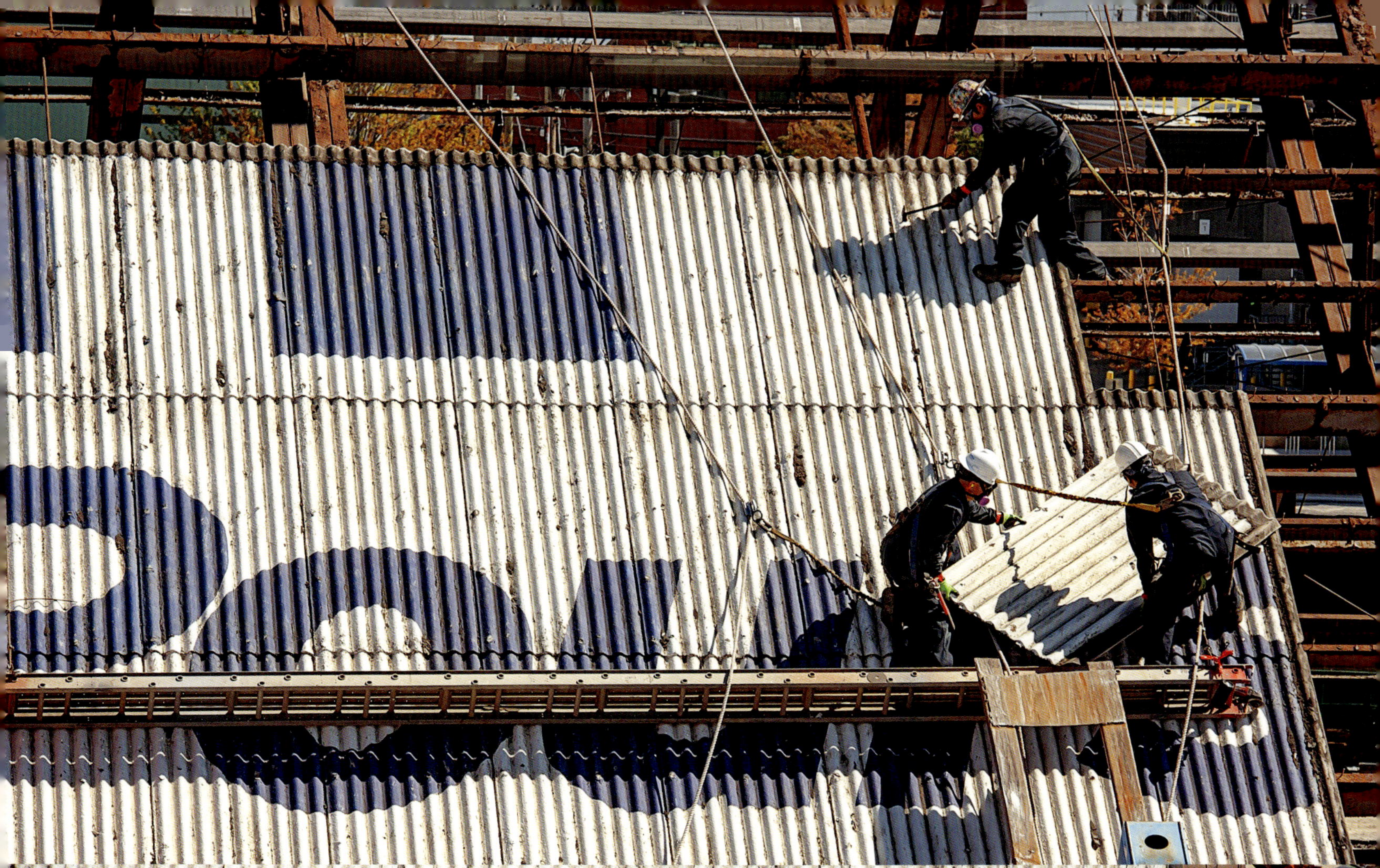

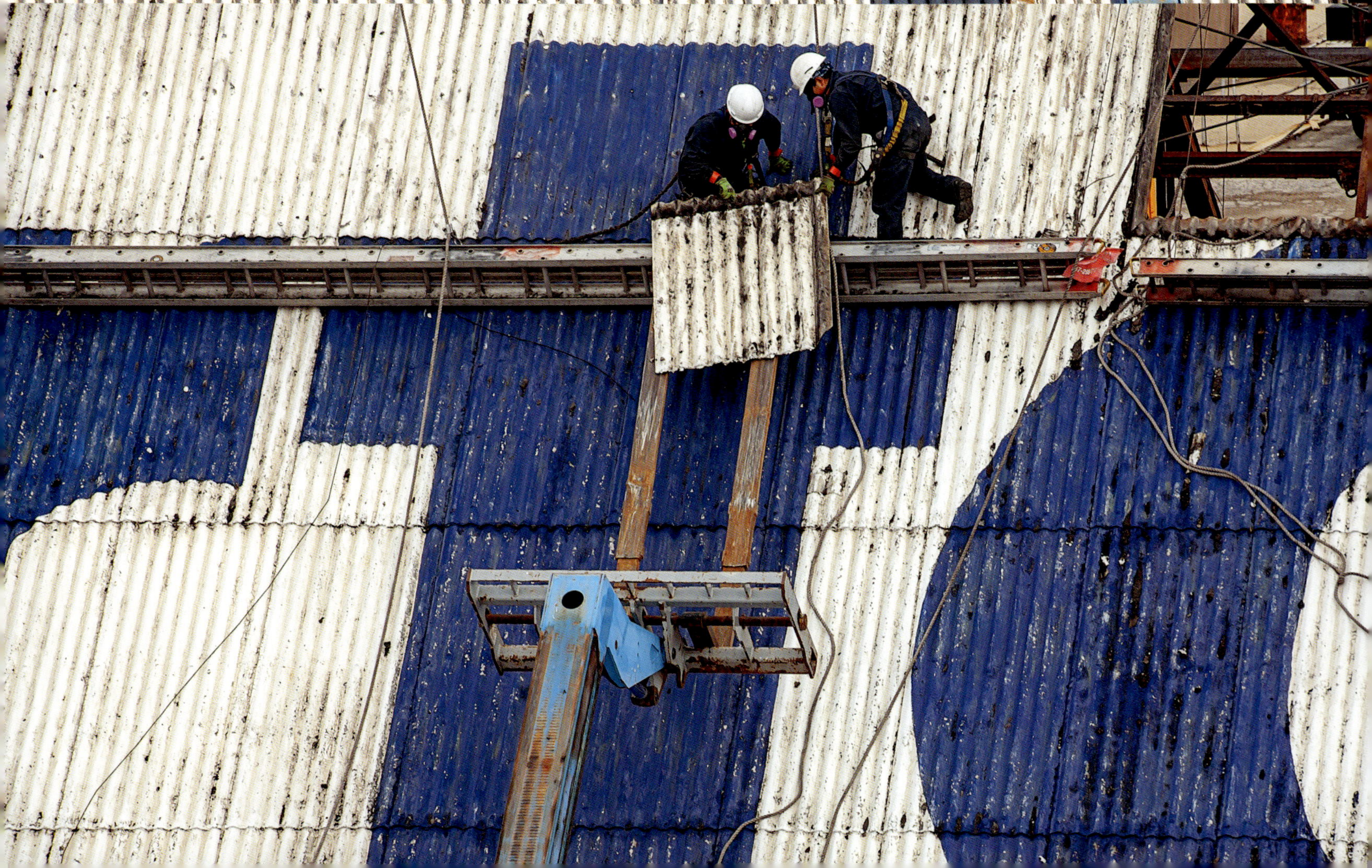

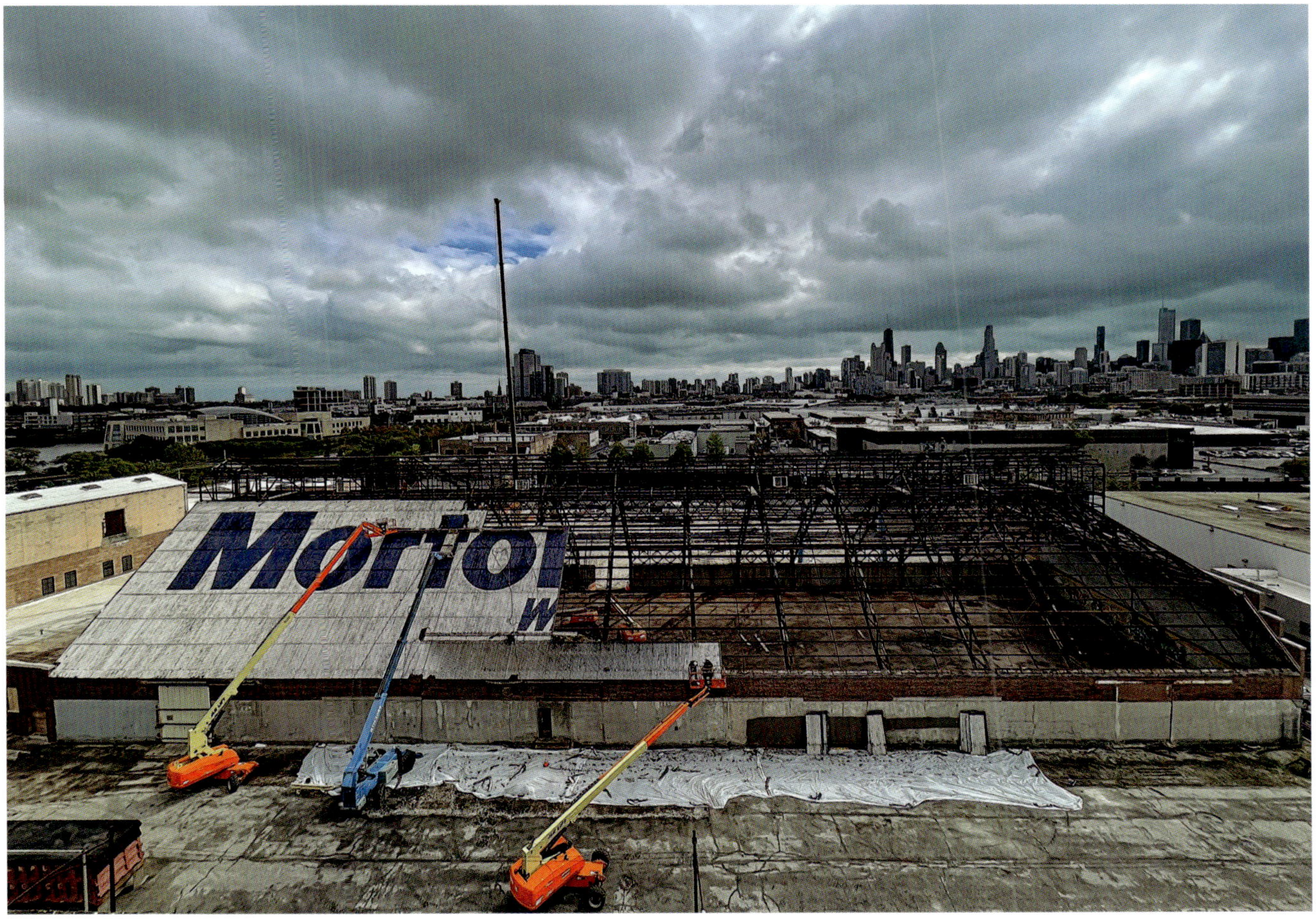
Morto
W

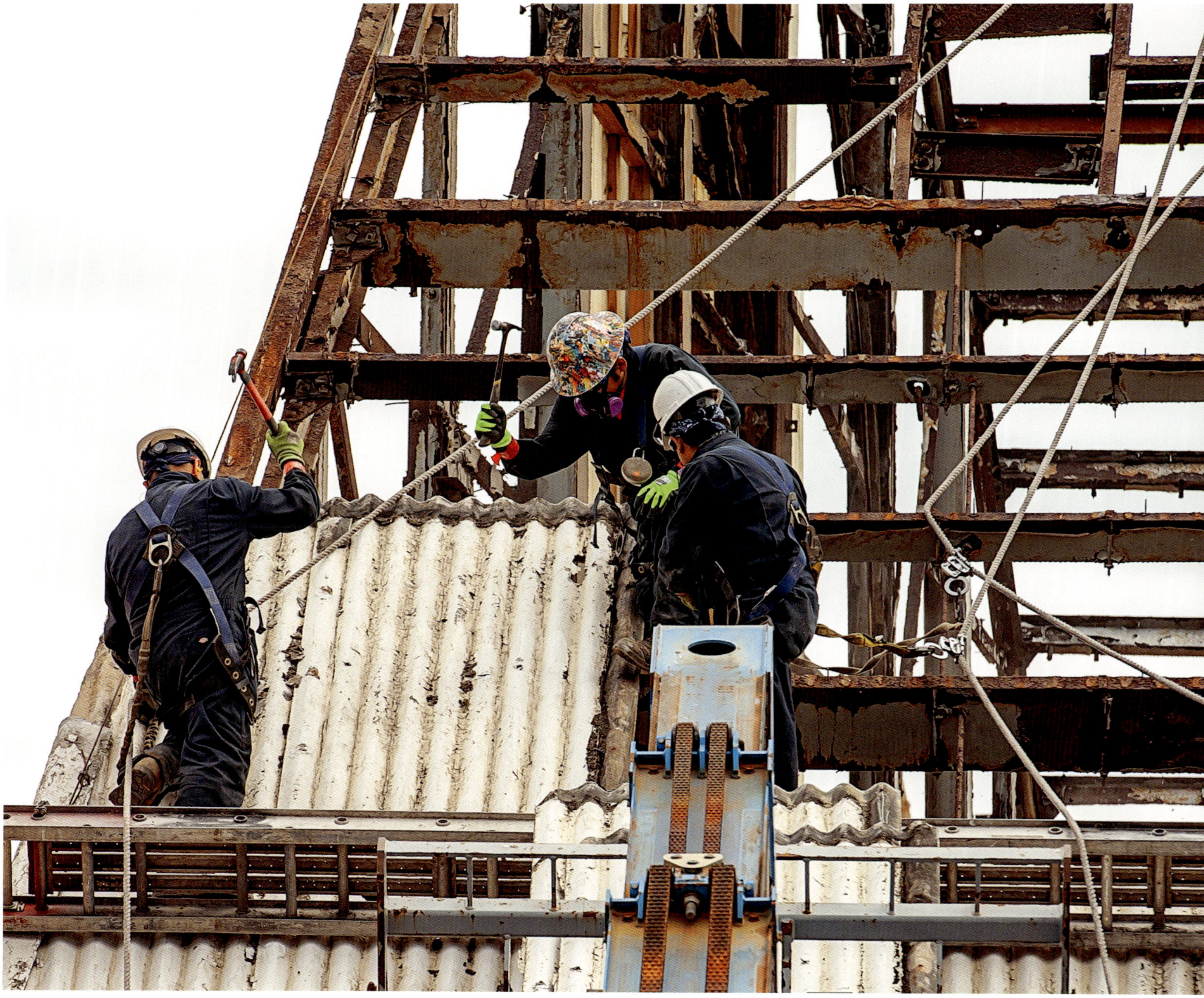

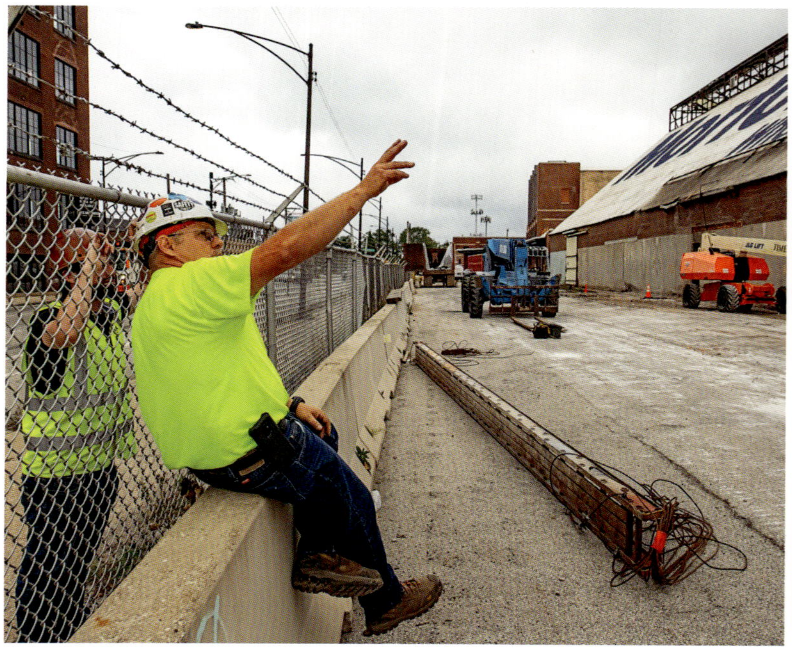

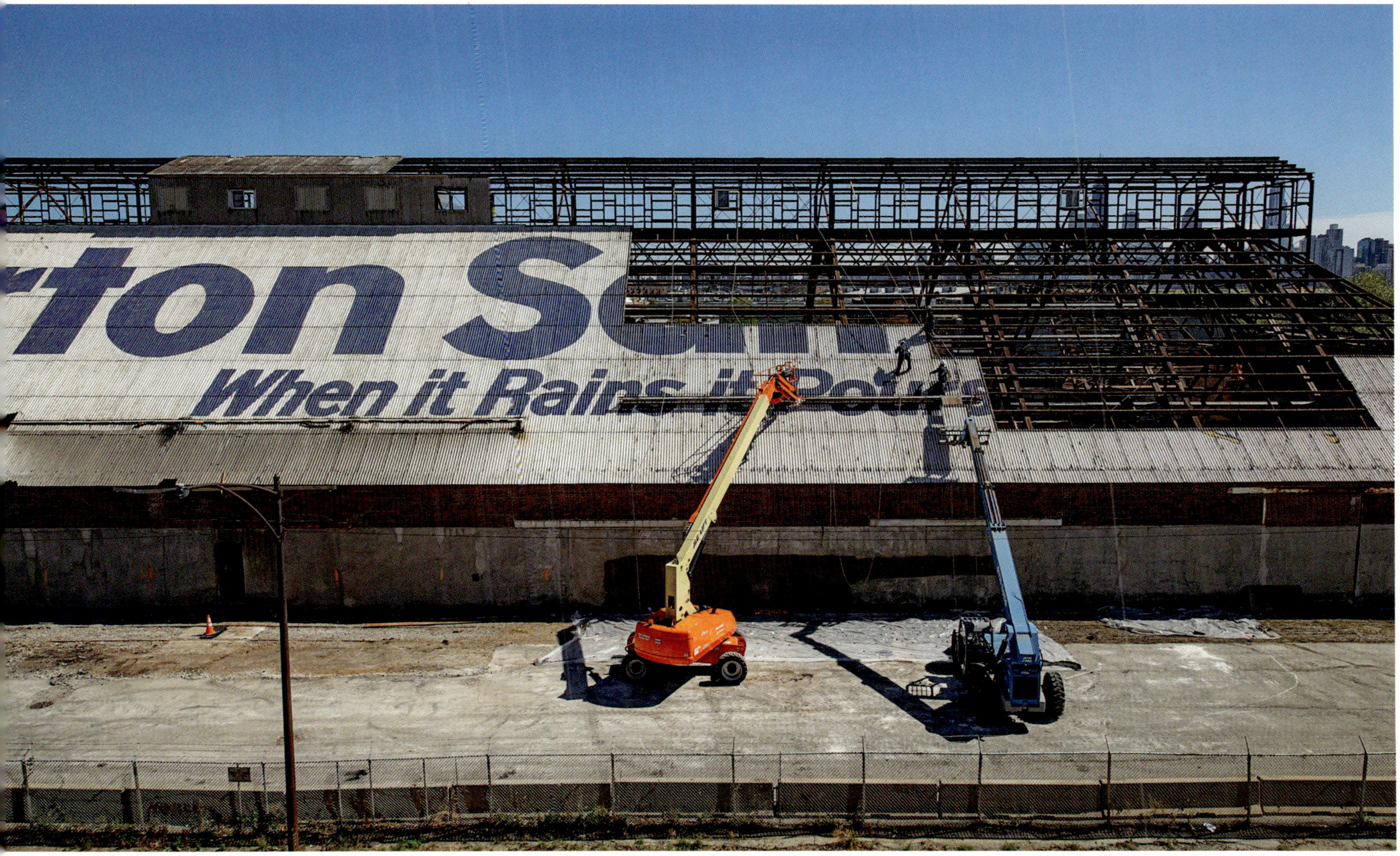
When it Rains

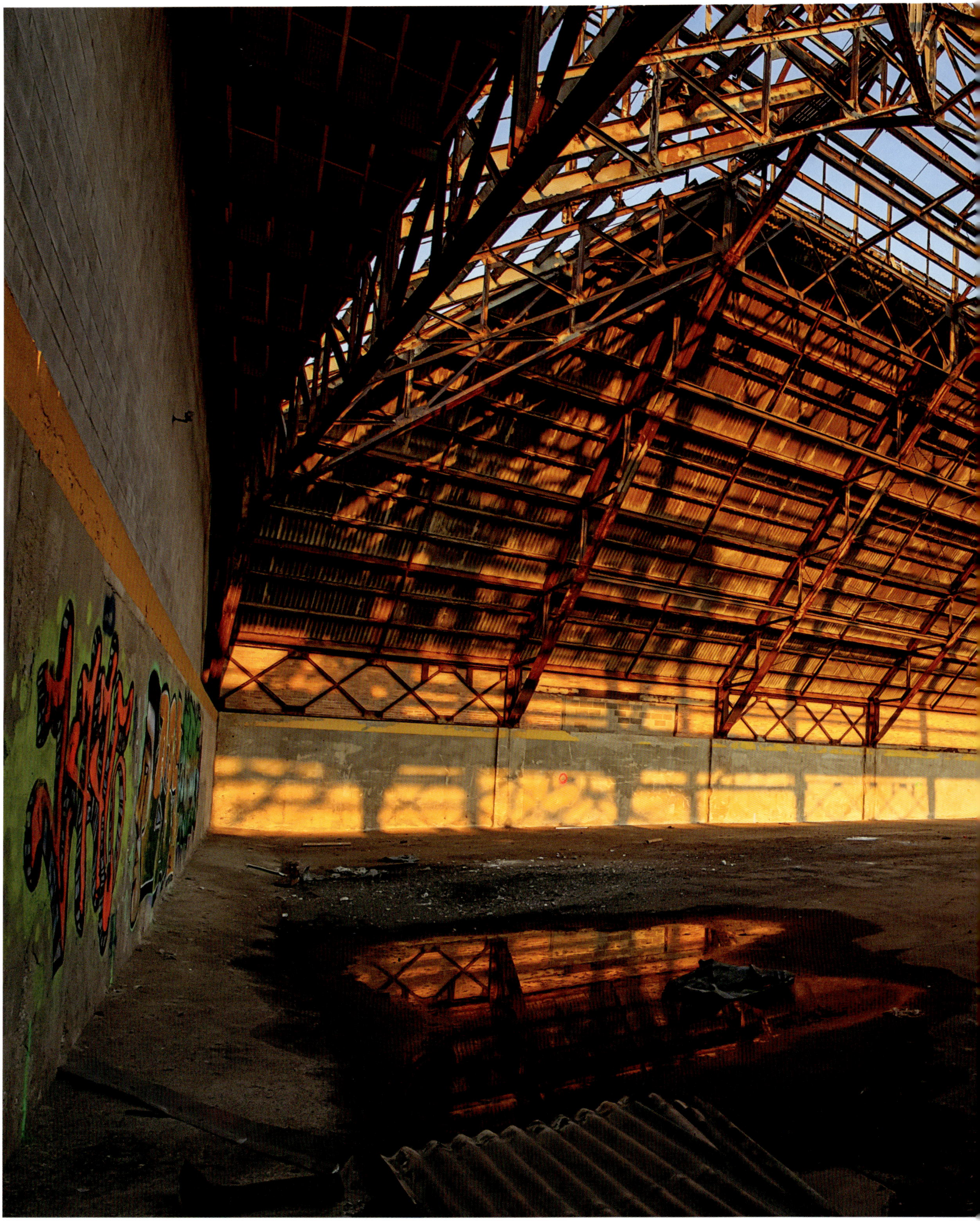

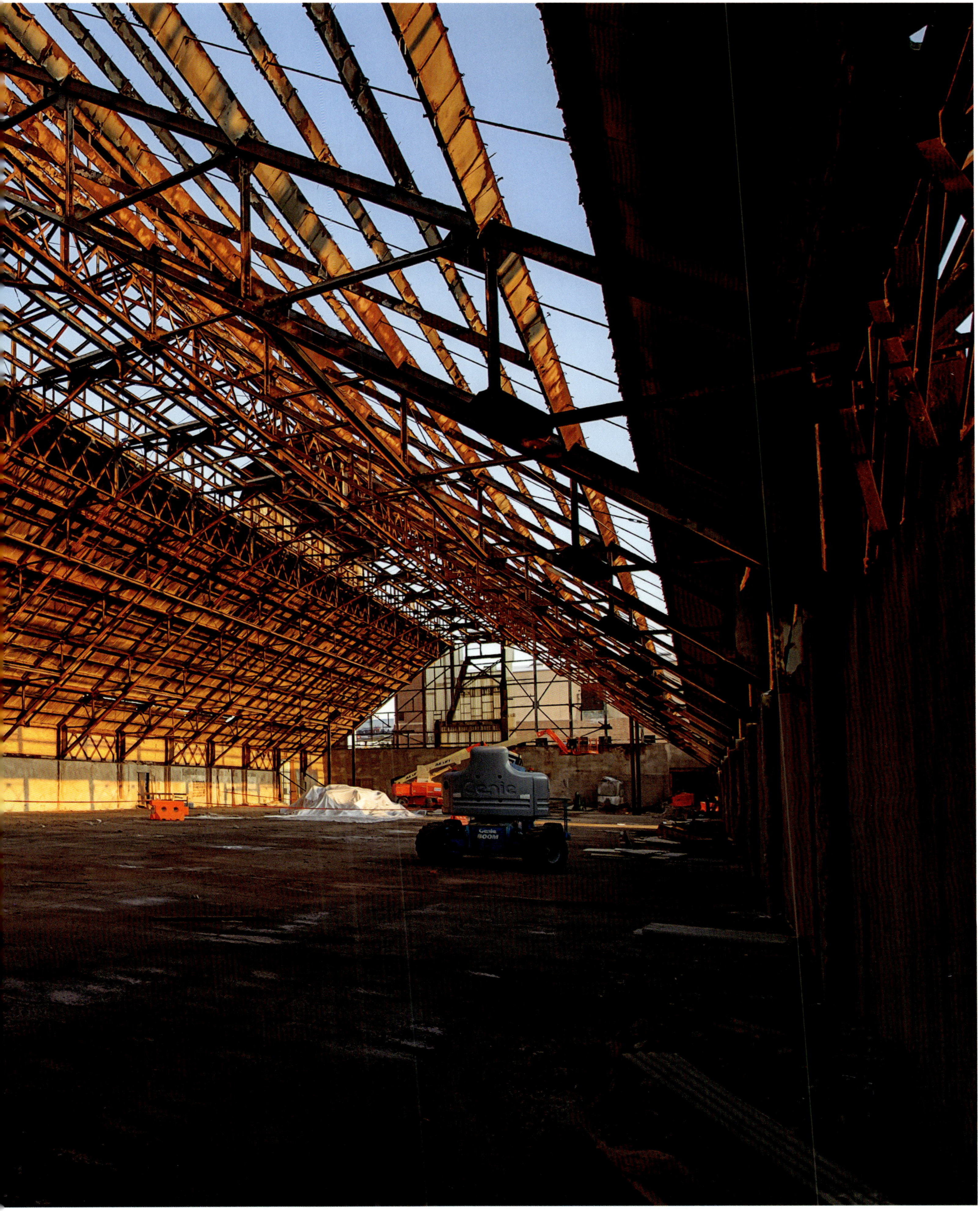
Genie
Genie
BOOM

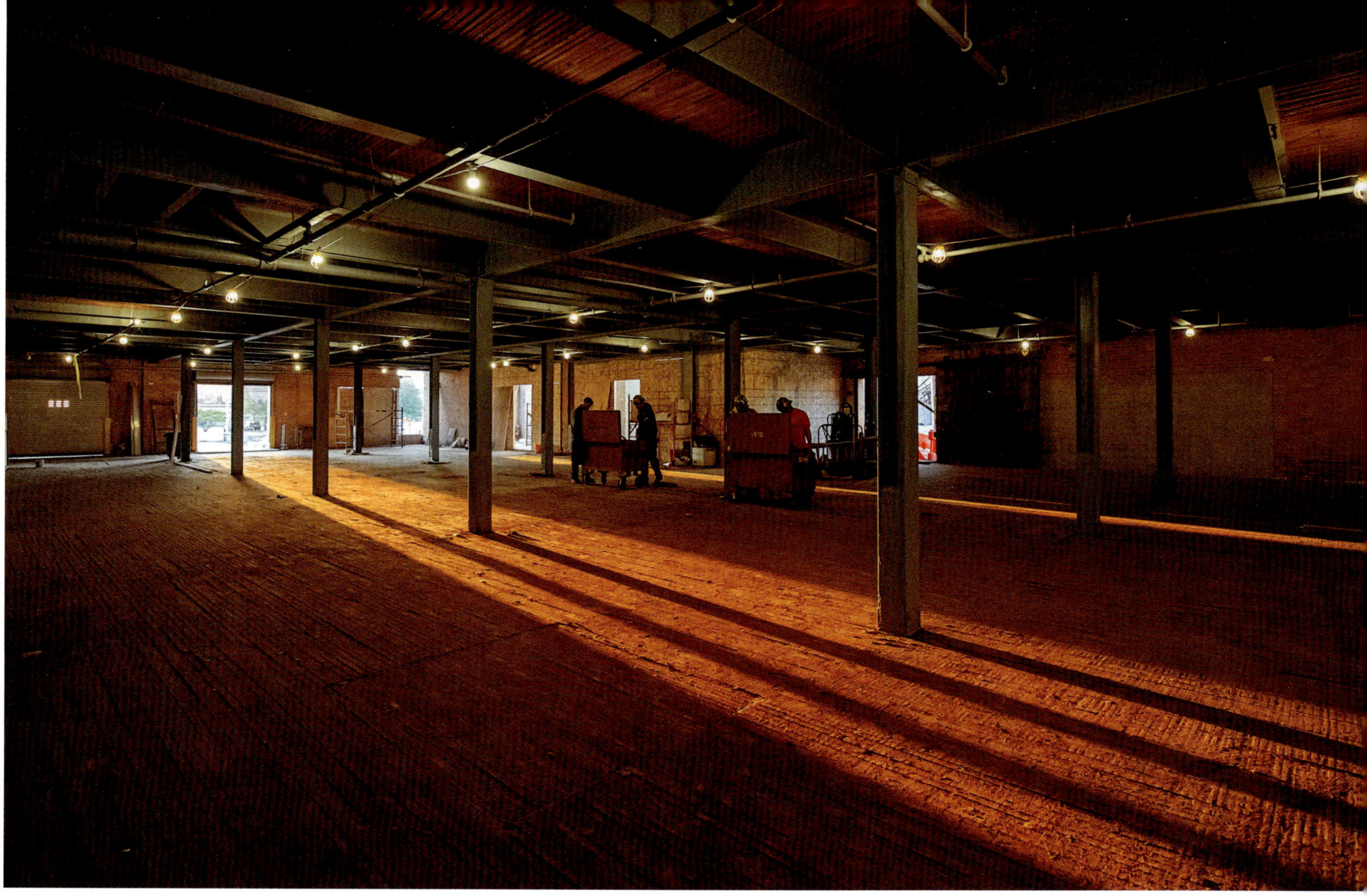

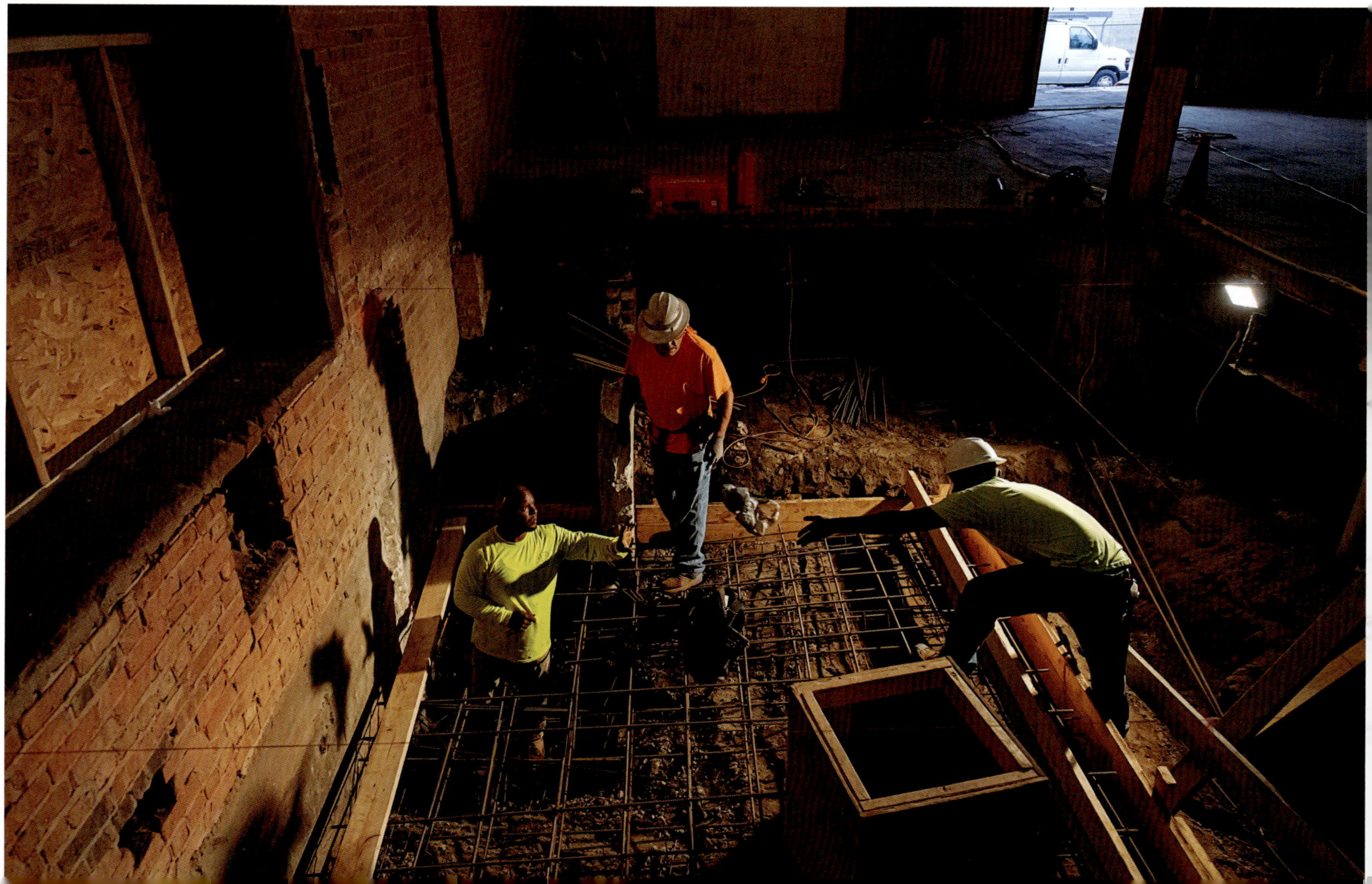

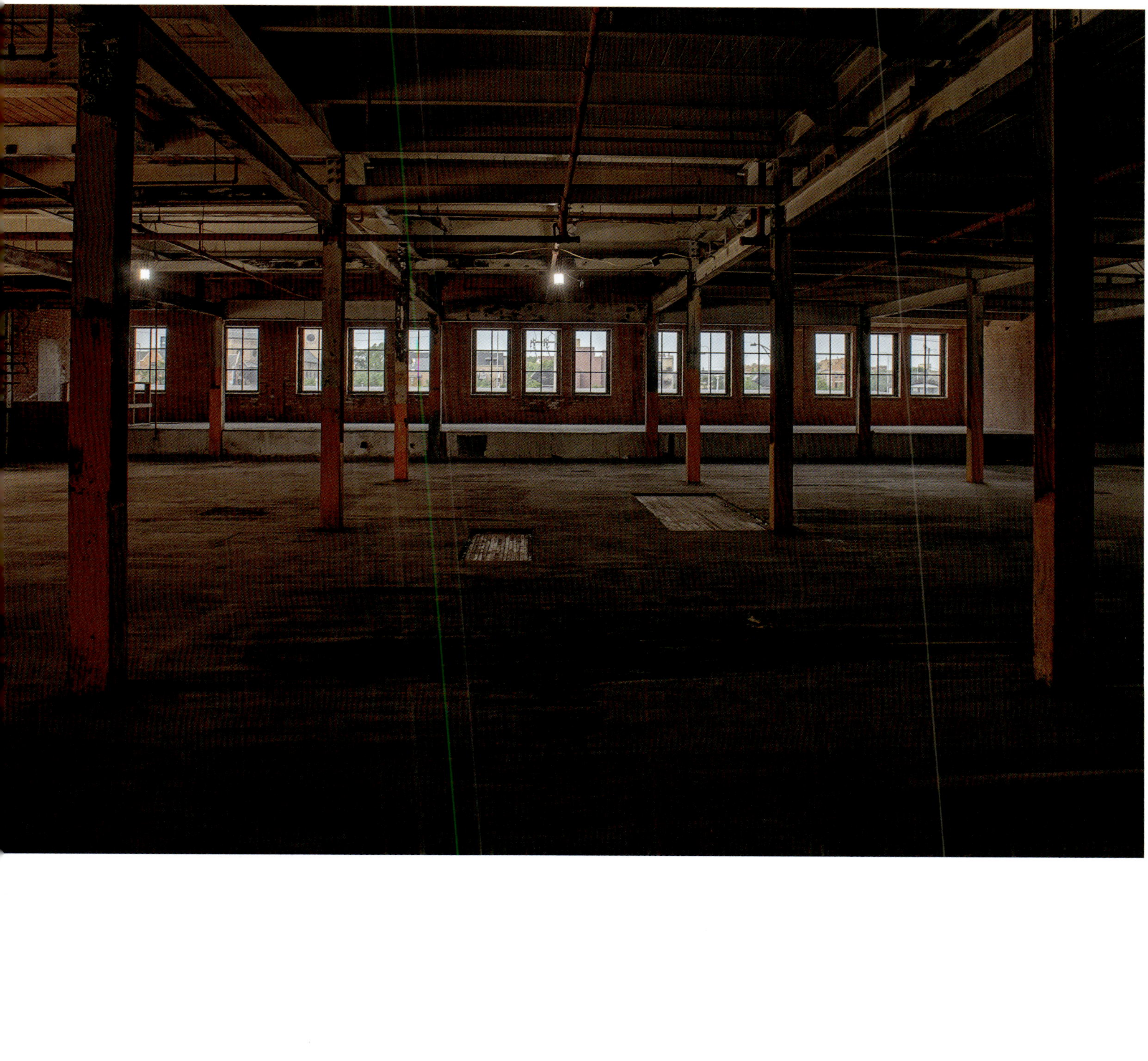

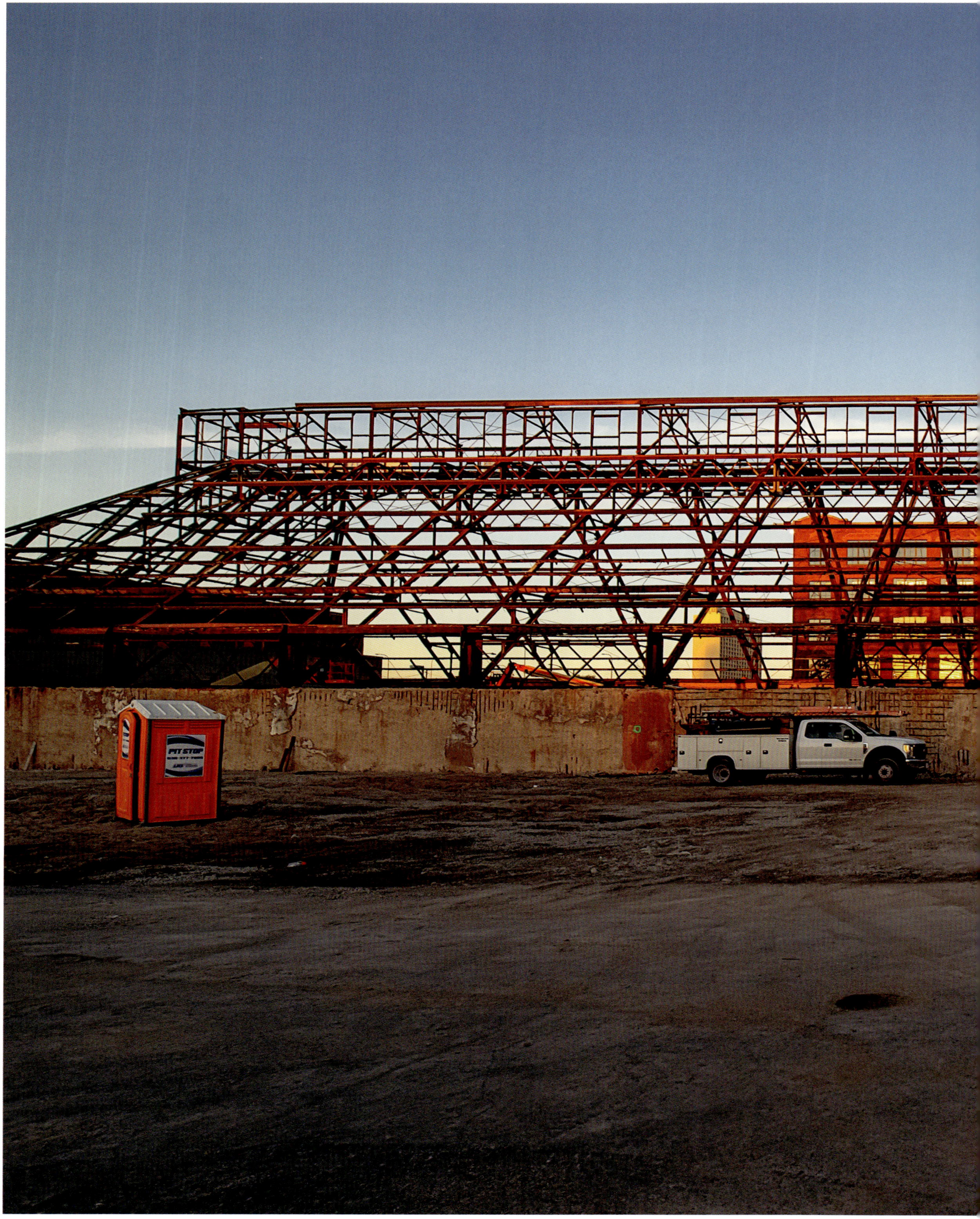
PIT STOP

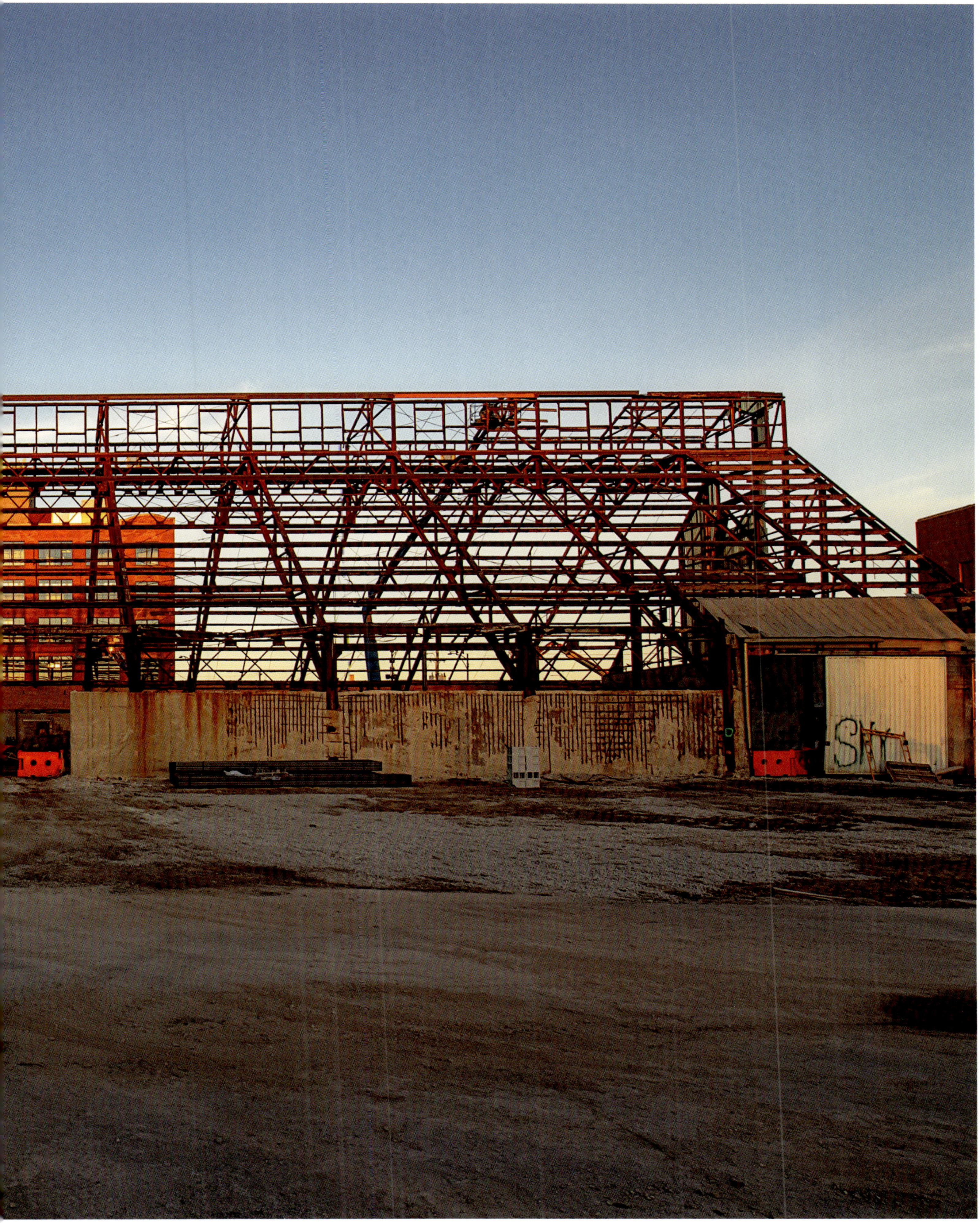

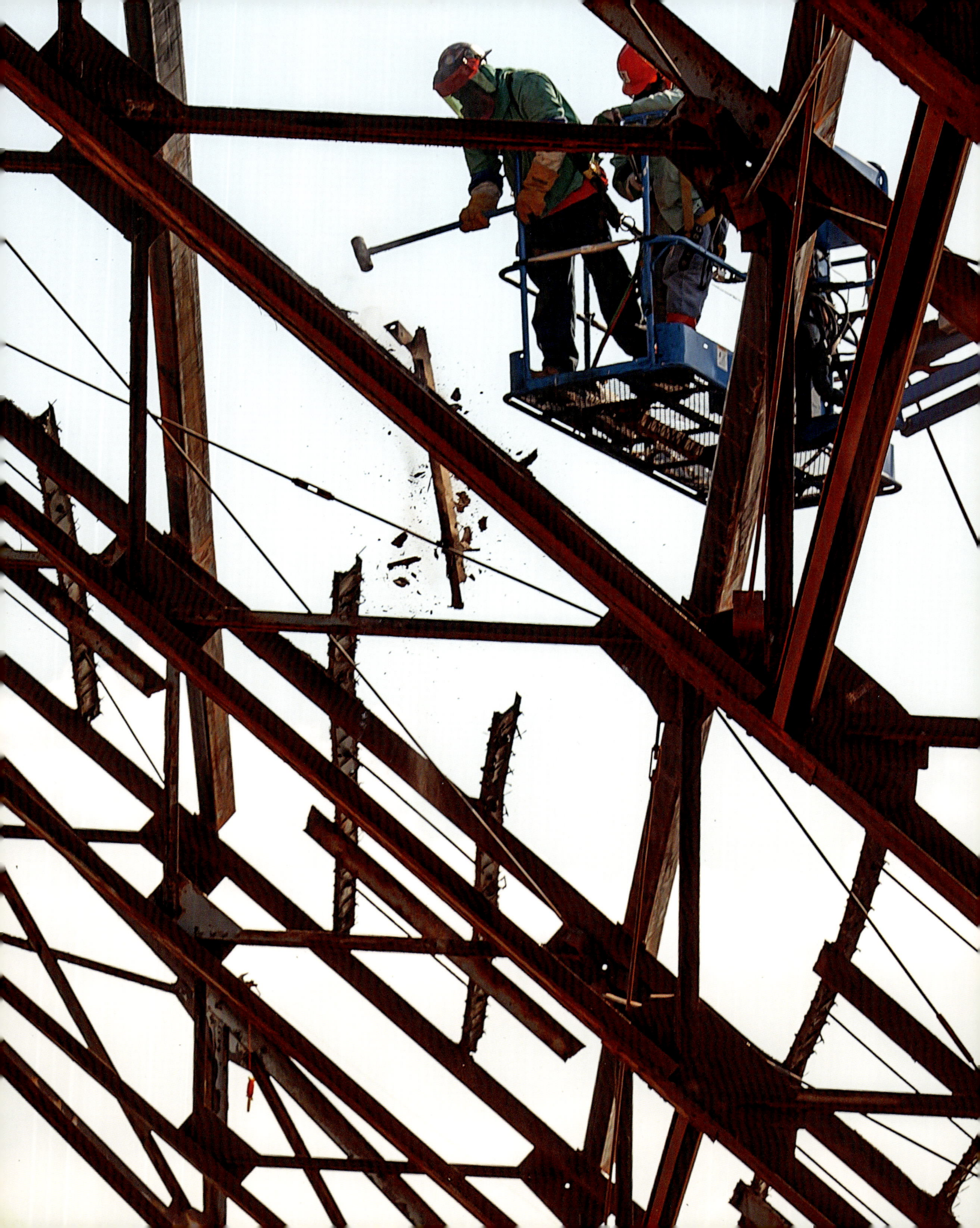

As ironworkers we appreciate the design and craftsmanship of the steel shed. We know the strength and energy it takes for steel to be able to span these distances and create this type of building. The steel they used a hundred years ago was incredibly high quality. We found holes in it and a lot of corrosion, but it was still stronger than what we have available today, and so we were able to repair a fair amount of it. Restoring a historic building is more challenging and expensive than tearing it down, but it's worthwhile, because once something like this is gone, it's gone forever. This is a beautiful building, a piece of art.

~ Stephen Felty + Raul Fiero, ironworkers

Nº 2
STEEL

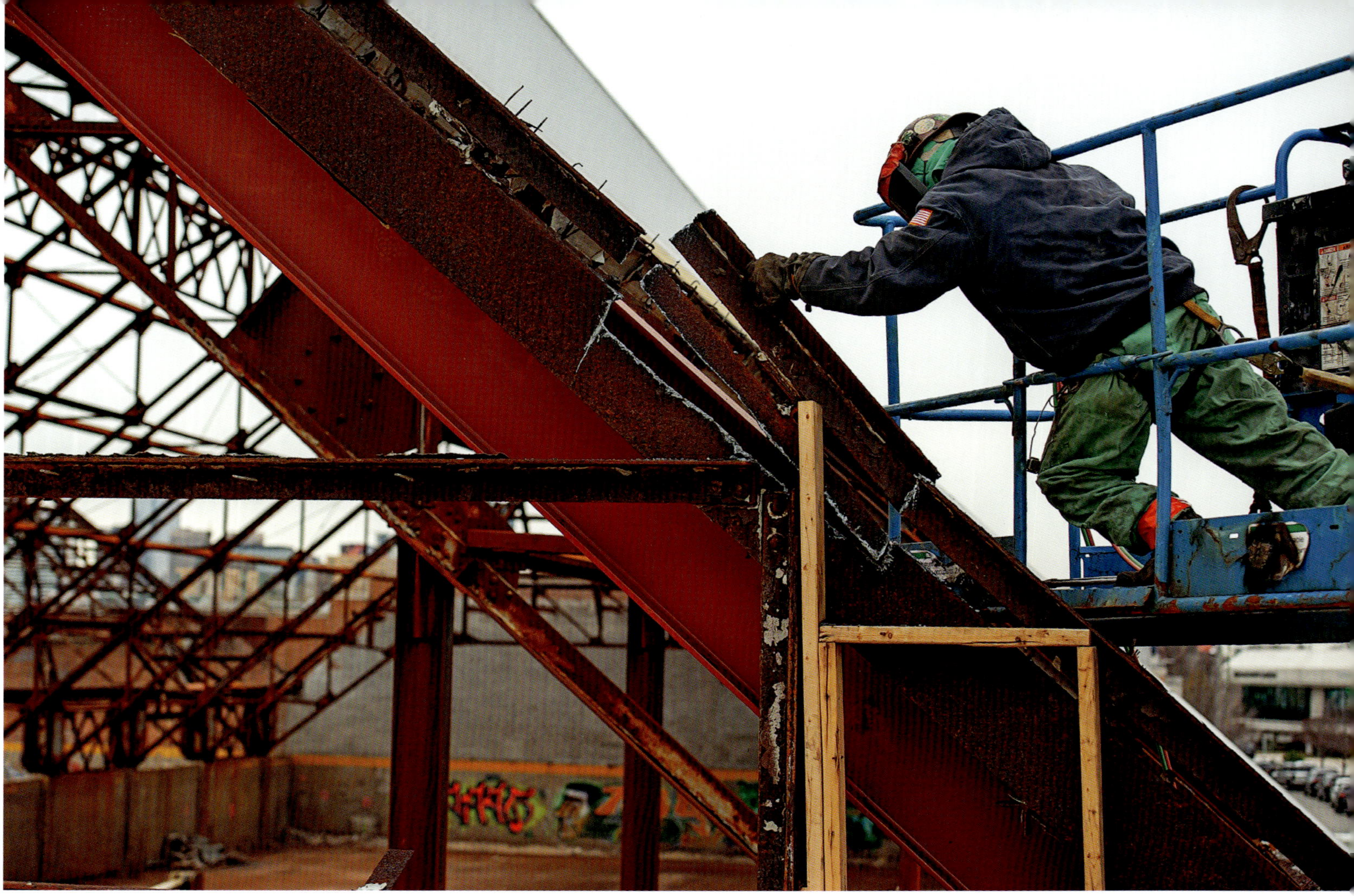

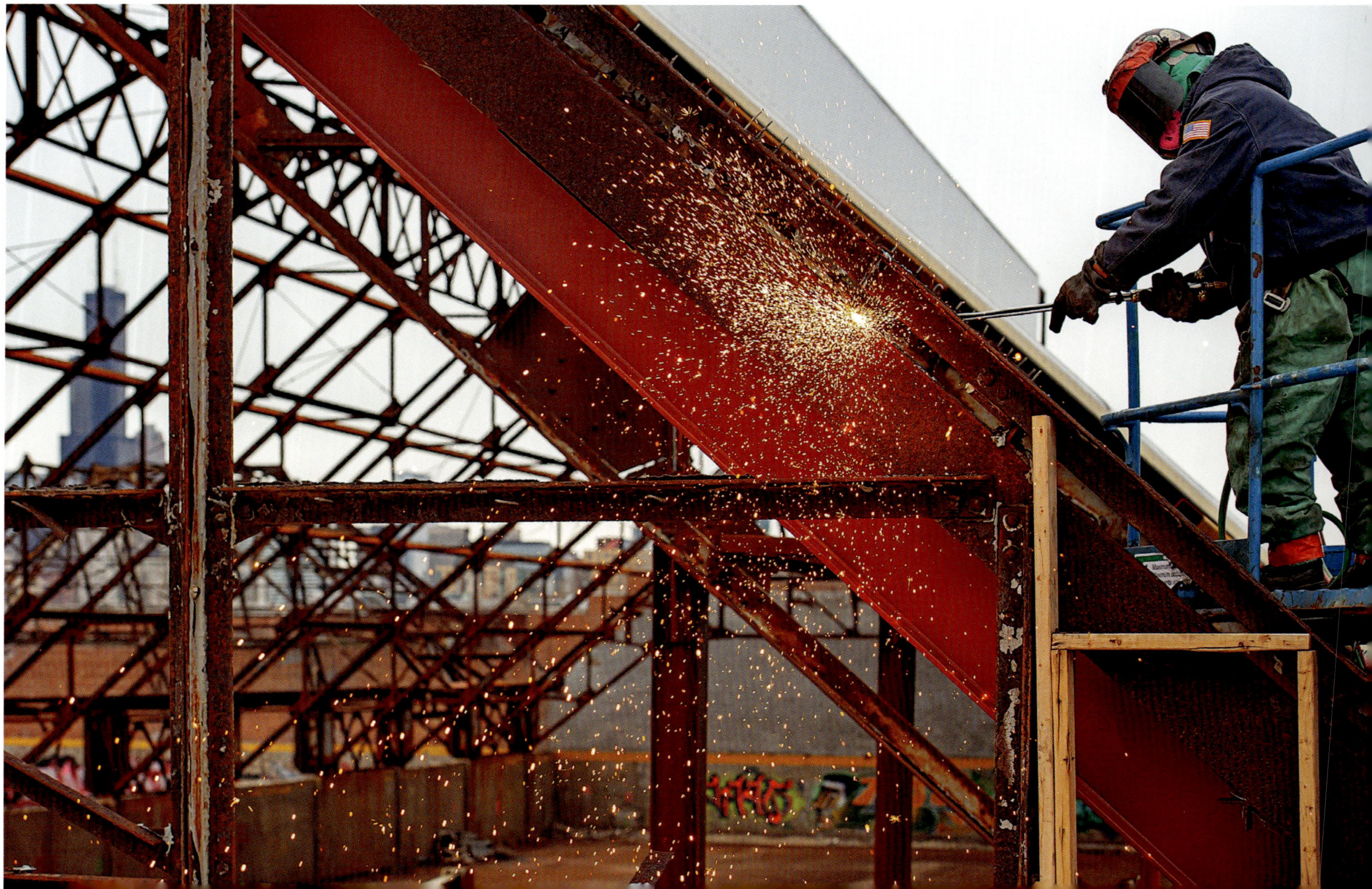

Steel

An Architectural and Structural Innovation

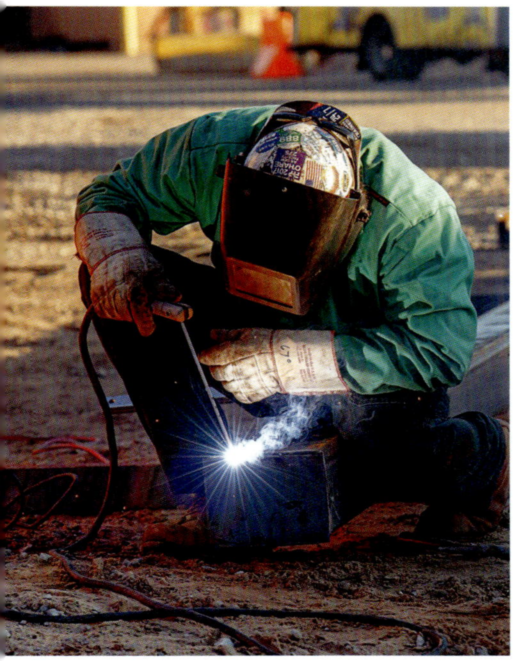

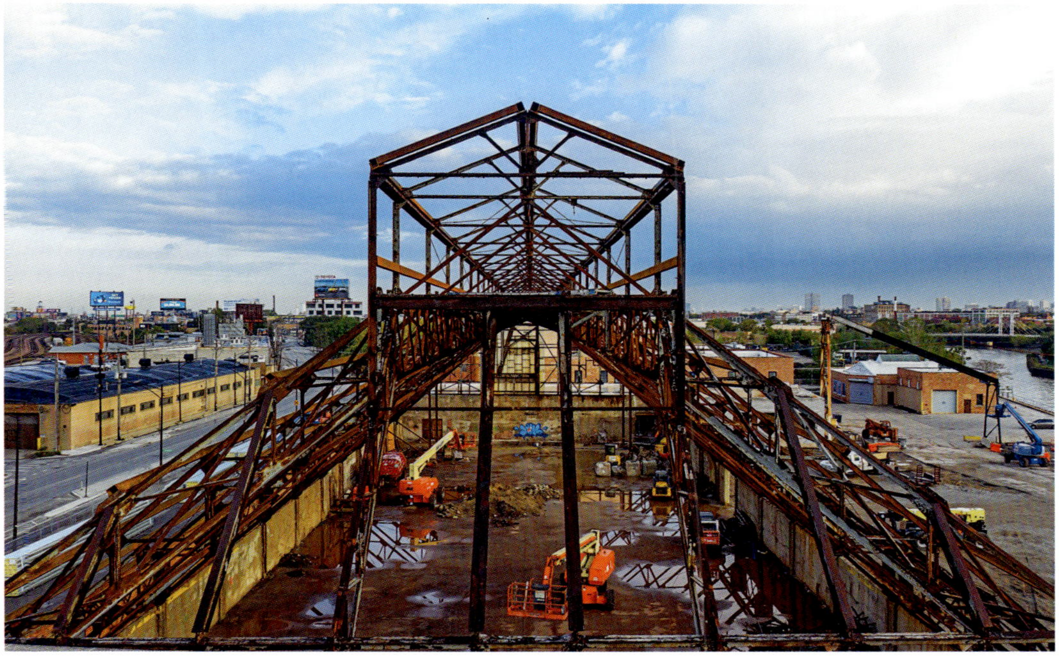

The early morning light showcased the Morton site's industrial beauty. East of the river, the rising sun lit the tops of trees and buildings. Inside the packaging building, light shone through the windows, laying down bright rectangles on the old wood floors. But when the sun made its way to the shed, it lit up the steel frame in gorgeous pinks, reds and oranges.

When construction began in 1929, Morton Salt's massive steel framed shed was architecturally and structurally innovative. The steel truss design allowed for wide spans that created expansive, ventilated, and light-filled workspaces. Original architectural drawings required the building's roof to be constructed at an angle of forty degrees to accommodate tall salt piles, which naturally form at about thirty-two degrees. This production shed was built to be efficient and to last. But after almost 100 years of daily exposure to salt, plenty of the steel in the west shed building was corroded. However, there was enough to save and restore, a testament to the integrity of the design and materials of the time. This sturdiness is at the heart of what both inspired and reassured the development team to take on this restoration project.

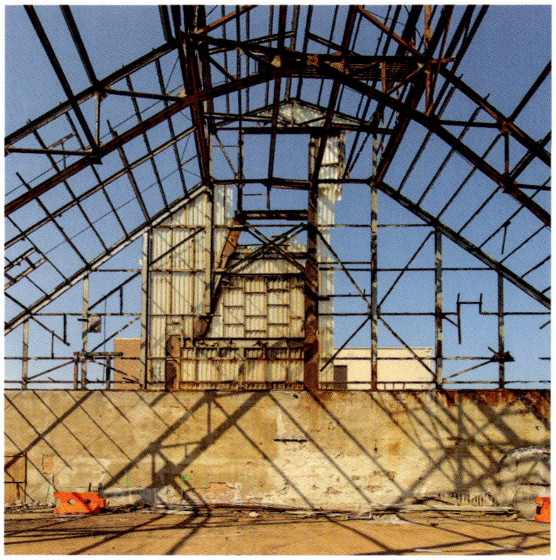

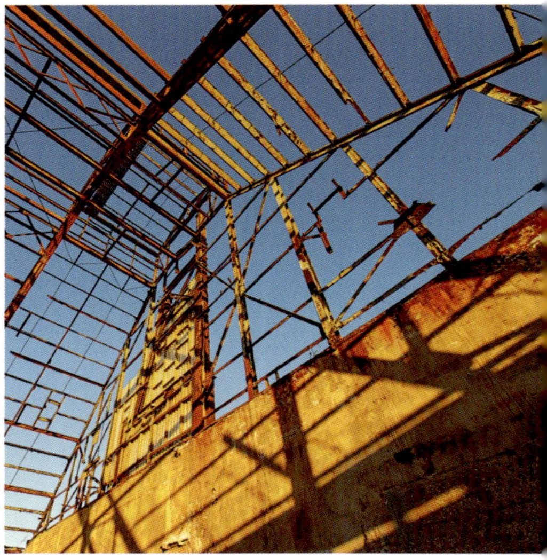

In the original construction, a "twin" east shed building was attached to the west shed, but that building was structurally beyond repair and had to be demolished. After that east side came down, the next task was to render the remaining shed (now the performance venue) sound enough to be safe to work in. After measuring the corrosion on every steel beam by hand, structural engineers called for temporary shoring towers to be installed from floor to ceiling. Some beams had over two inches of salt layered on top, requiring sandblasting before workers began the long process of repairing and replacing hundreds of steel beams, bracings, and other parts.

I was still learning my way around the construction site, watching where I walked and searching for the best vantage points from which to photograph. Each day presented new challenges as access to areas changed daily or weekly. As a documentarian, I photographed what happened in front of me, without asking for changes or accommodations. I didn't want to interfere.

Through trial and error, I discovered how to follow the rhythm and sequence of the labor and how to capture the drama of the process. Everywhere I looked, work was taking place against quintessential Chicago backdrops—the river, the bridges, the skyline, and Elston Avenue. Inside the shed, the steel frame presented its own spectacular scene.

Steel

An Architectural and Structural Innovation

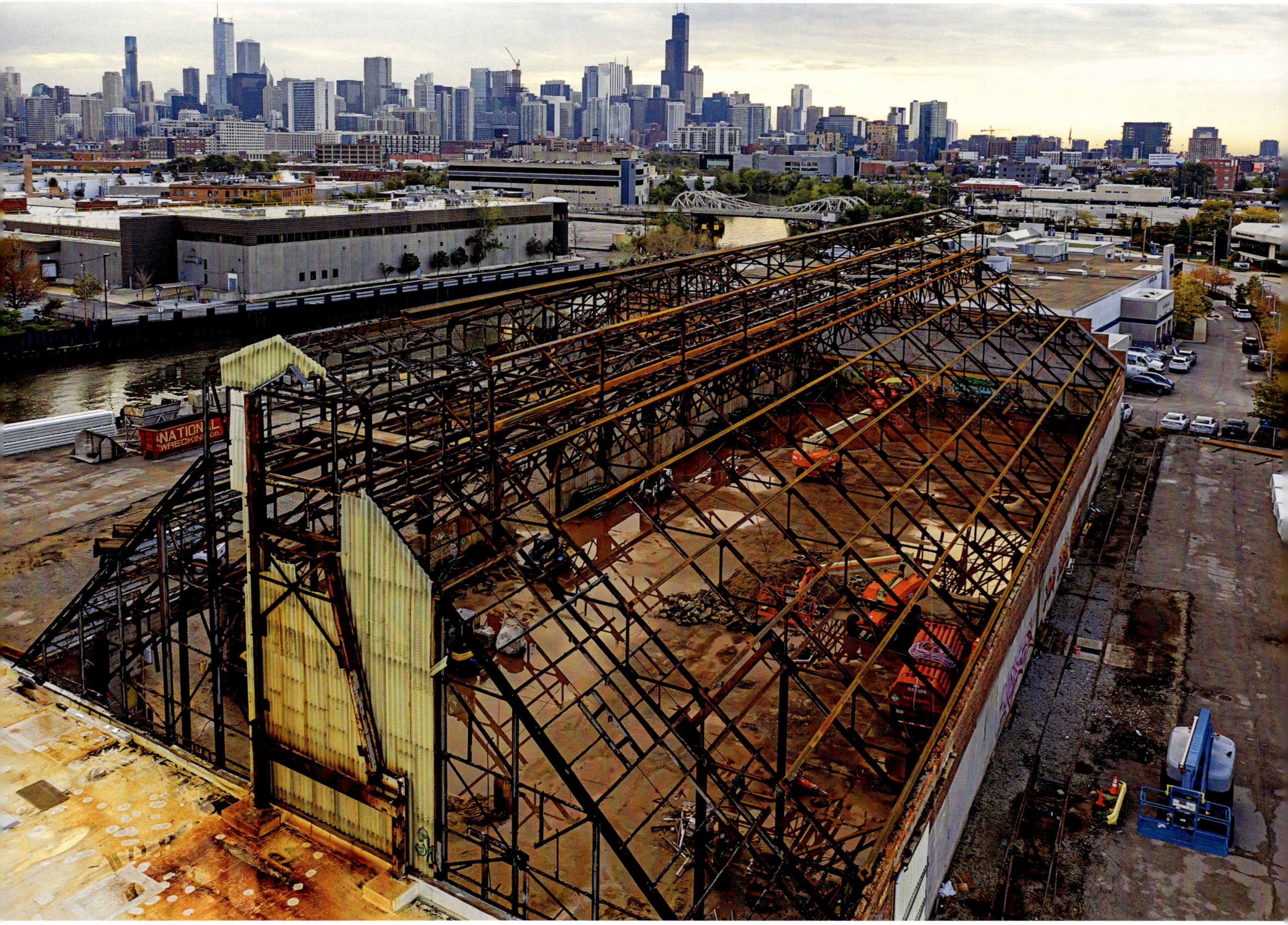

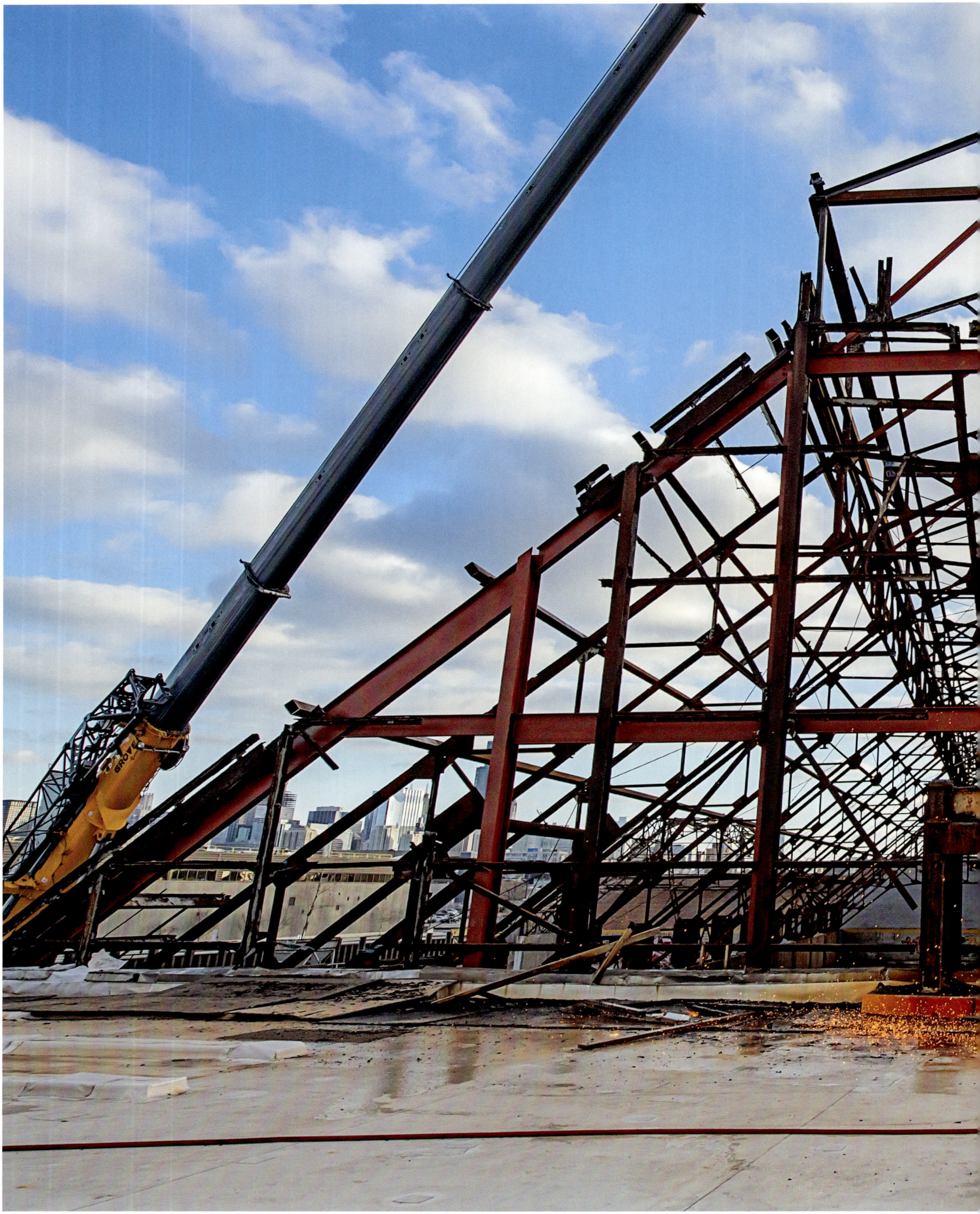

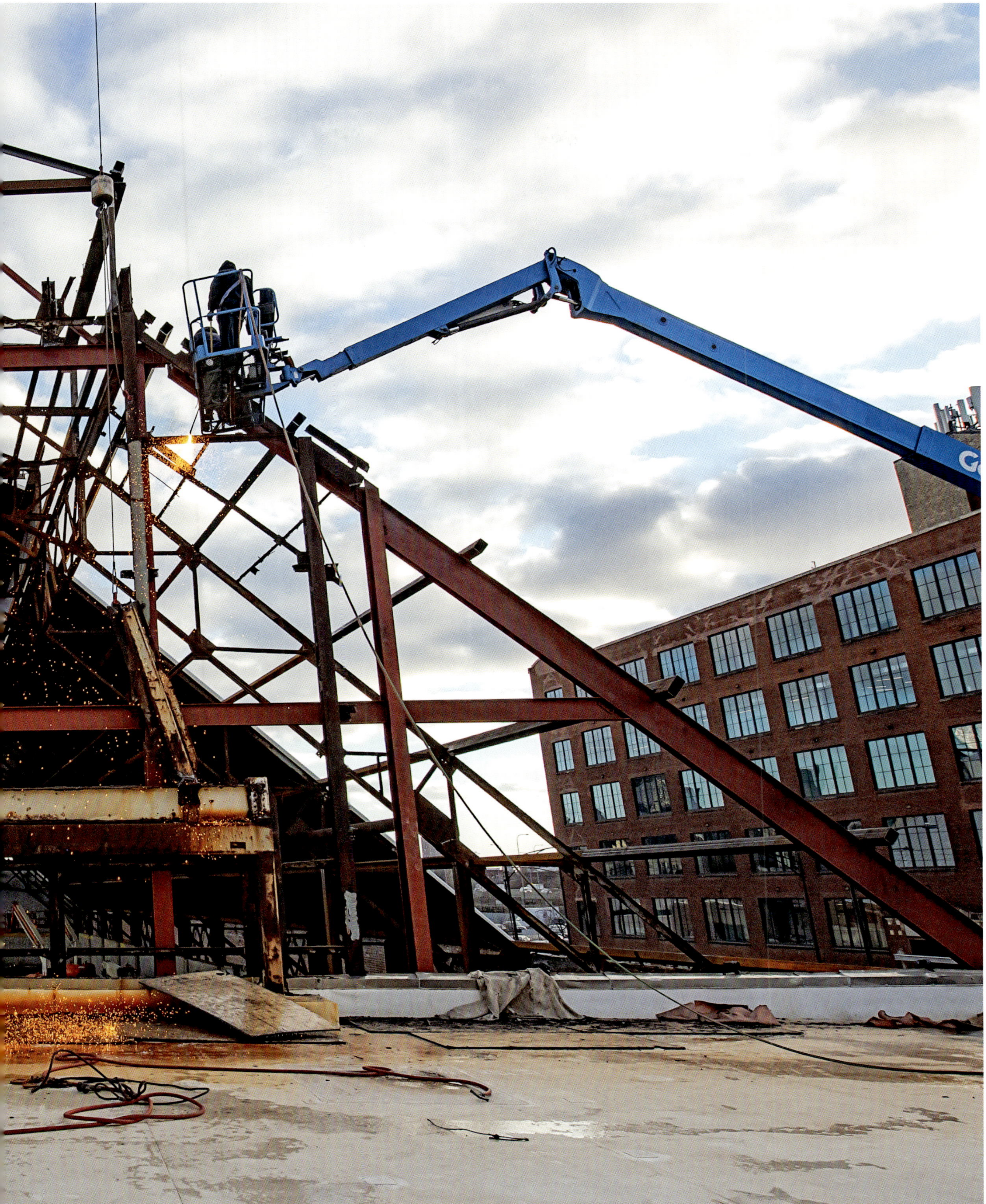

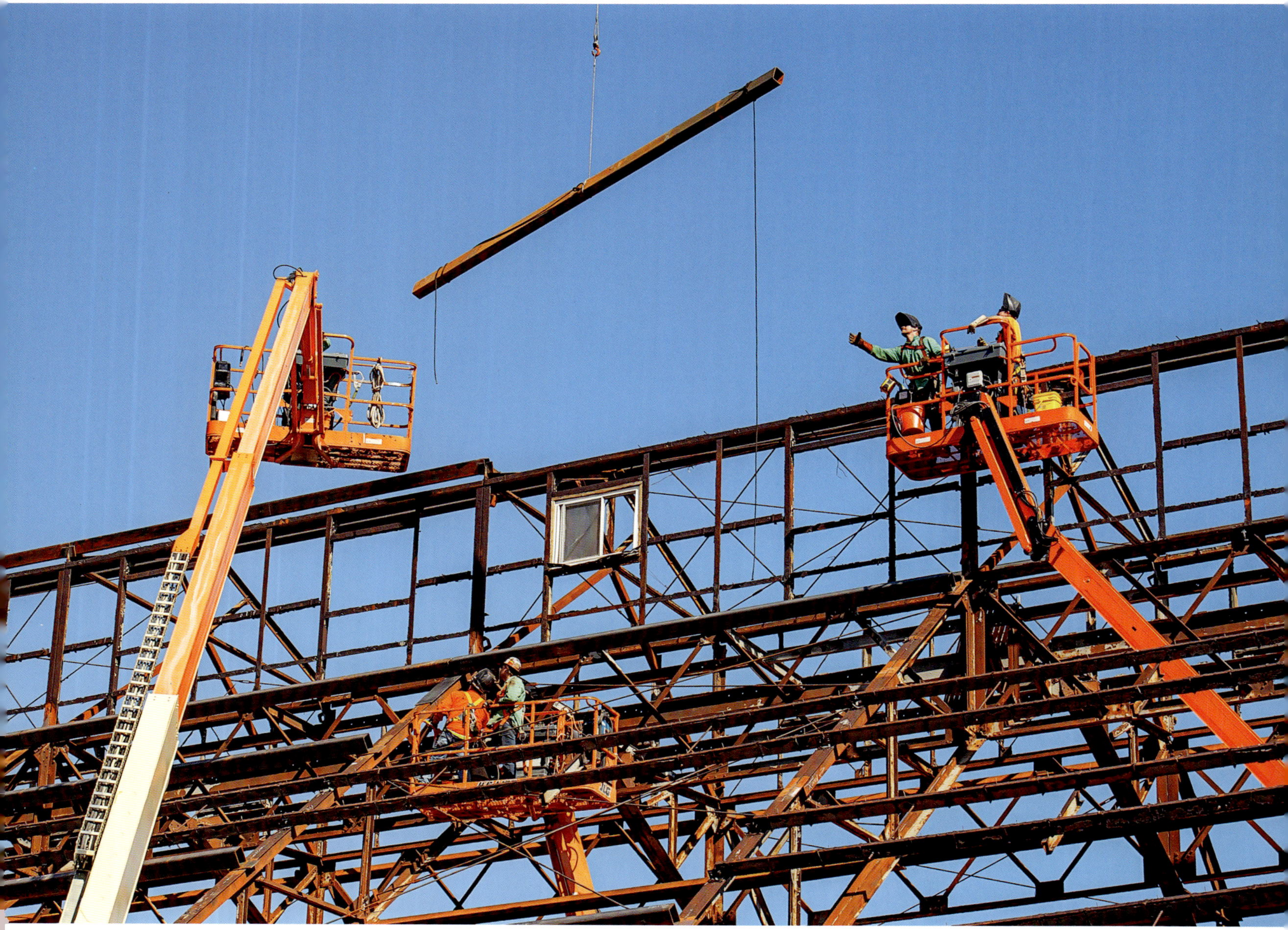

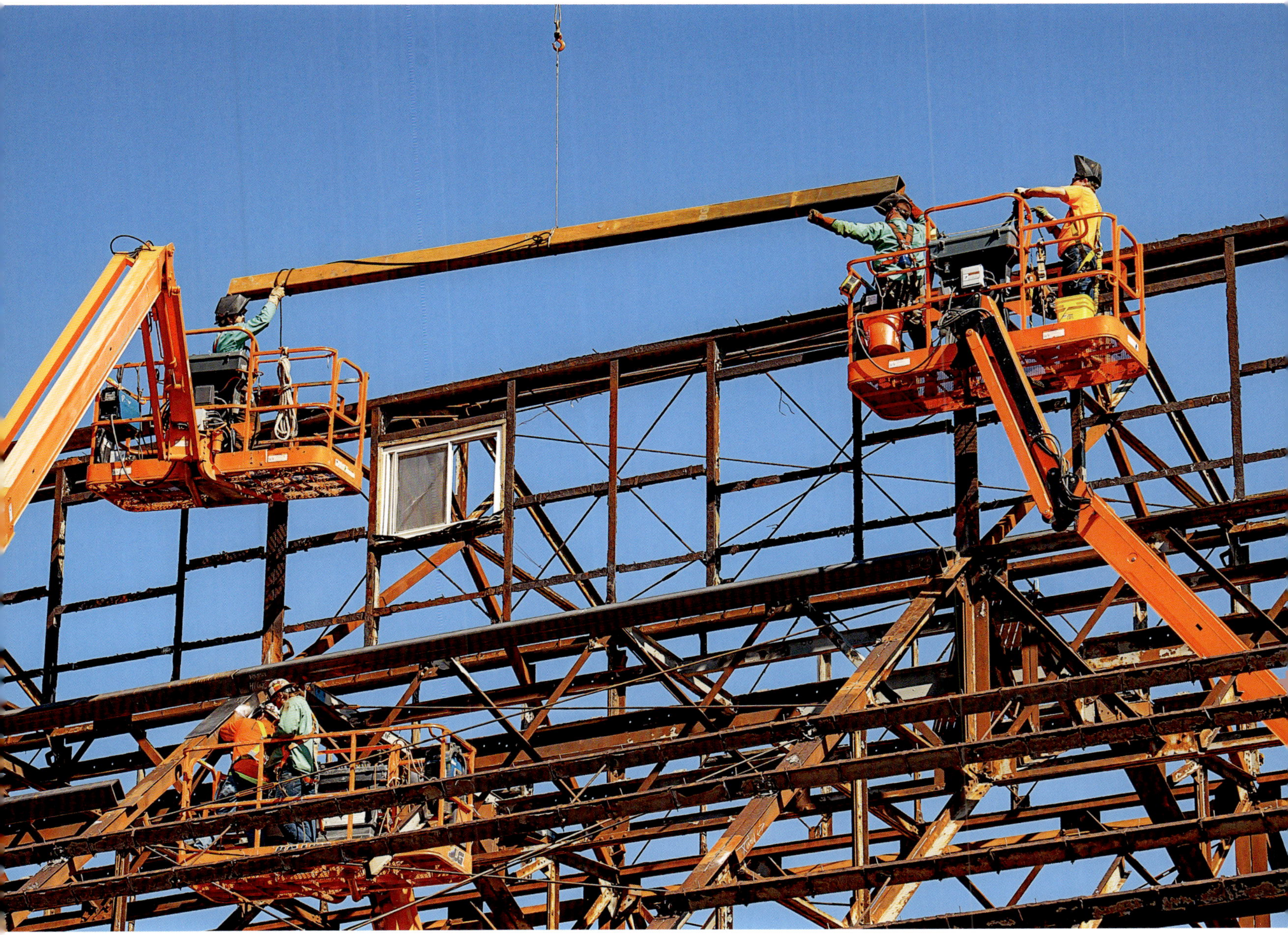

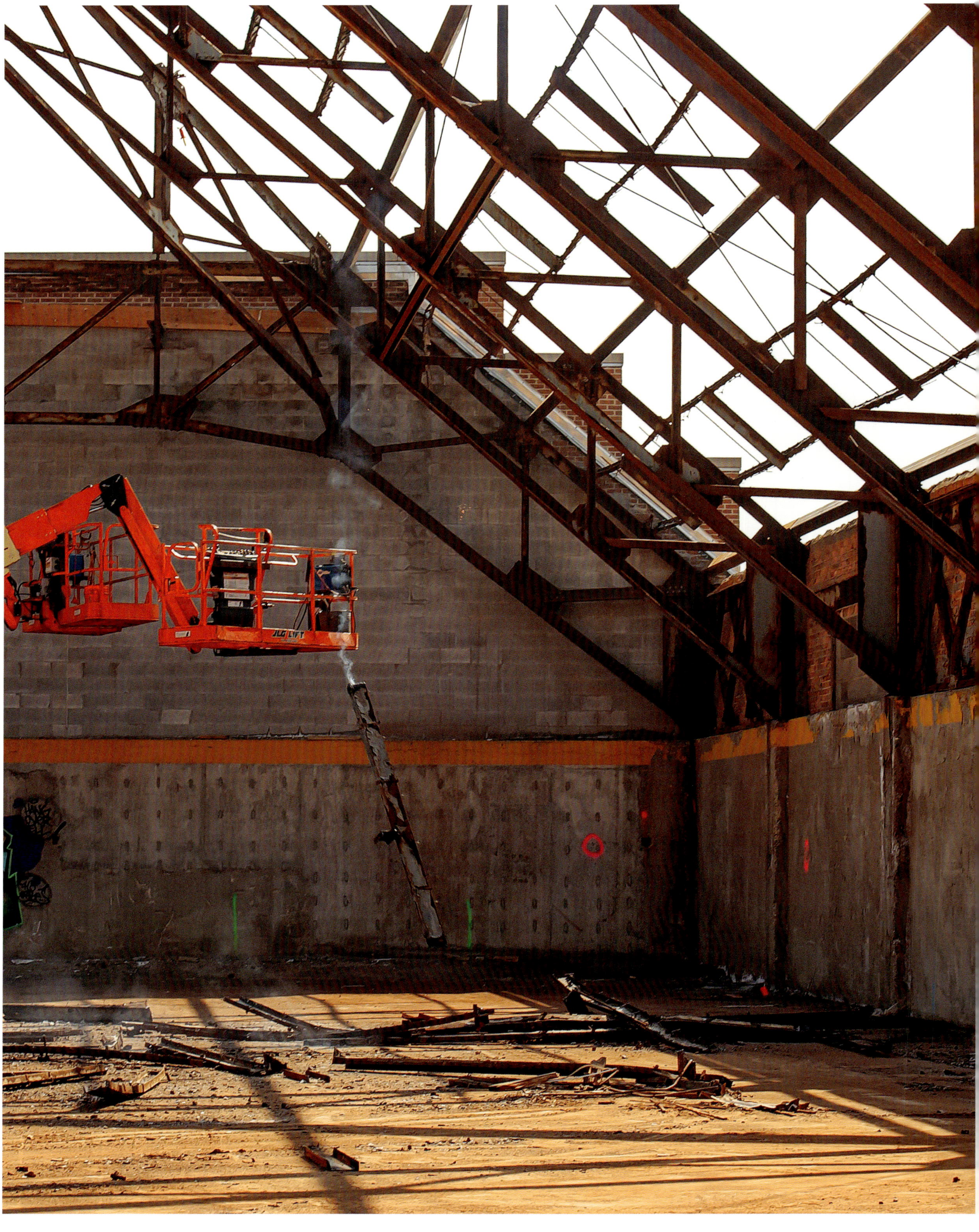
JLG LIFT

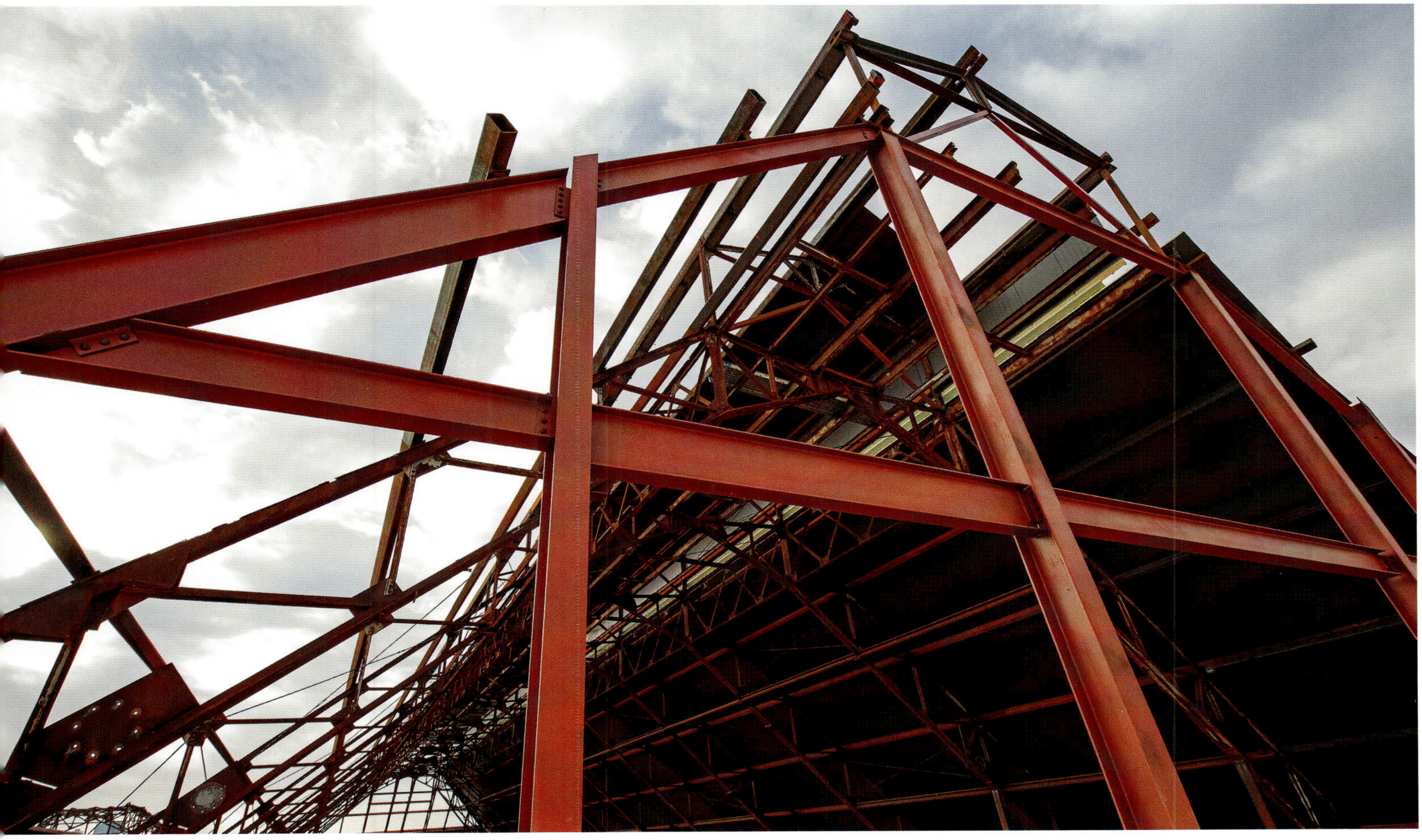

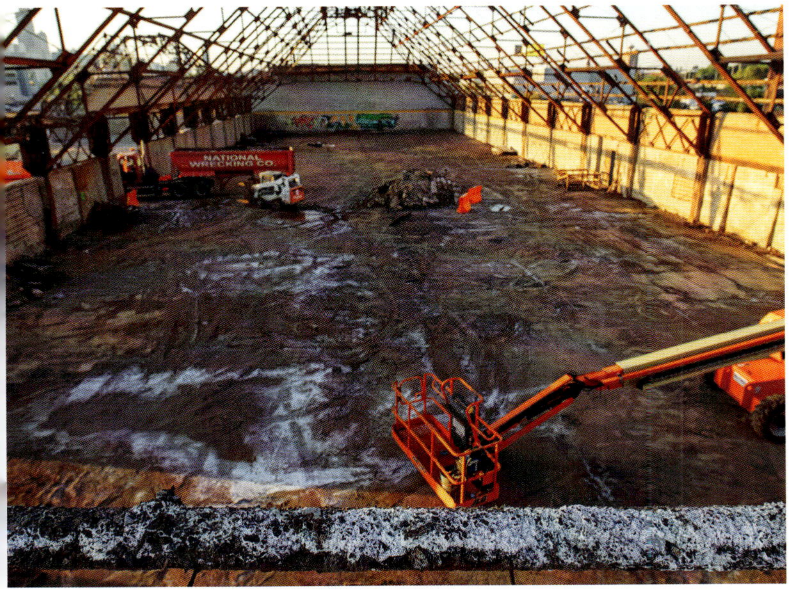
NATIONAL
WRECKING CO.

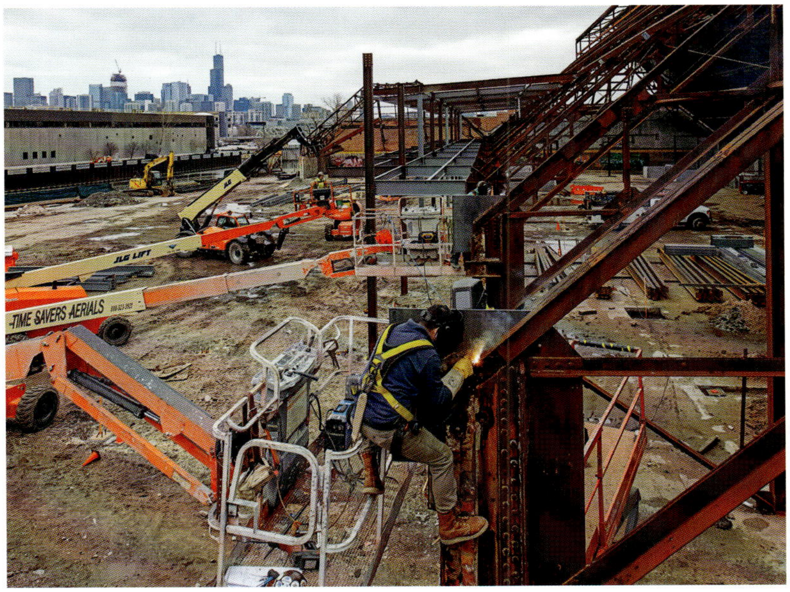
JLG LIFT
TIME SAVERS AERIALS

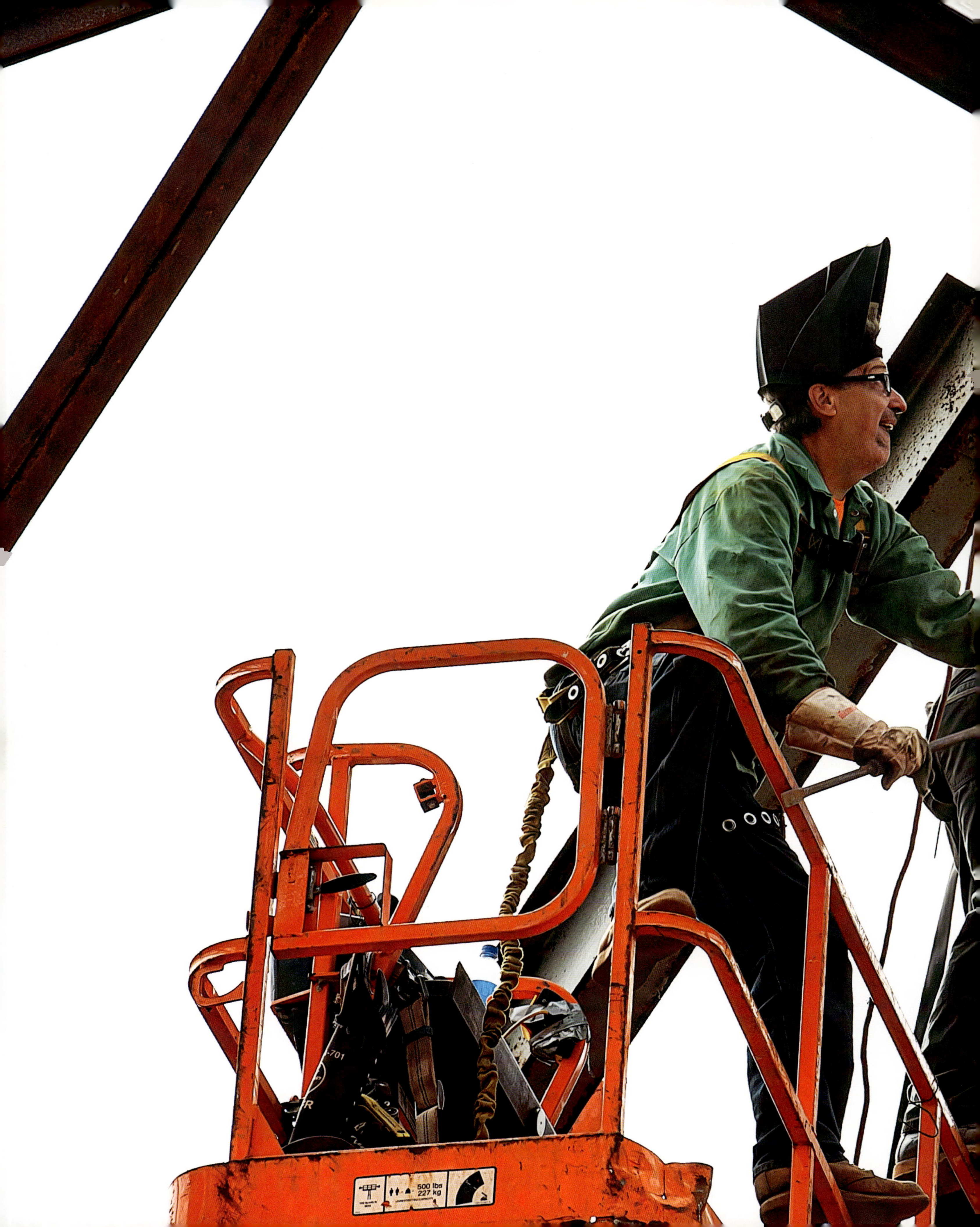
500 lbs
227 kg

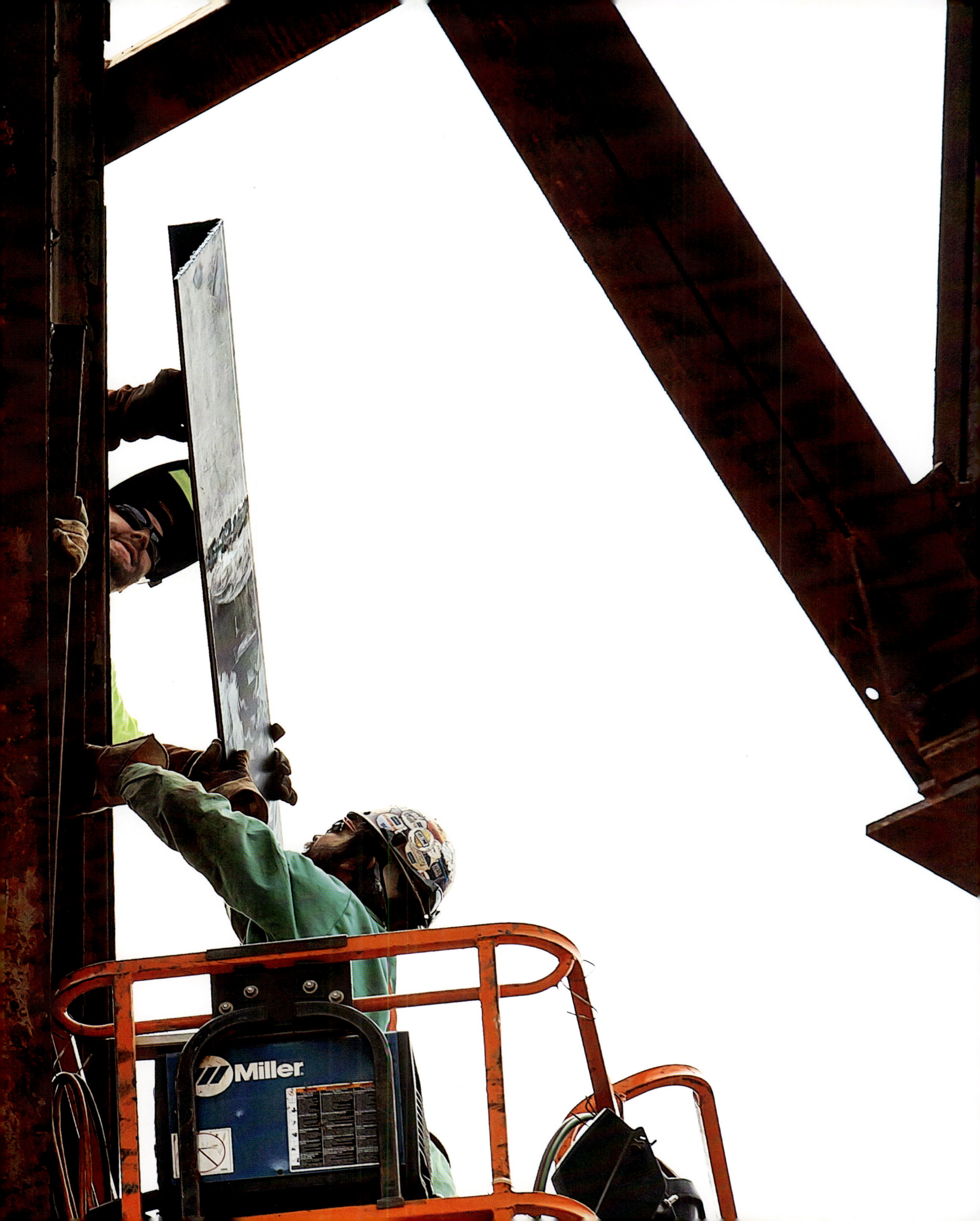
Miller

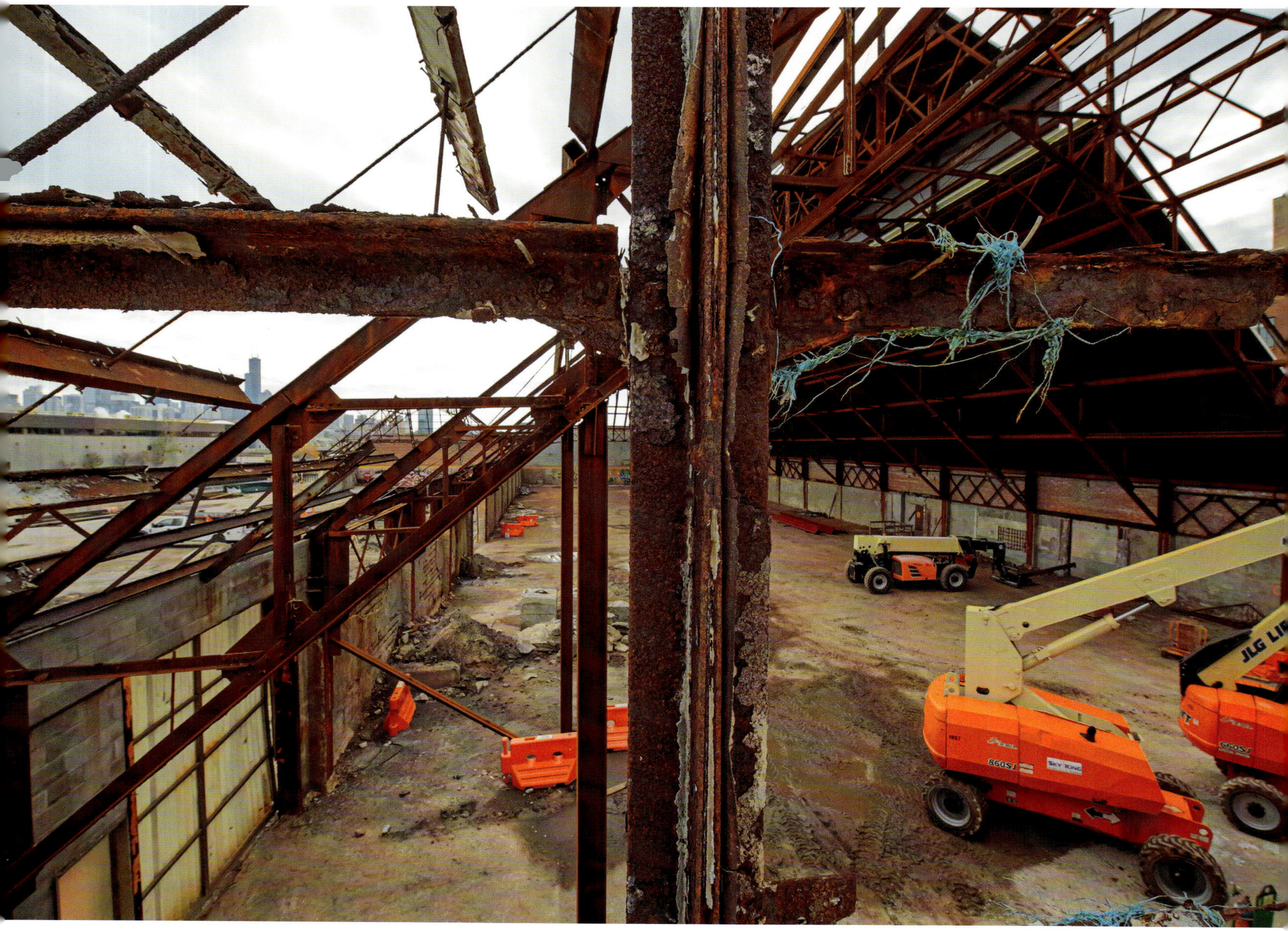

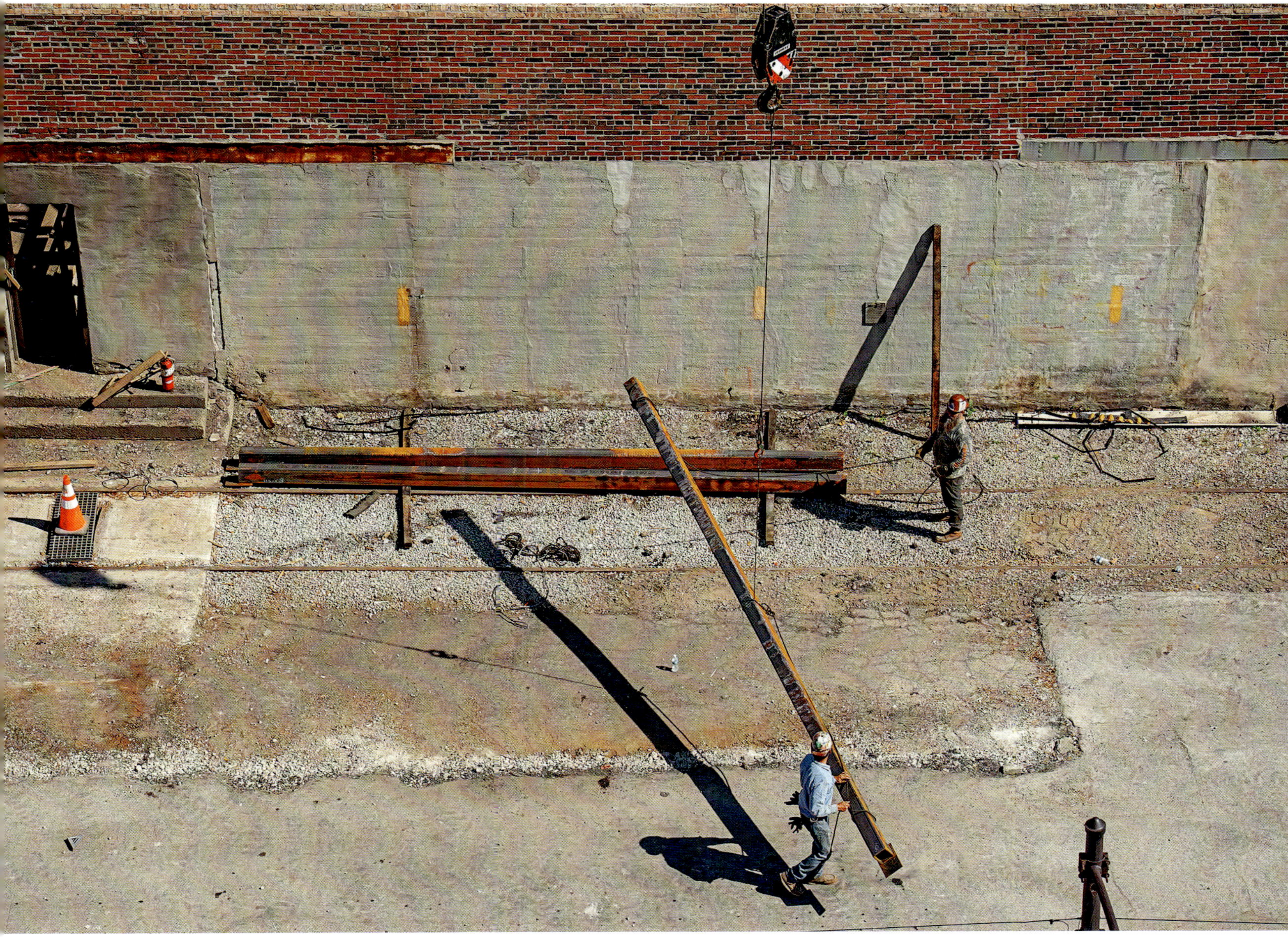

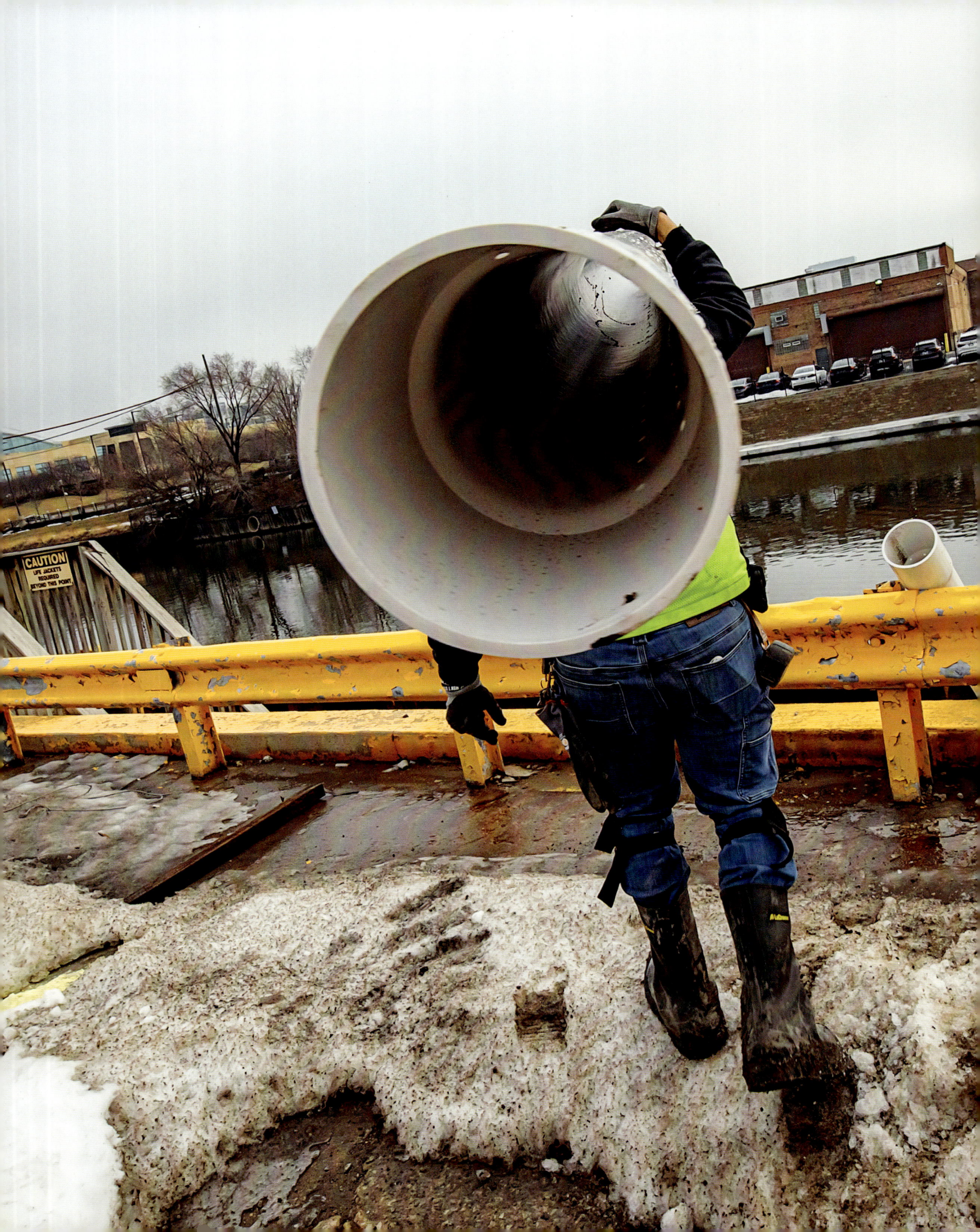
CAUTION
LIFE JACKETS
REQUIRED
BEYOND THIS POINT

Cities evolve and buildings are replaced, but to tear down entire urban fabrics is a theft from future generations. To keep them is to restore our sense of place.

What were these cathedrals of industry suited for, if not places of mass assembly? The structure that gave the Salt Shed's interior its character was compromised by decades of exposure to salt, requiring reconstruction to support the roof panels—not unlike the vaults of a cathedral that serve an ornamental but not a structural purpose.

When one of these structures is demolished, you lose not only the embodied energy of the materials and construction, but their history and character are then gone forever. The loss of this building would have erased a familiar landmark, as well as the memory of the work that was undertaken there and in the surrounding environs.

~ Aric Lasher, architect + retired president and director of design for HBRA Architects

Nº 3 WINTER

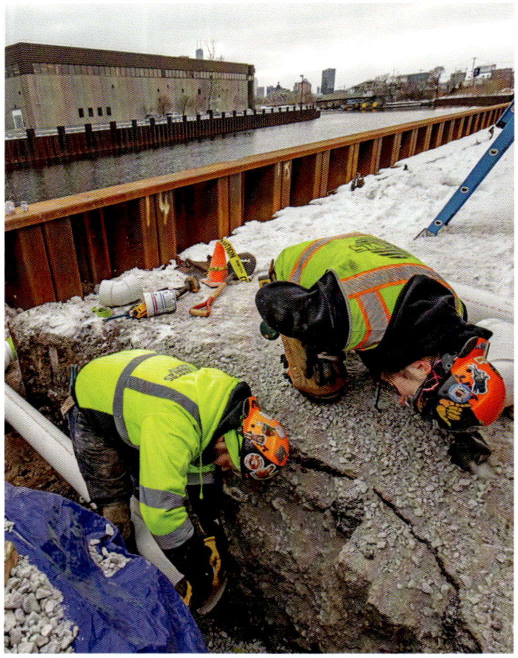

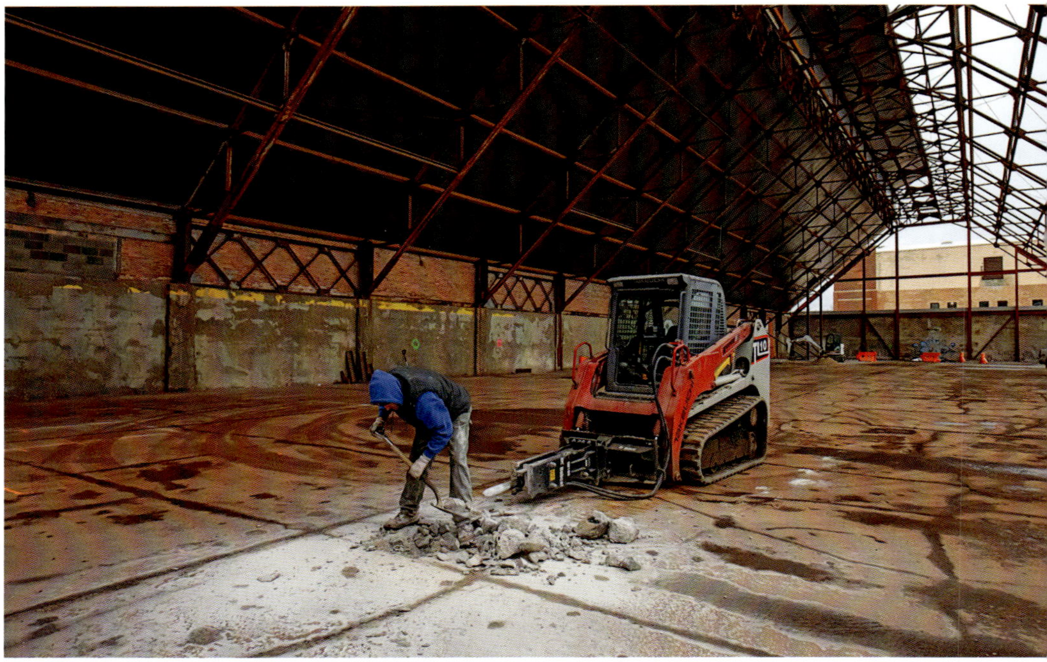

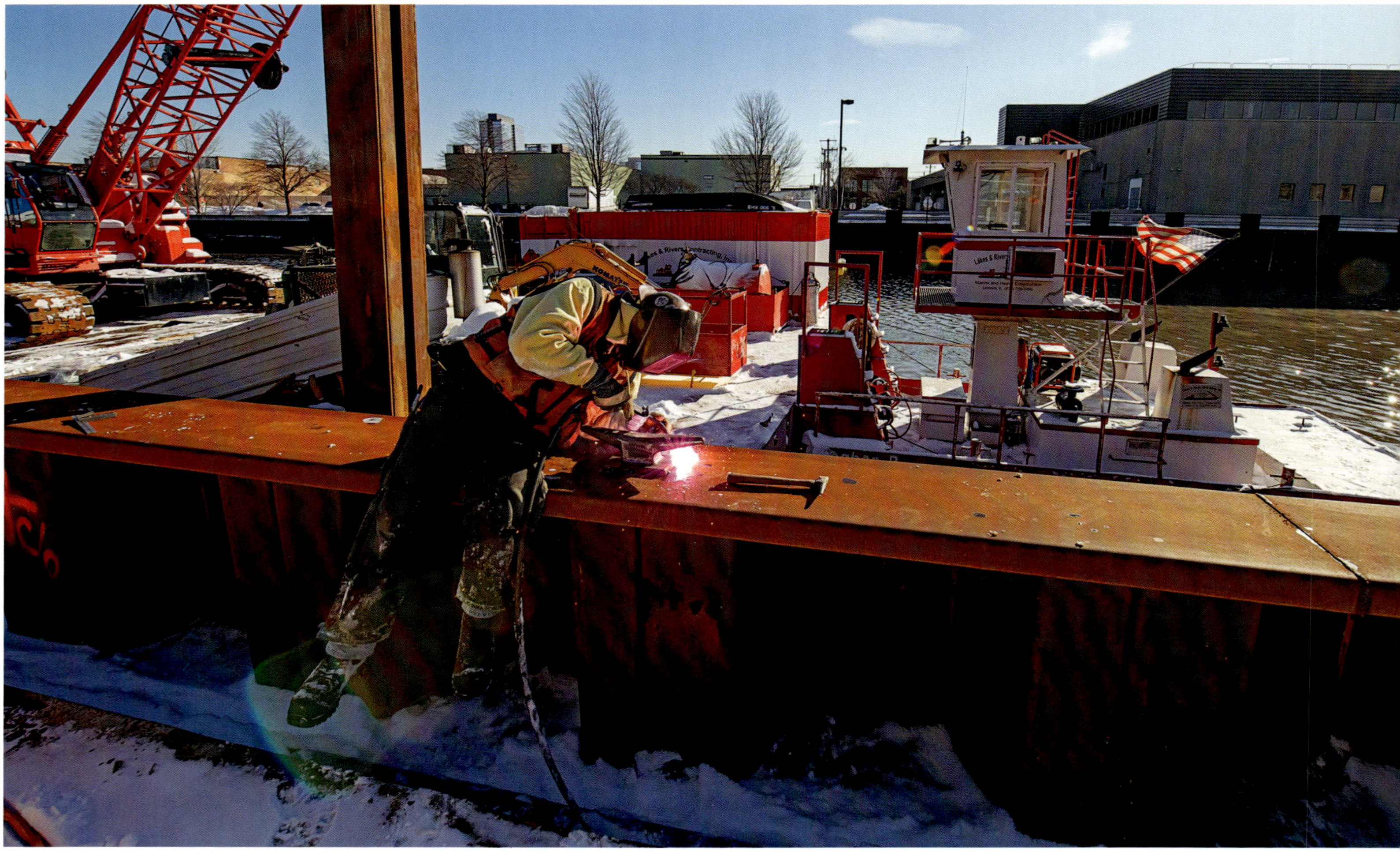

Winter

A Year-Round Renovation

On a cold January day, excavation for the stage and back of house area began inside the shed, with one man, one shovel, and one compact digger.

Winter had arrived. It became clear that the work wouldn't slow down because of the season. There were deadlines for opening the new music venue spaces, both inside the shed and out on the grounds. I continued to photograph. If workers were out there, I was out there.

As the focal point and crucial area of the performing arts venue, the Salt Shed stage was designed for the south end of the shed, facing the packaging building to the north. It took several weeks on the coldest days of the year to excavate and build the complex forms for the stage area and the back of house foundations, walls and elevator pit. Work on the south end continued all winter with multiple concrete pours, and on other spaces that had been mapped out on the shed floor for excavation and construction. At the opposite end, ironworkers and carpenters reinforced and then rebuilt the north shed wall, which had also undergone considerable corrosion from exposure to salt.

Along the river, the plumbing crew worked on laying pipes out in the snow. In late winter they began to dig tunnels in the shed floor, preparing to install indoor plumbing for the venue's bars and bathrooms. One snowy morning, a barge appeared on the river carrying welders to repair the steel cleats along the sea wall. The torch flames looked pink and blue in the frigid air. Electrical, concrete, carpentry and masonry work all continued, from the tunnels underground up to the tops of the bow trusses. Ironworkers spent more time finishing the restoration work on the east side of the shed to prepare for the installation of new panels that would finally complete the roof, later in the spring.

Winter mornings were dark. It was demanding just to move around safely and stay warm while keeping up with the excavation and construction in the mud, snow, and cold. The workers faced greater challenges and dangers than I did, of course. But I kept my ears open and heard tips on layering and handwarmer packets and plastic grocery bags over shoes. As one of the ironworkers commented, it's not how many years you have left—it's how many winters.

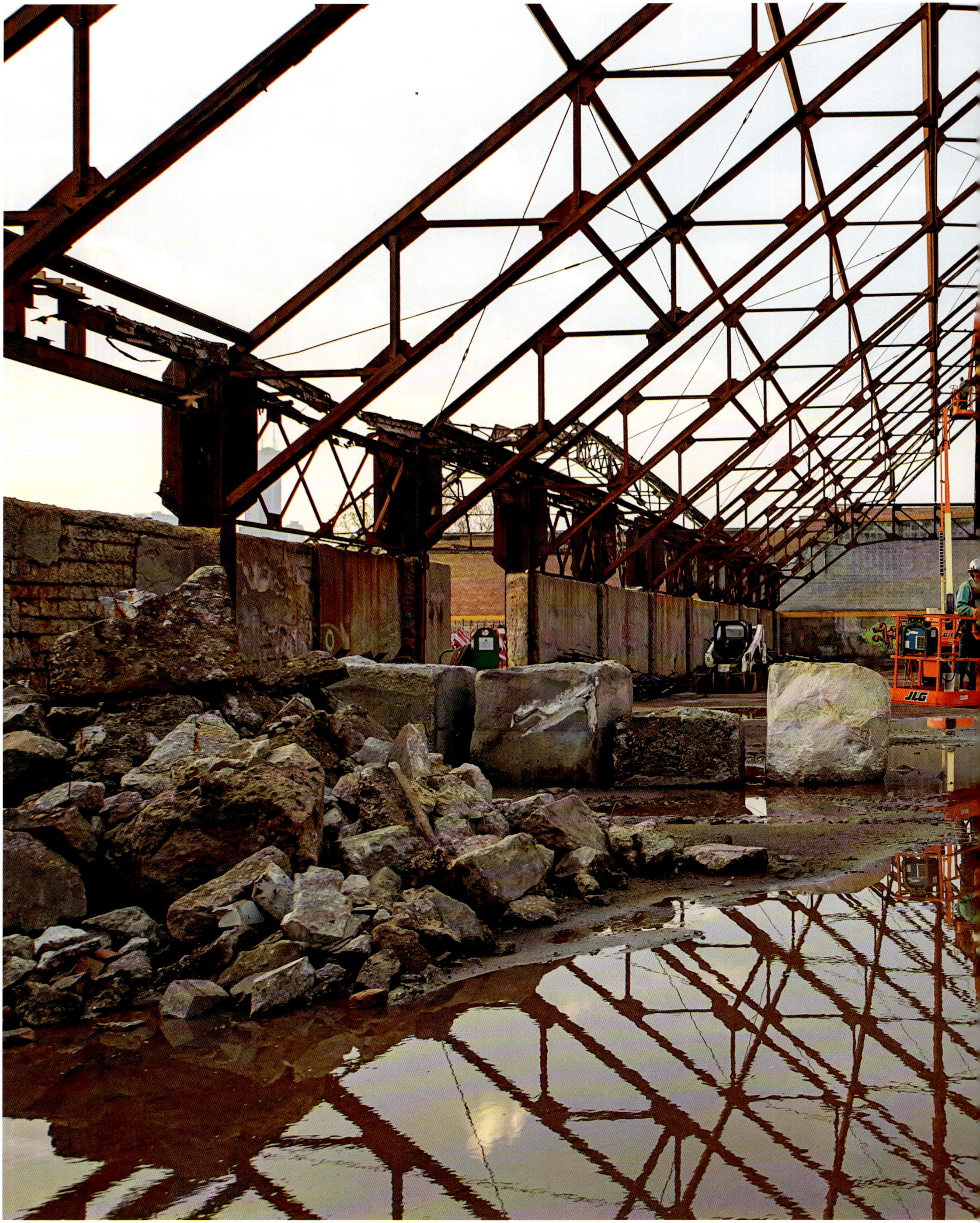

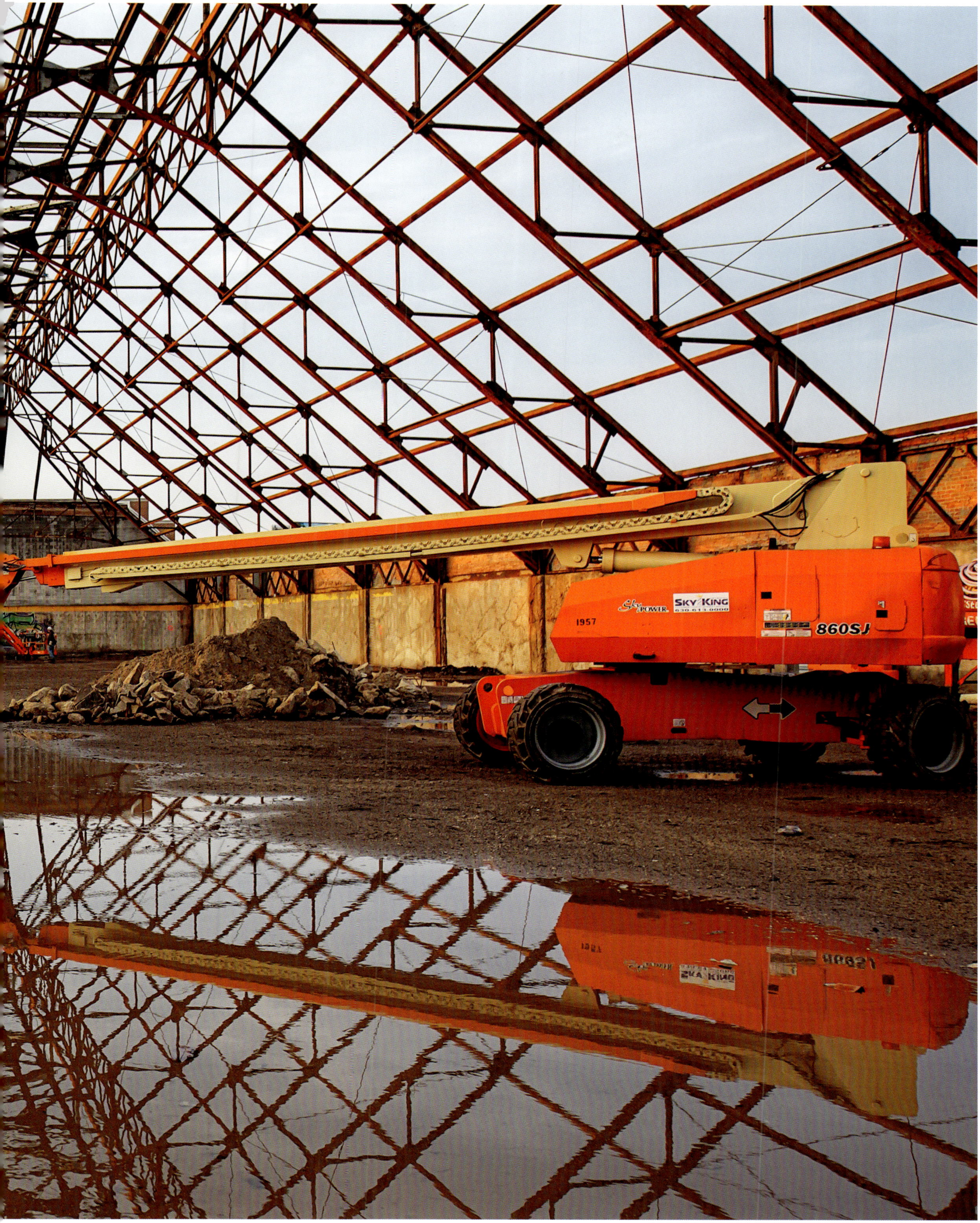
SKY KING
1957
860SJ

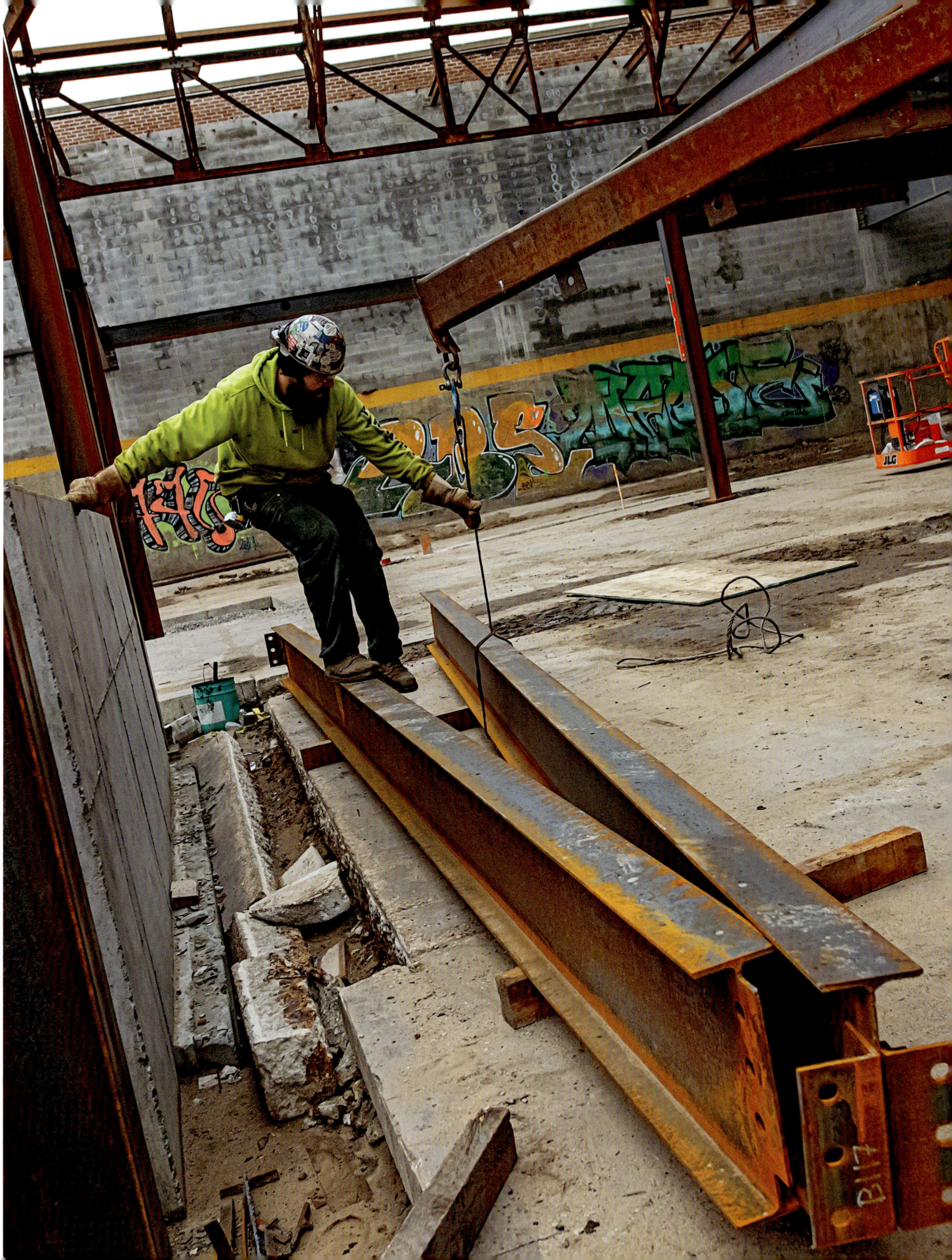
JLG
B117

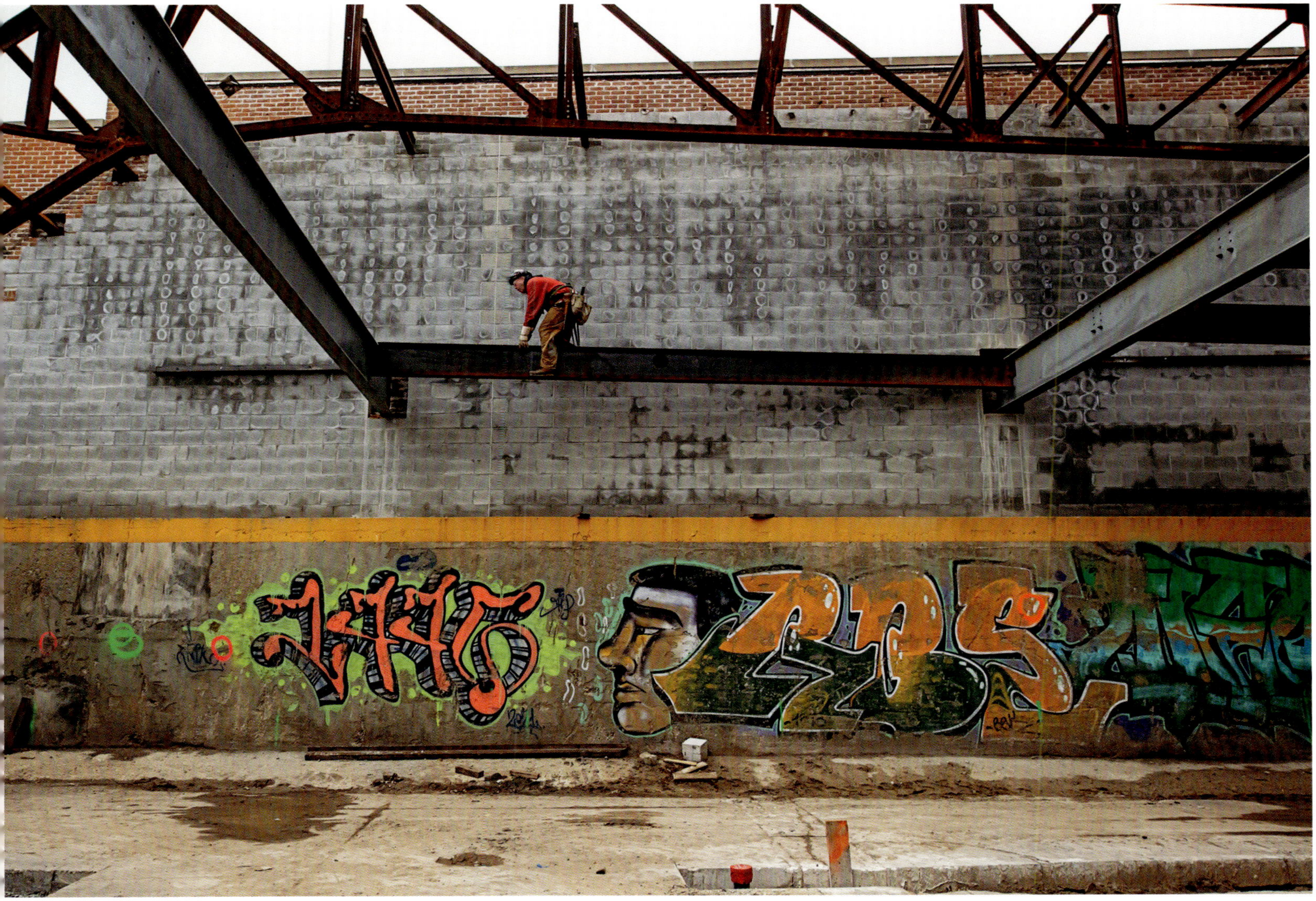

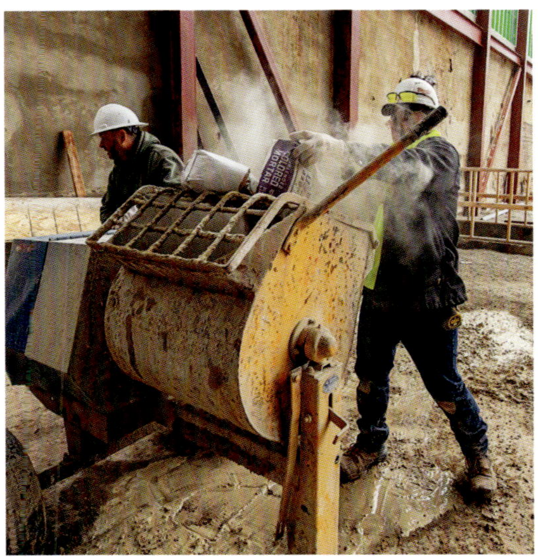

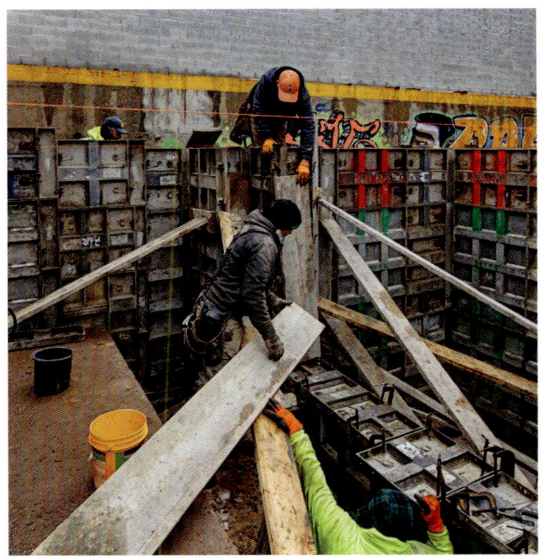

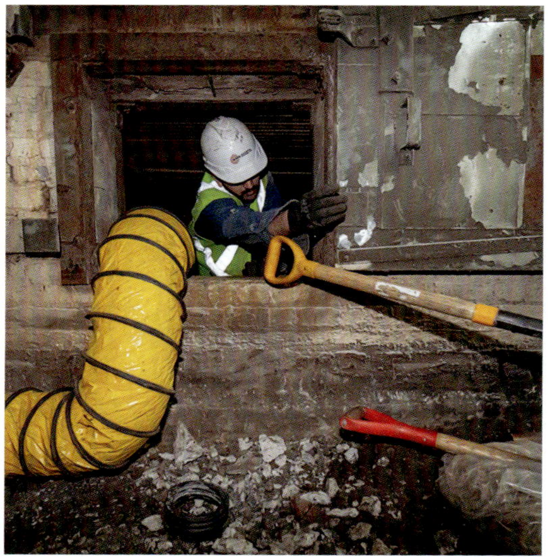

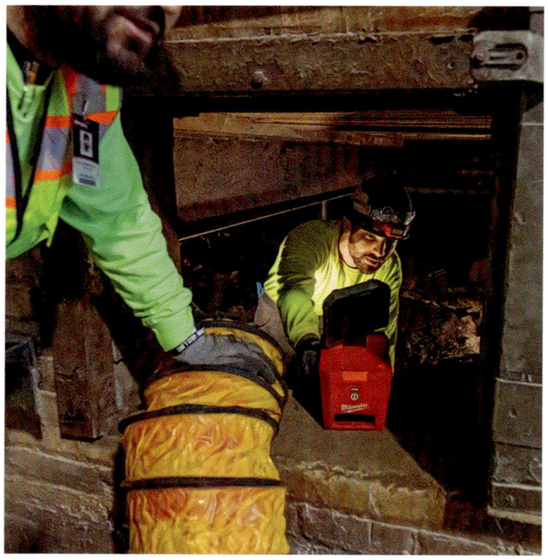

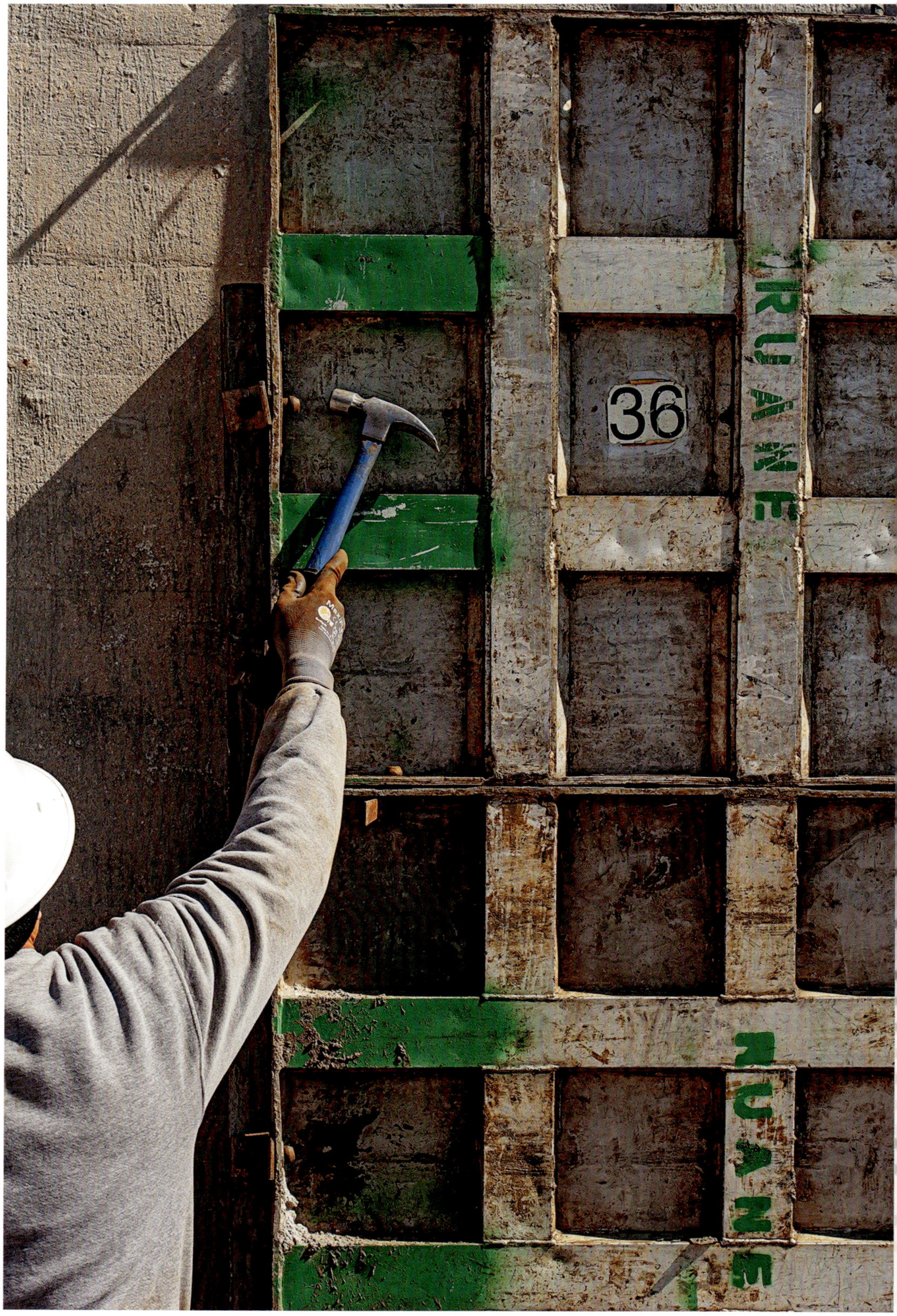
36

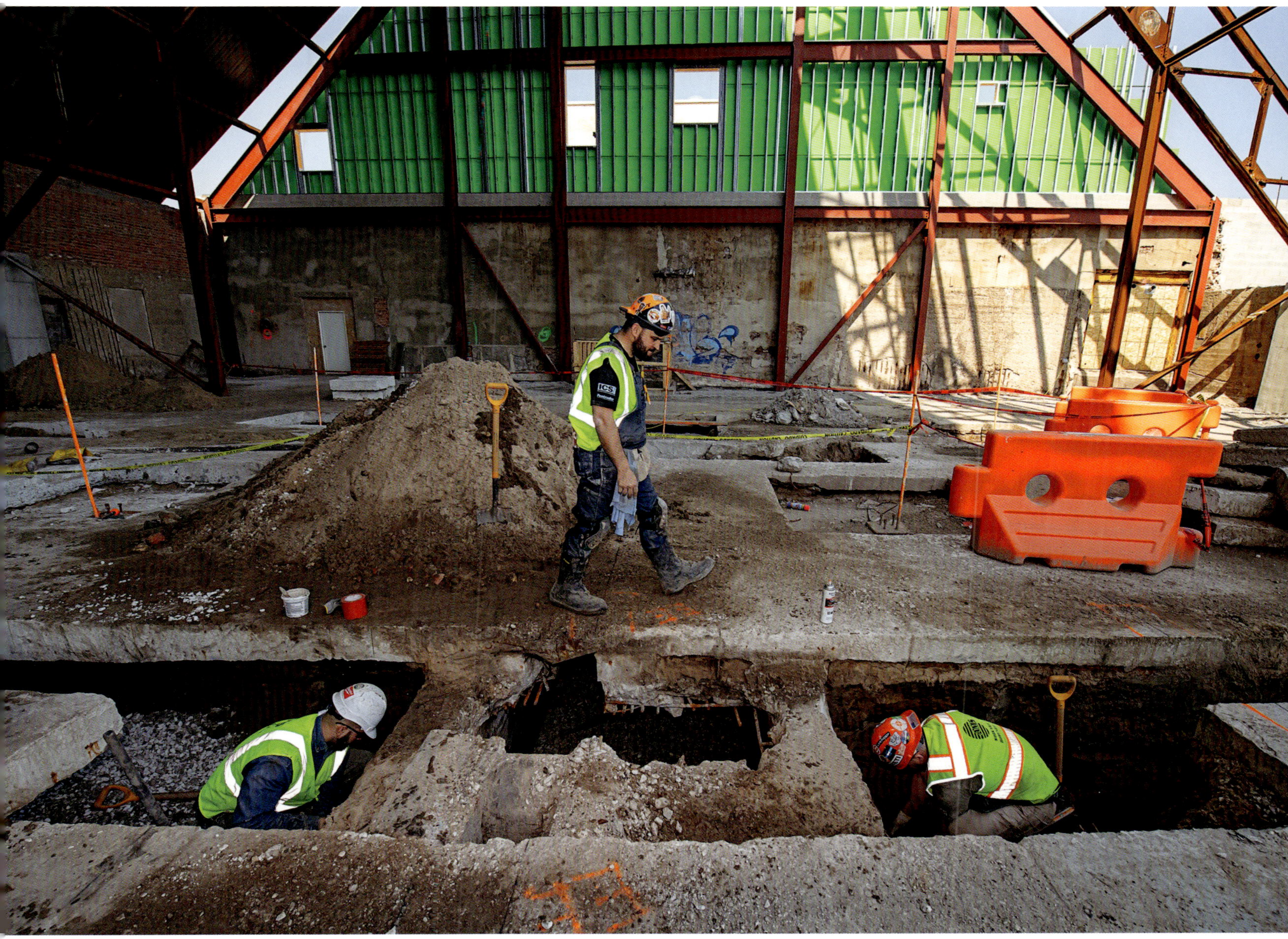

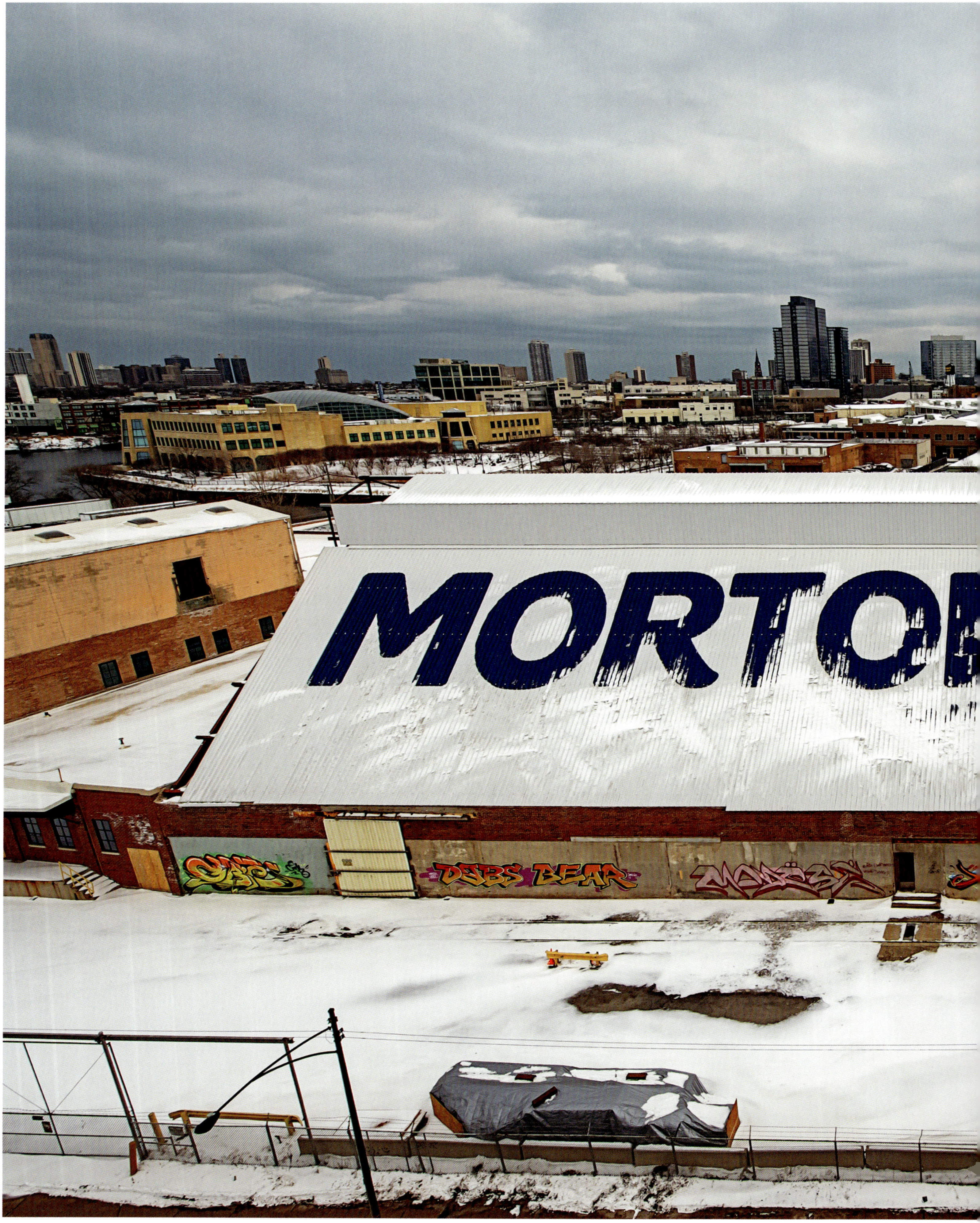

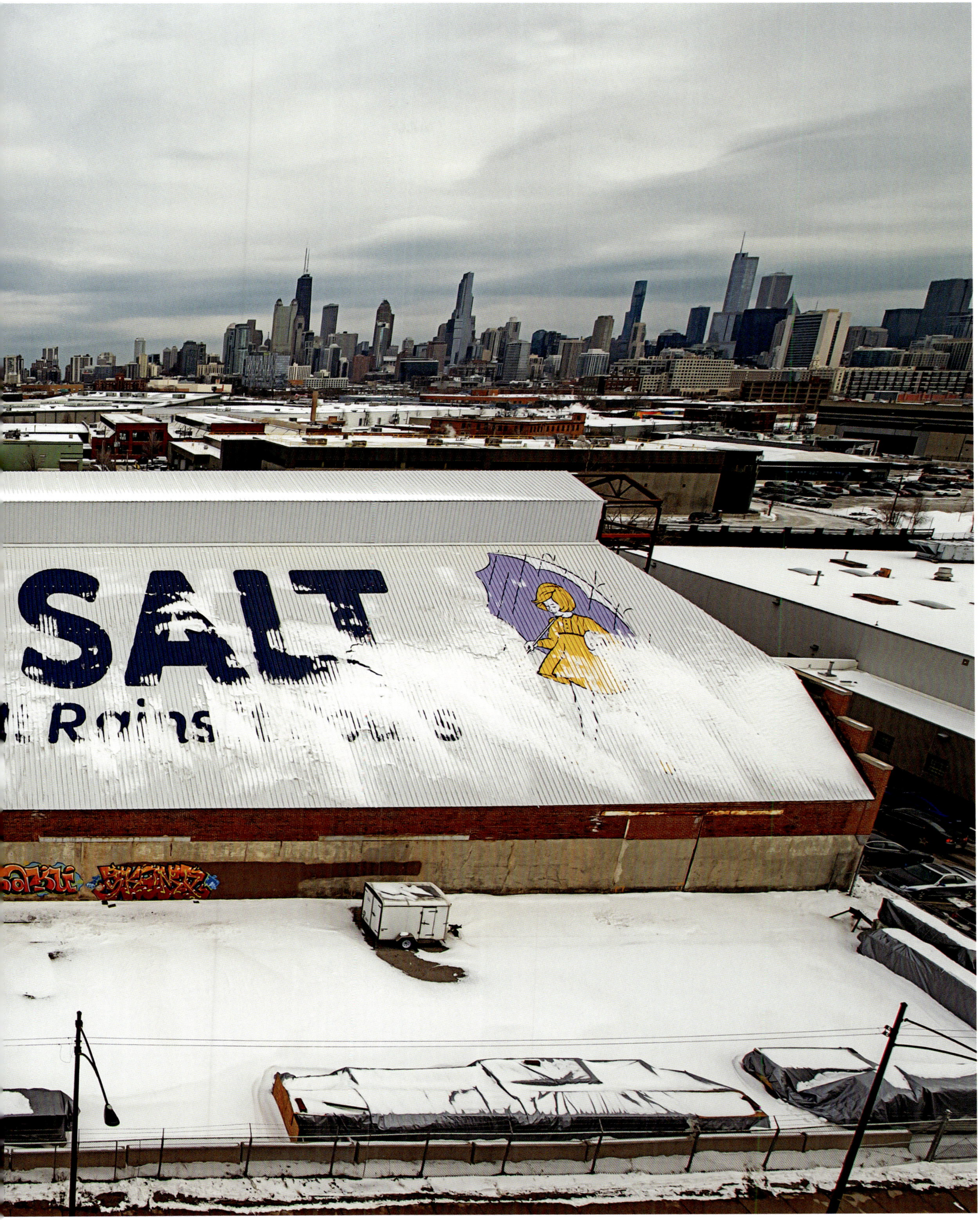
SALT

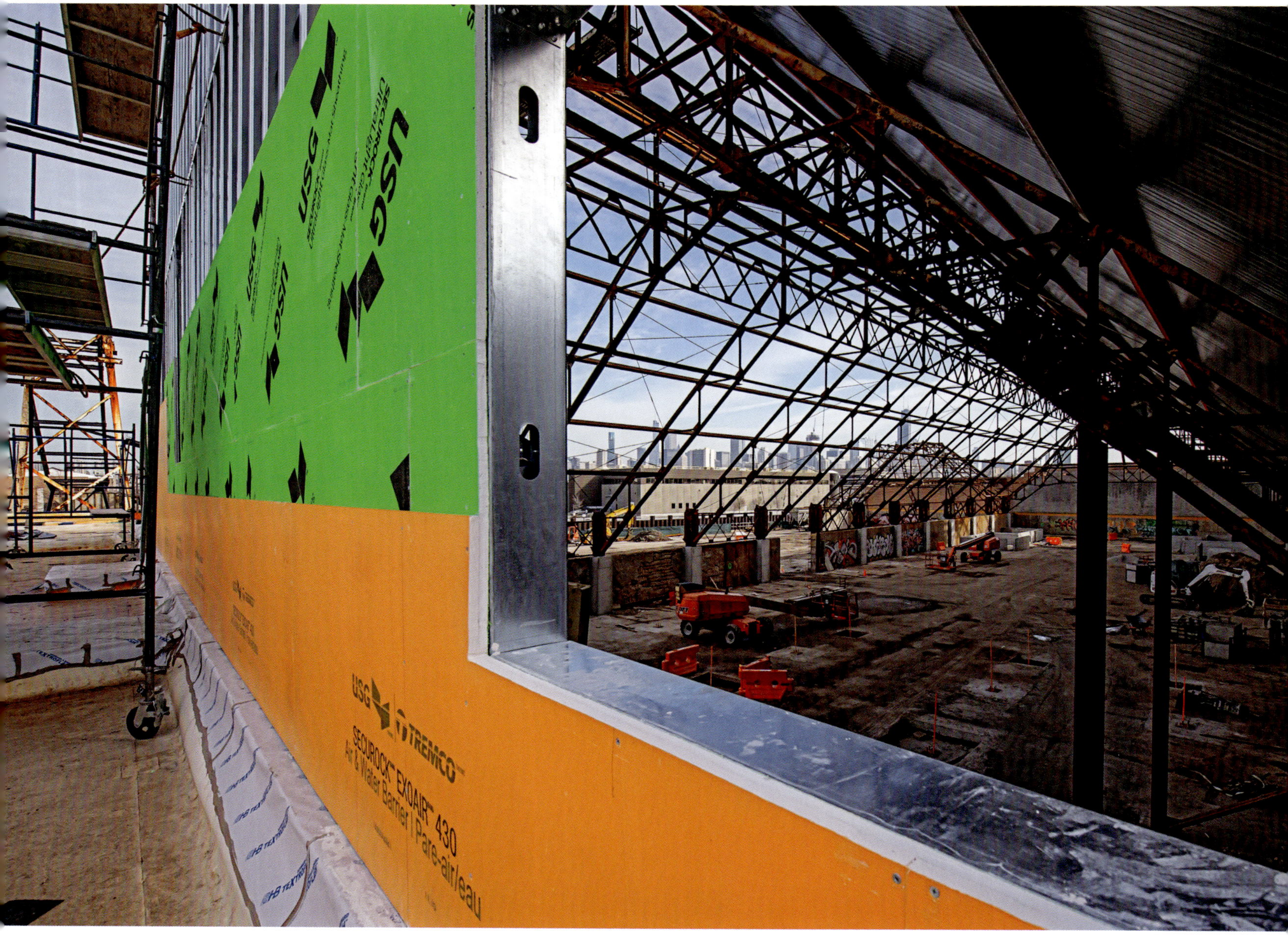
USG
TREMCO
SECUROCK EXOAIR 430
Air & Water Barrier | Pare-air/eau

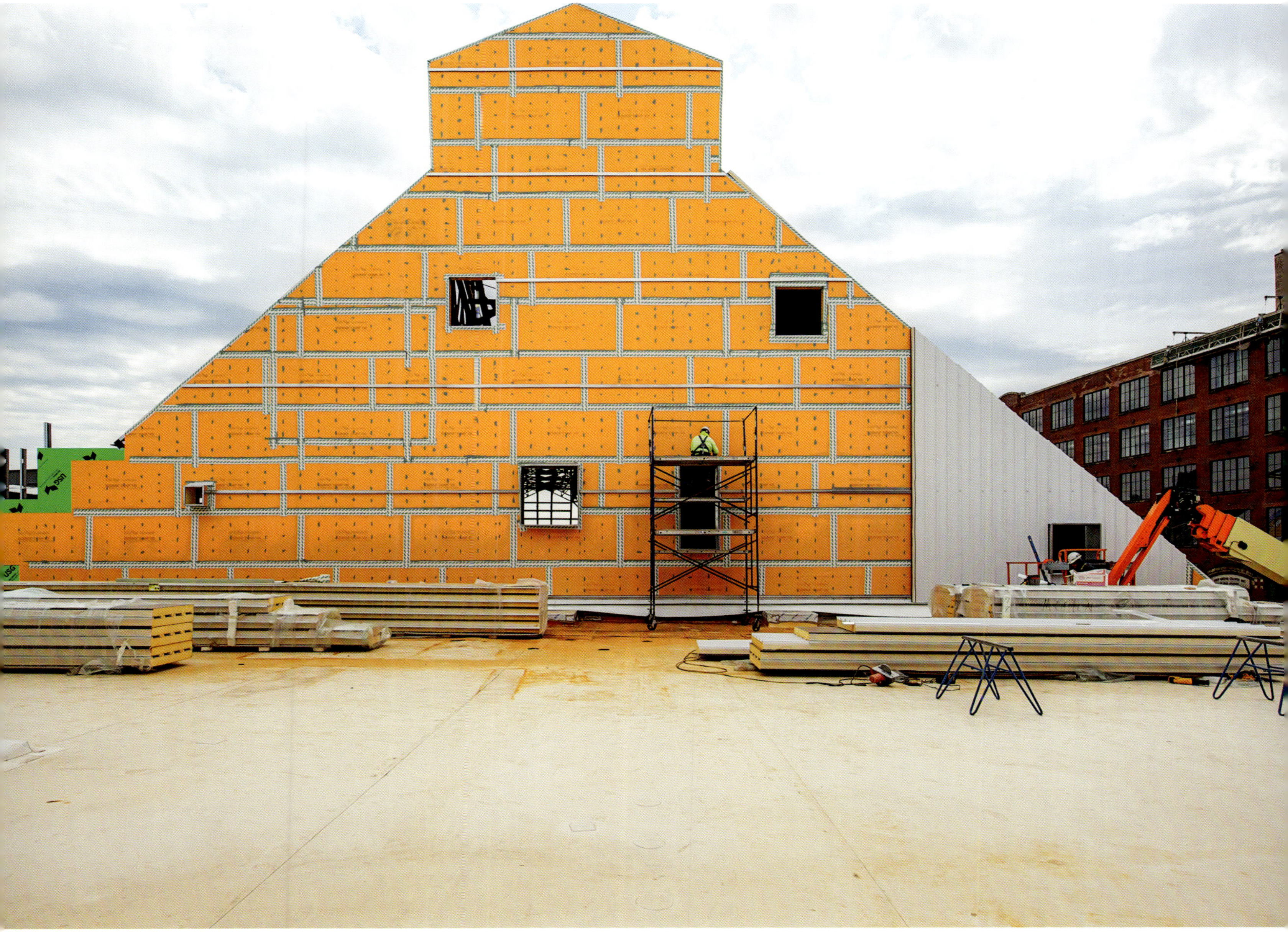

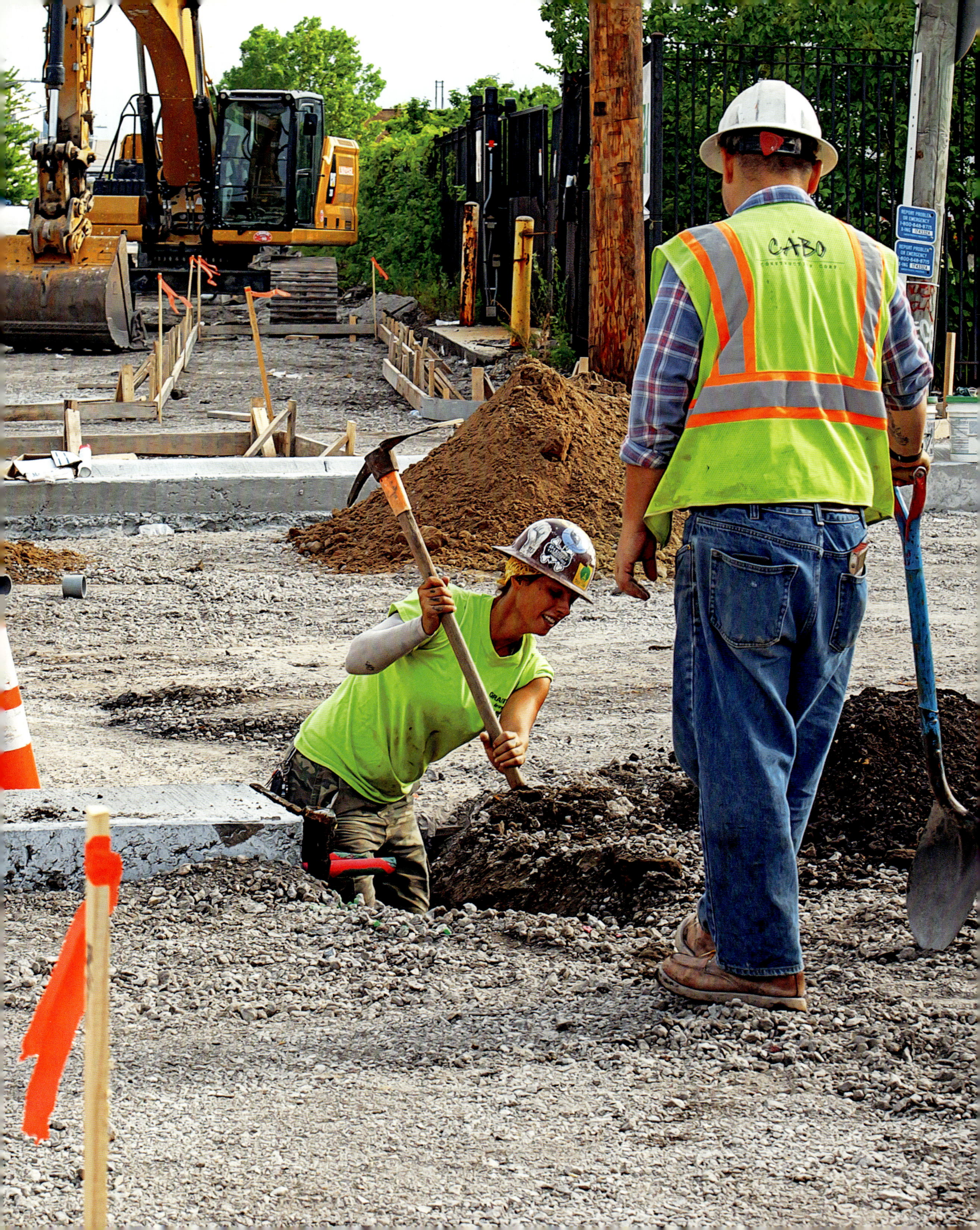
CABO

I remember thinking about the people who filled the salt bags and what their workday might have been like. There was a chute in one of the packaging buildings and you could imagine someone filling a salt bag and sewing it shut and then sending it out. Reflecting on the daily activity and the feeling of being in an environment filled with salt, walking through there, with all the natural light, which may have been a luxury back then. It seemed important to visualize what it would've been like to work there at the time.

~ Sarah Hitchcock, principal, Lamar Johnson Collaborative

Nº 4
PEOPLE

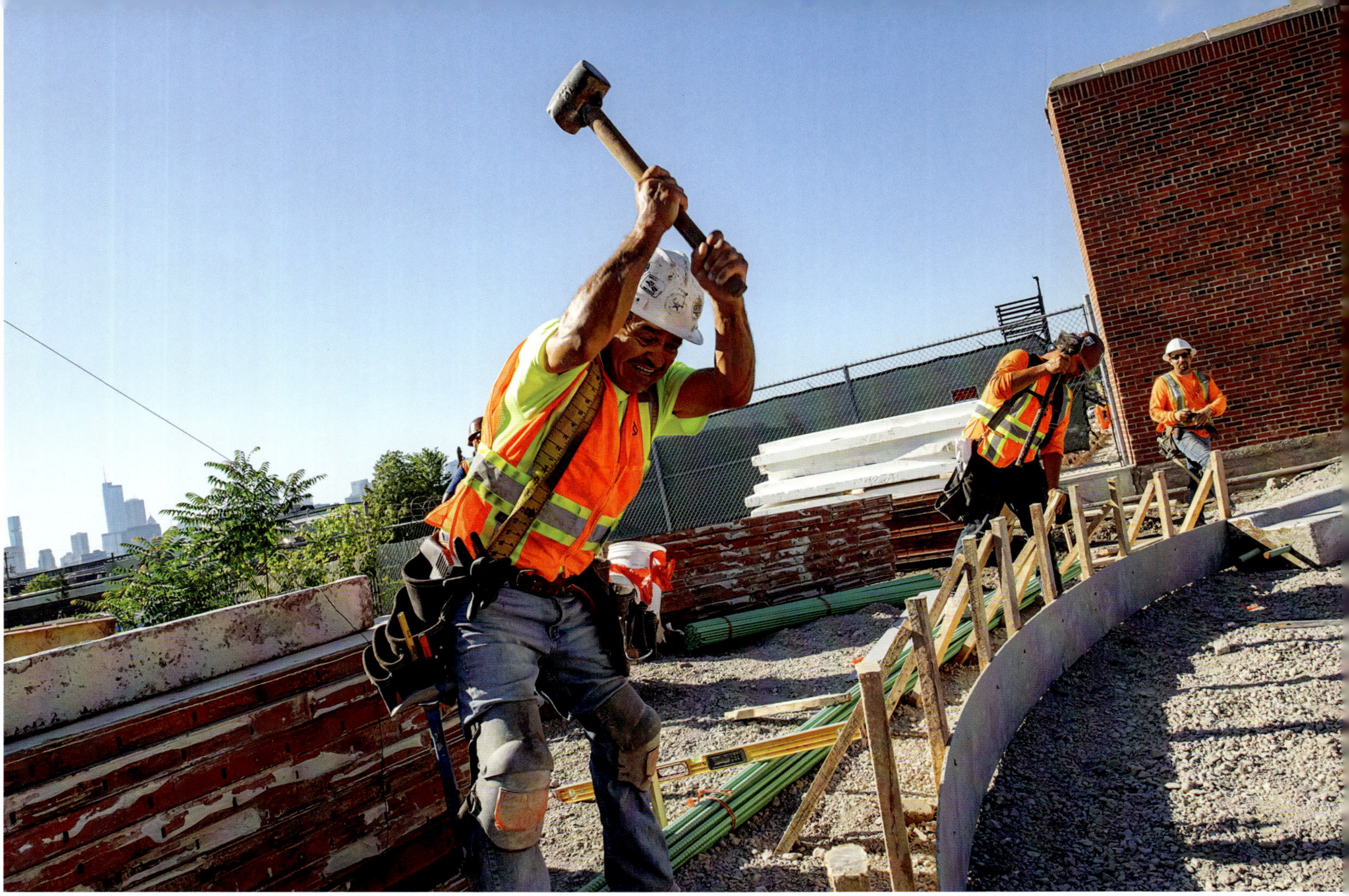

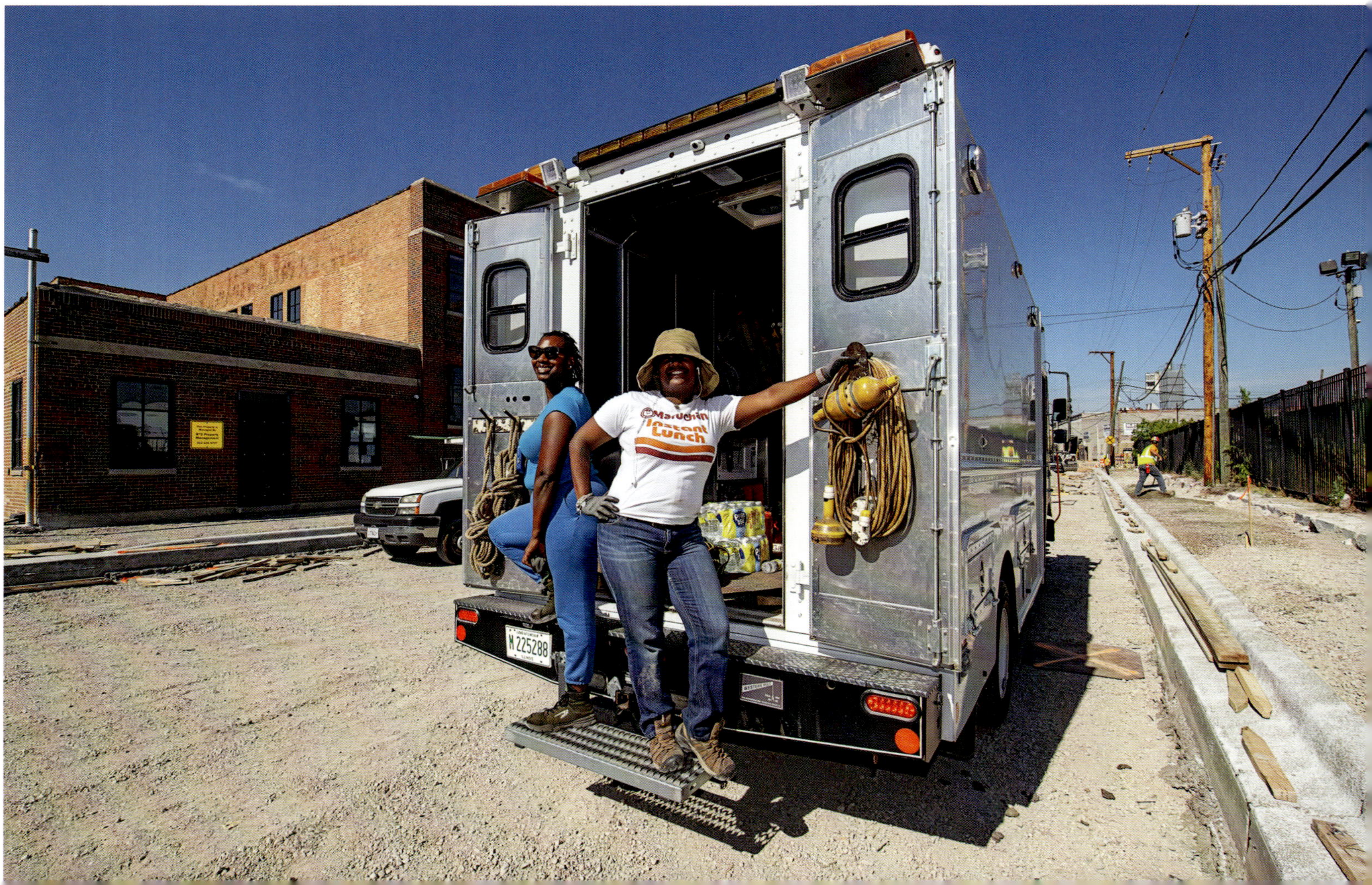
Maruchan
Instant Lunch

People

The Human Touch is Everywhere

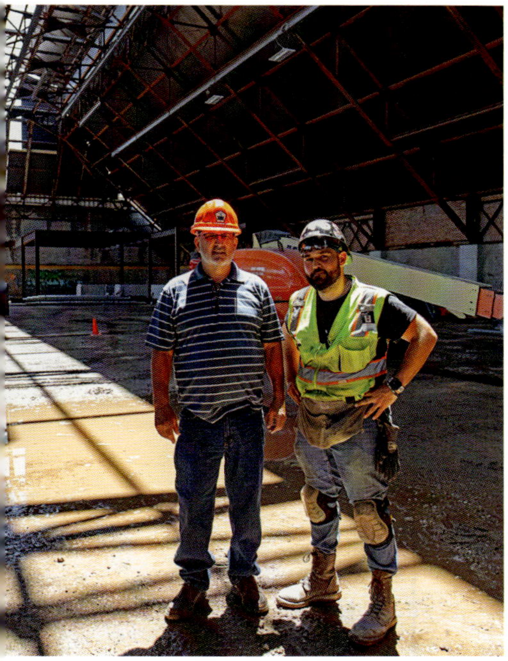

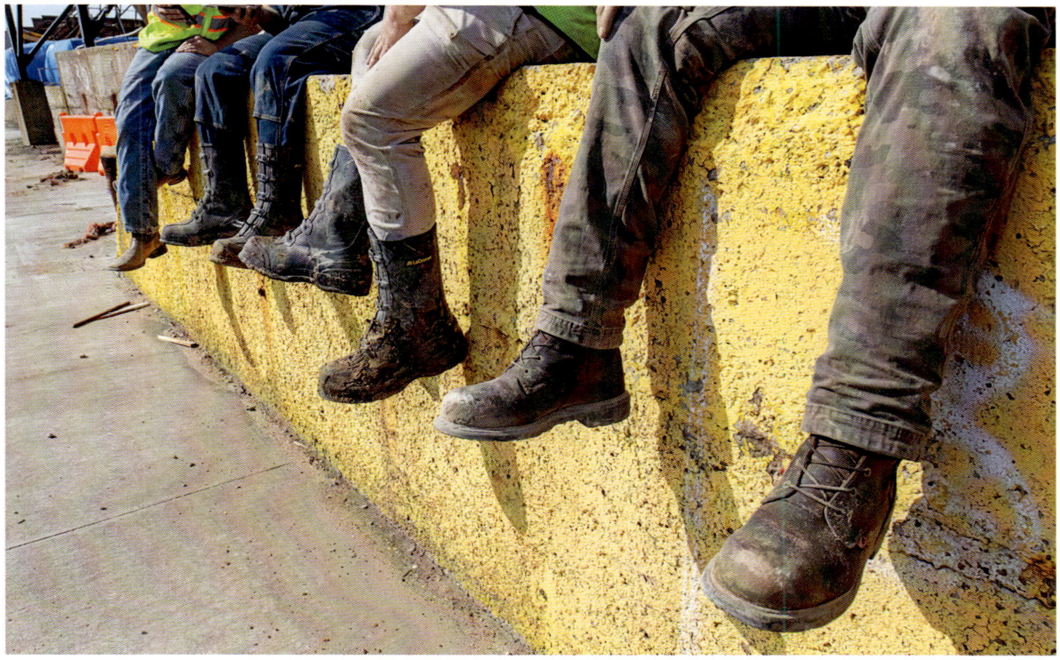

Despite the use of modern machinery and technology, a great many phases of constructing buildings, roads, and bridges are still done by hand, often using old-fashioned techniques and time-tested approaches. The human touch is everywhere.

Every day I observed attention to small details and an immense pride in craft. The jobs of tradespeople and manual laborers, it struck me, are often undervalued. They work in harsh weather conditions, doing the muddiest, grimiest jobs, with the constant presence of danger. Yet once the project is done, most of us don't know what went on behind the scenes or notice the skills and care that went into those tasks.

A small utility company excavated eight feet below ground on Elston Avenue to bring water service to the site, while contending with underground safety issues and maneuvering in dangerous traffic. Cement masons moved like dancers as they poured and leveled concrete and meticulously finished their work with hand trowels. Two Chicago artists painted the giant Morton Salt sign painstakingly by hand, with tiny brushes and narrow rollers. Plumbers laid pipes with precision, only to have them buried under loads of gravel and layers of concrete. When asked about their jobs, workers said over and over that it isn't as easy as it looks.

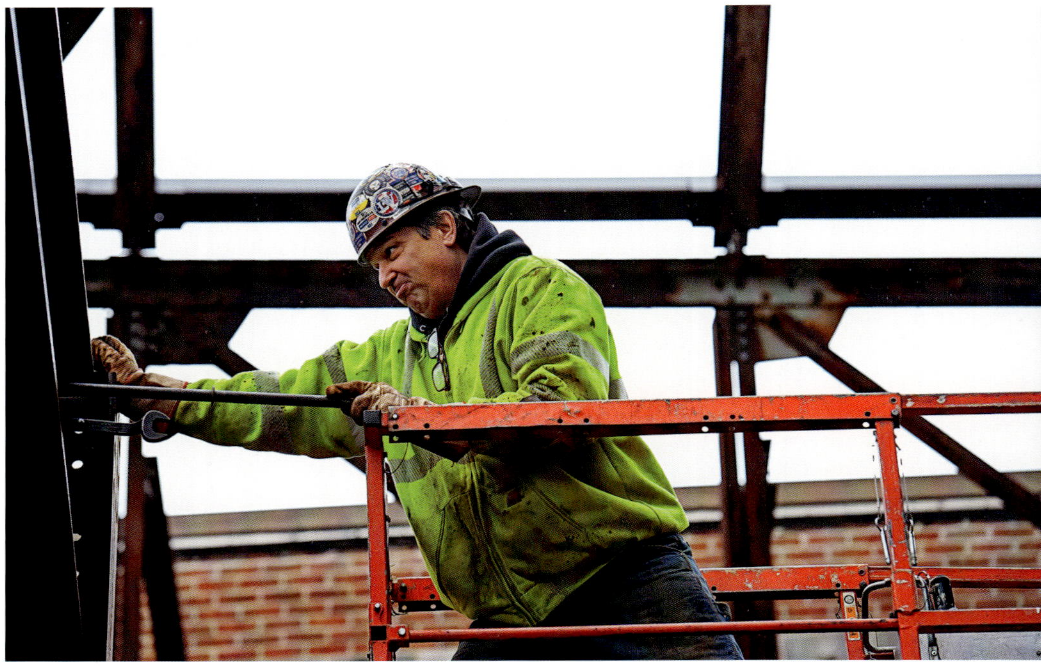

Many trades people get their start through the suggestion and encouragement of family members or friends, sometimes after feeling disengaged from school. One rare female laborer wielded a heavy pickaxe out on Blackhawk Street while skillfully navigating her place in the world of construction. A cement mason, smiling, remembered that his father had poured concrete at almost the same spot at the Morton site several decades before. Skills and solutions to tricky situations are passed along anecdotally. The plumbing foreman has daily chats with his father, a retired plumber, to solve problems or to go over the challenges and accomplishments of the job. Satisfaction, it seems, lies in building something by hand and creating what didn't exist before.

At break time, I'd walk the property. Workers would show me their lunches, made in homes rooted in cultures from around the world. Stories were told of family holiday traditions. One day, a note covered in colorful hand-drawn hearts and rainbows was pulled from a lunchbox. A sweet message from the pipefitter's ten-year-old daughter. A sheet metal worker came down from the roof panel installation to show off photos of the prized dahlias in his home garden. On a sunny day in early spring, I walked out to the river and found the plumbing crew sitting on the ledge, watching the seagulls dive and telling stories as they ate. With their muddy boots and dusty coveralls, they could have been workers from a hundred years ago, on break from unloading barges filled with salt.

People

The Human Touch is Everywhere

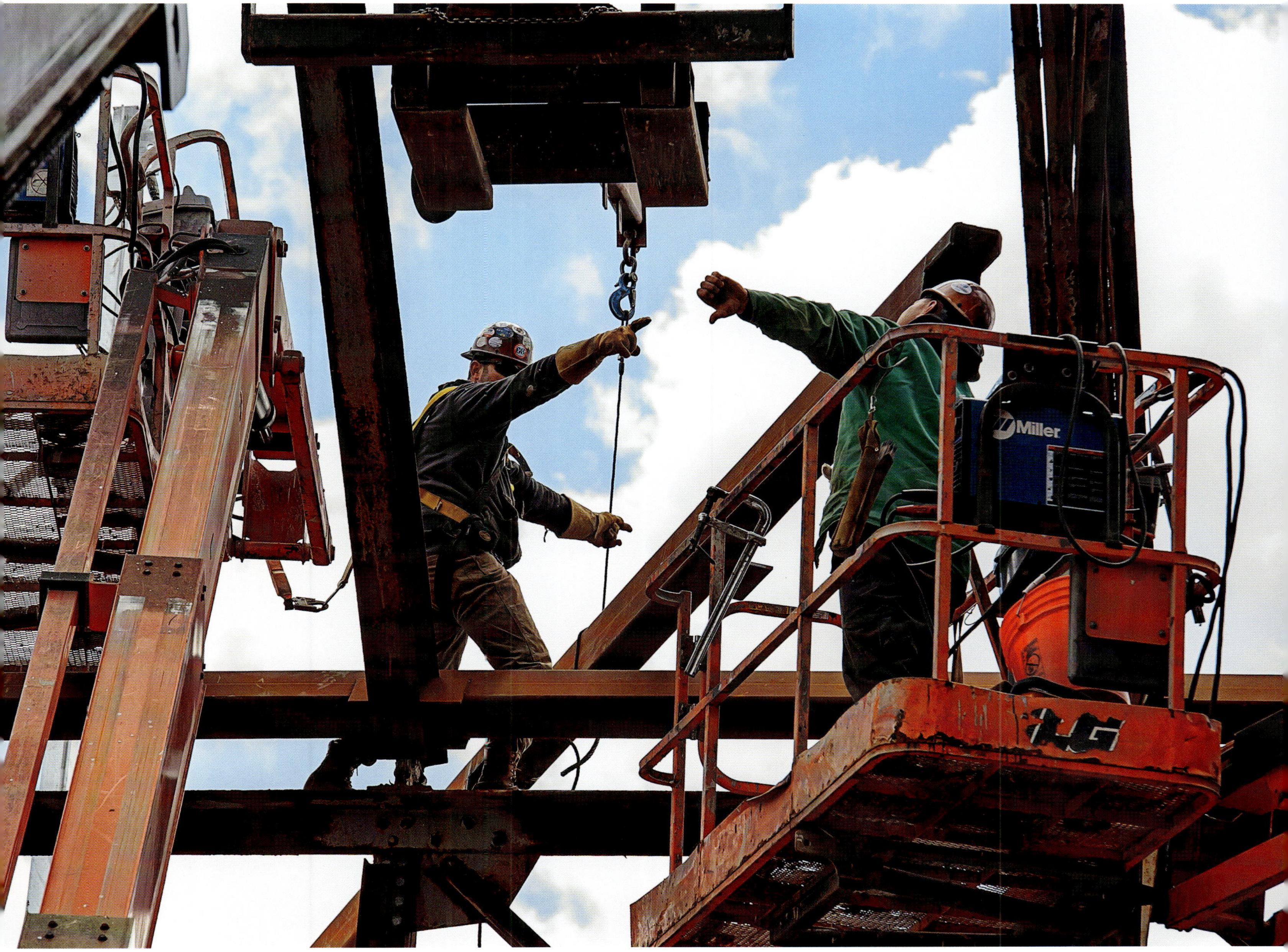

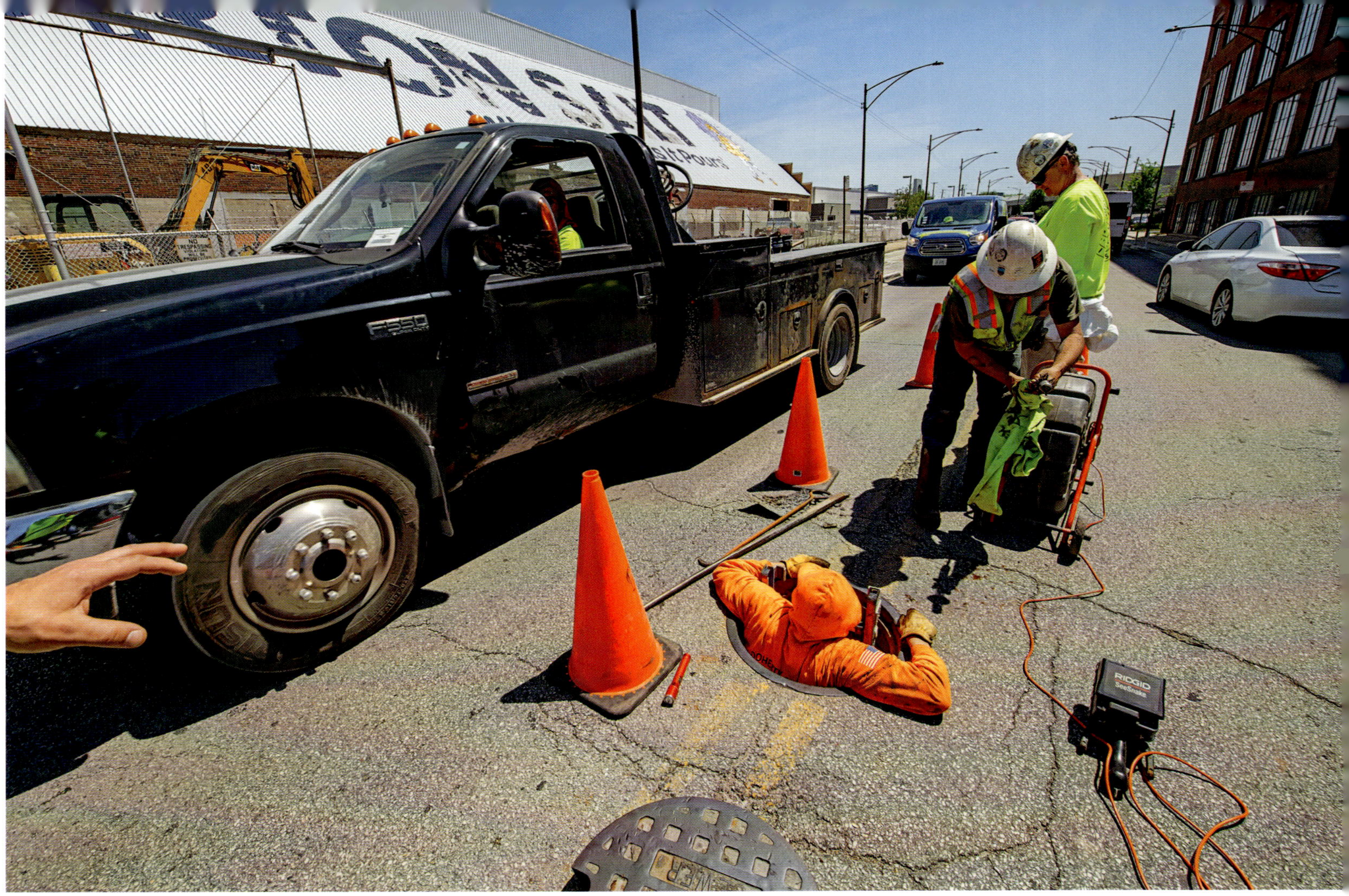

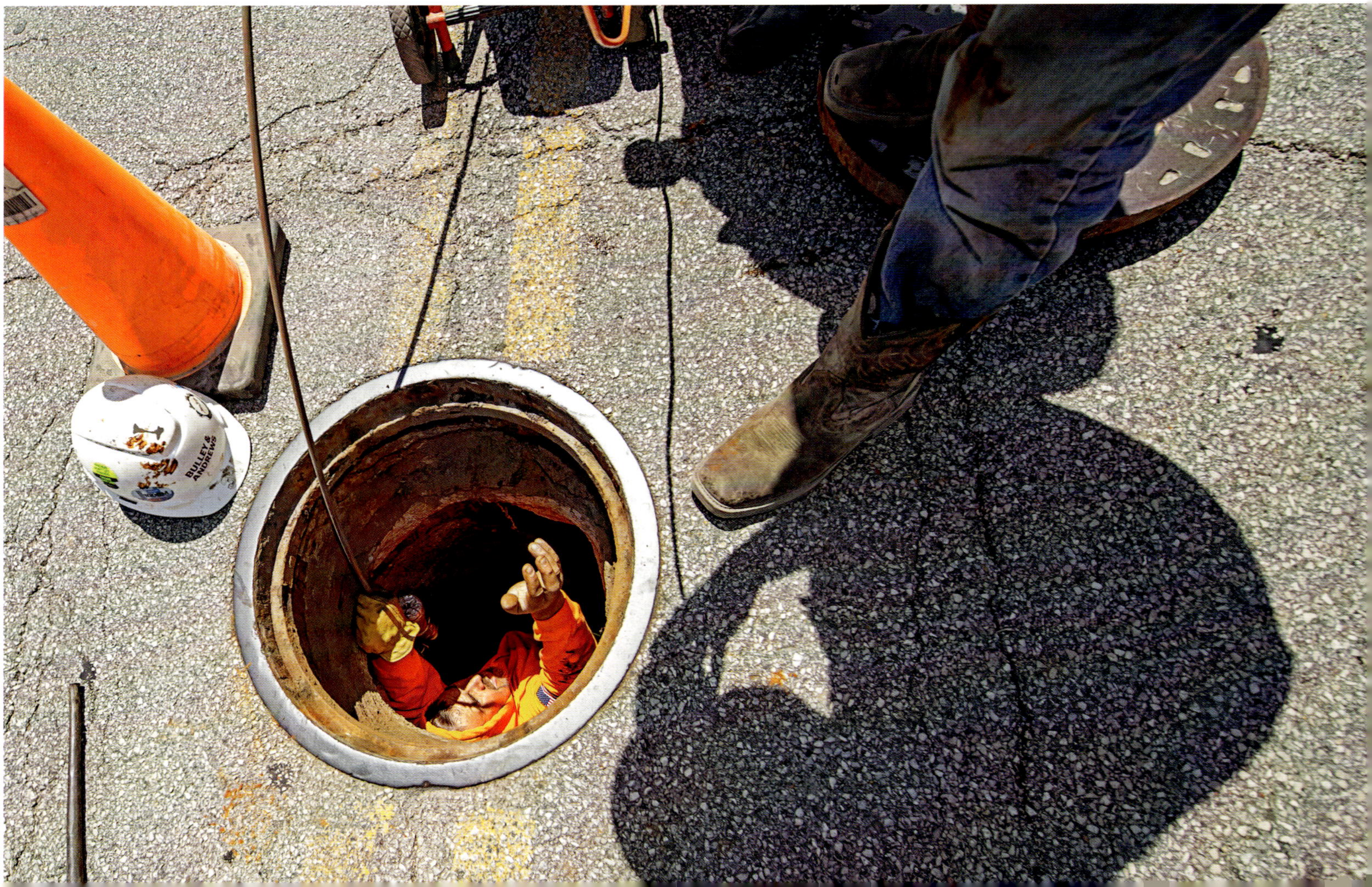

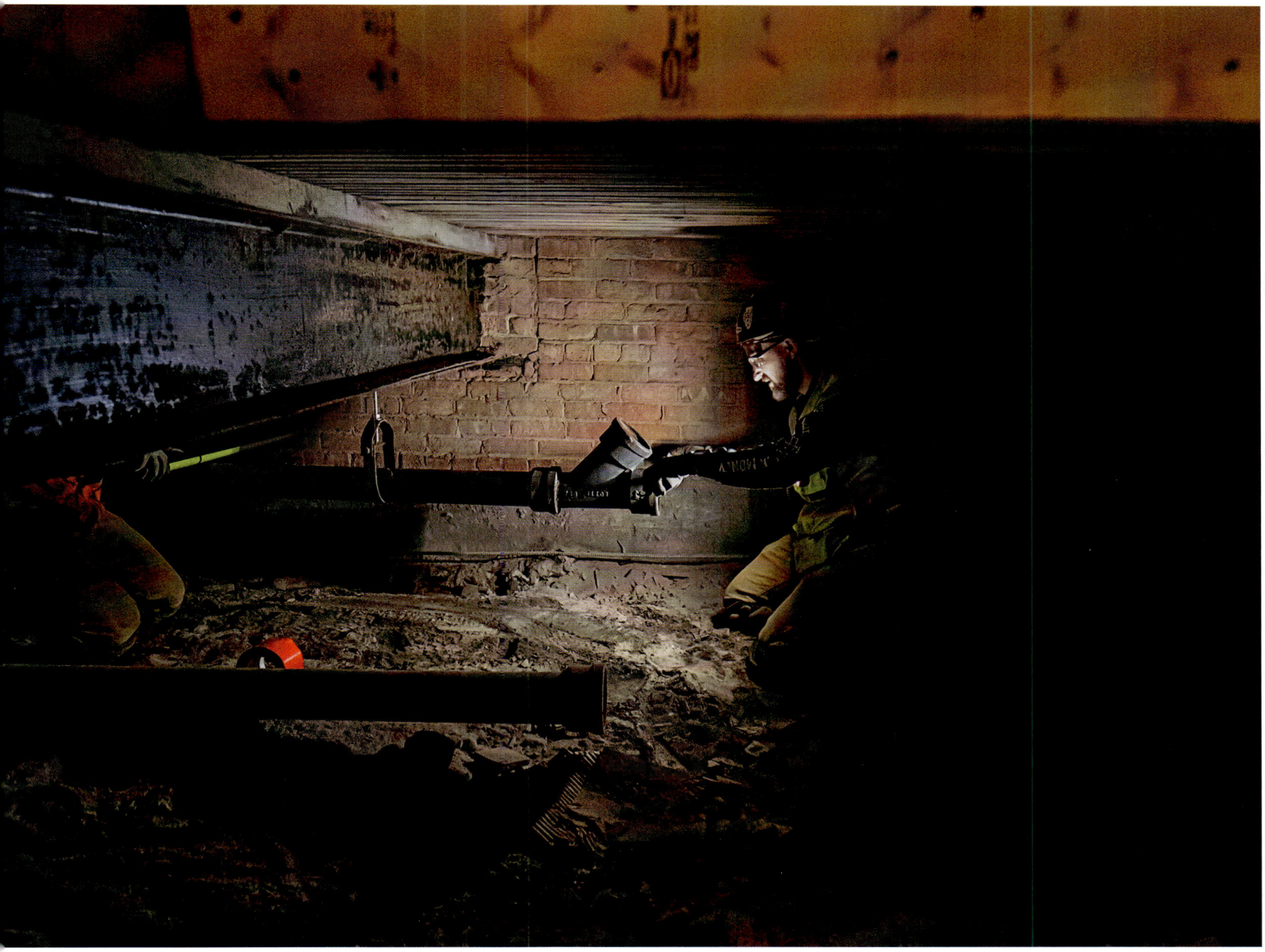

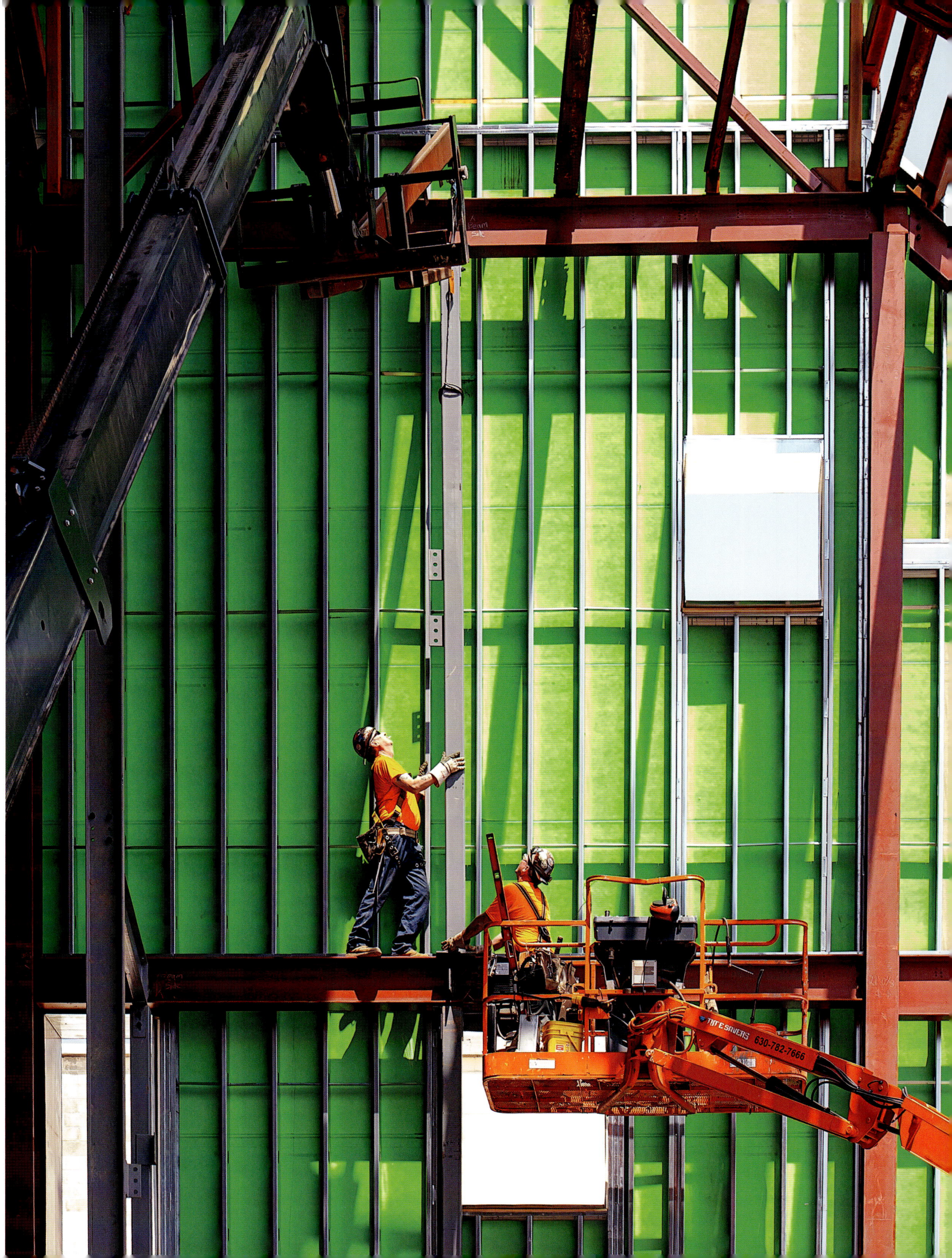
TIME SAVERS 630-782-7666

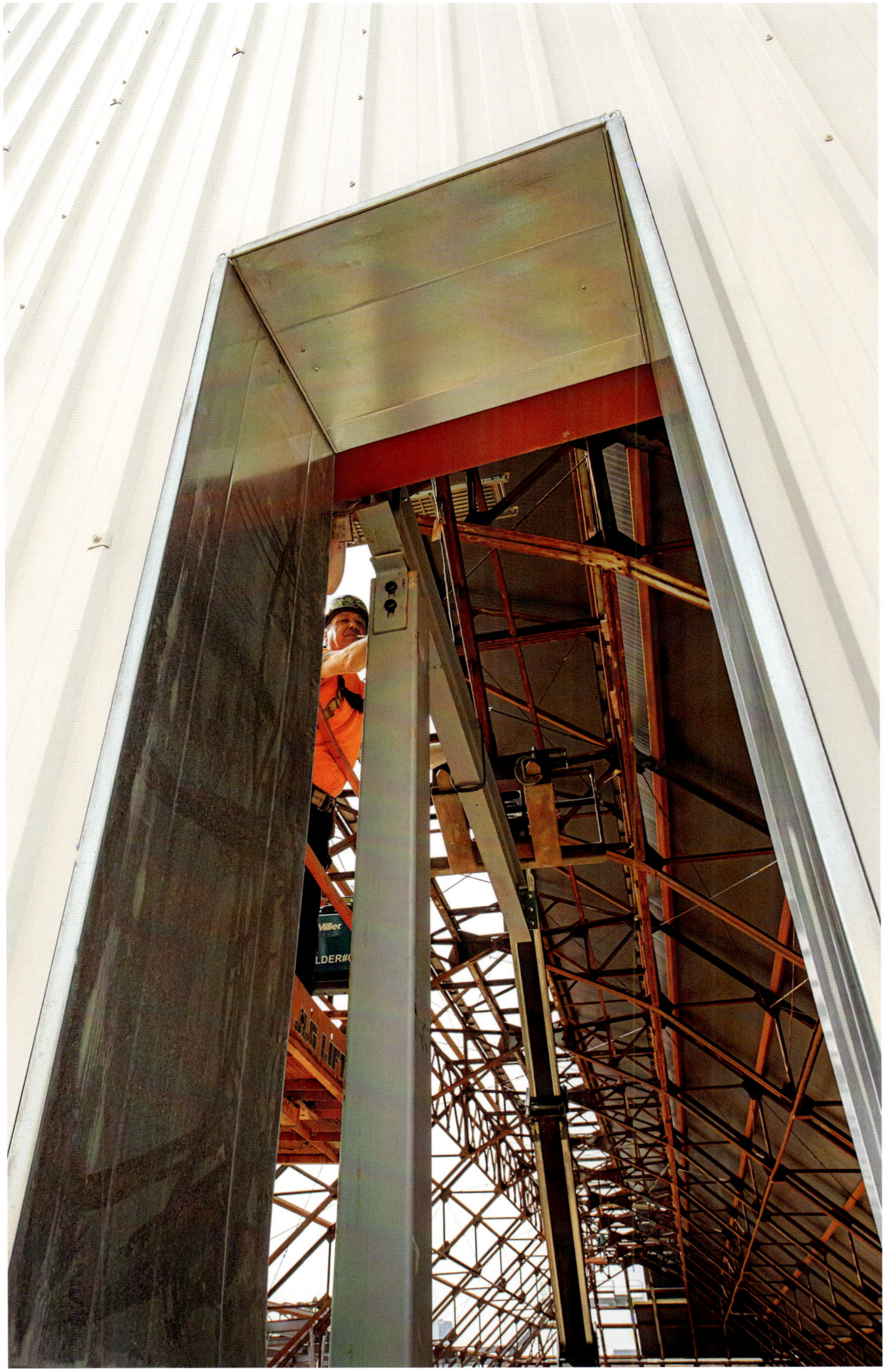

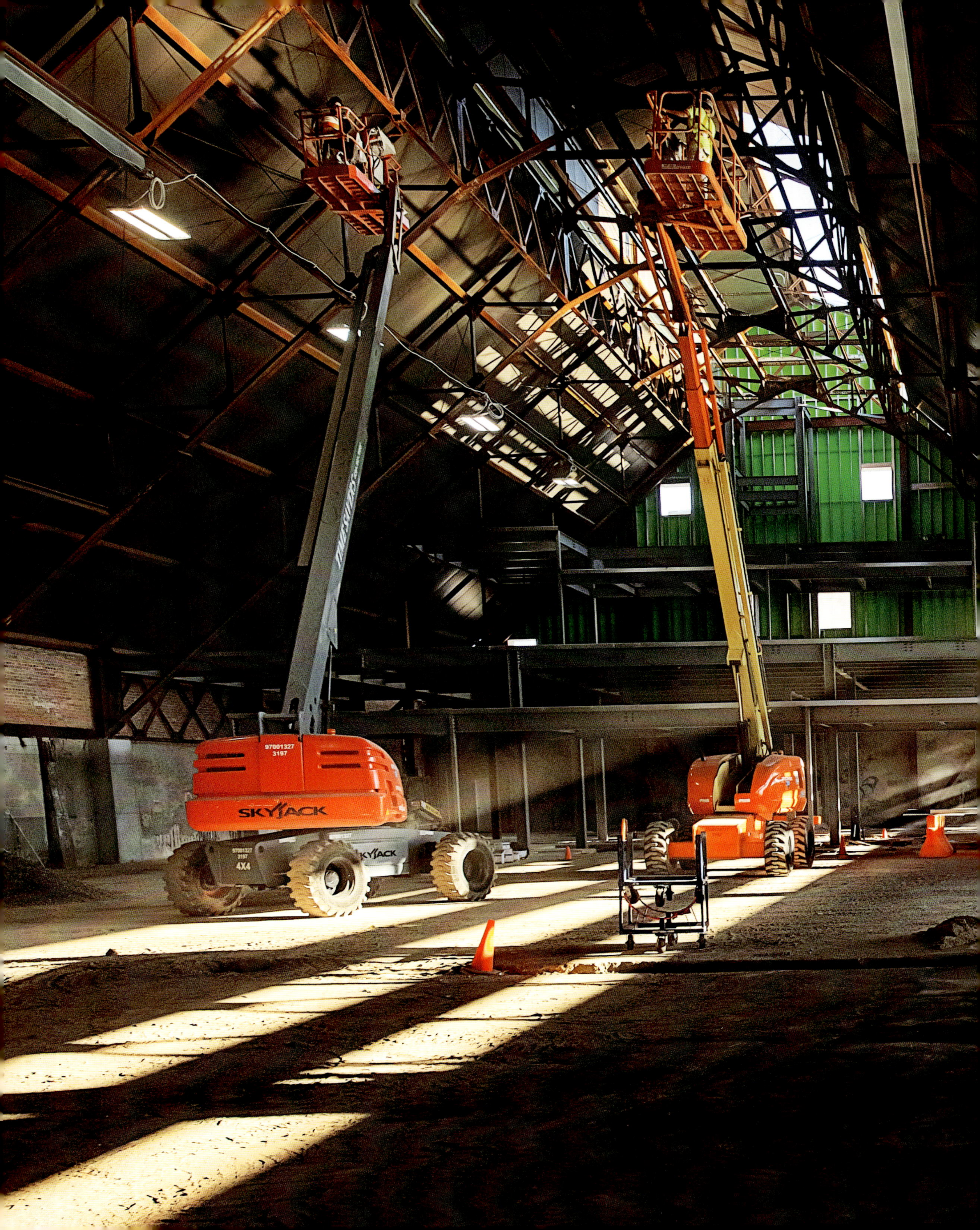
97001327
3197
SKYJACK
4X4

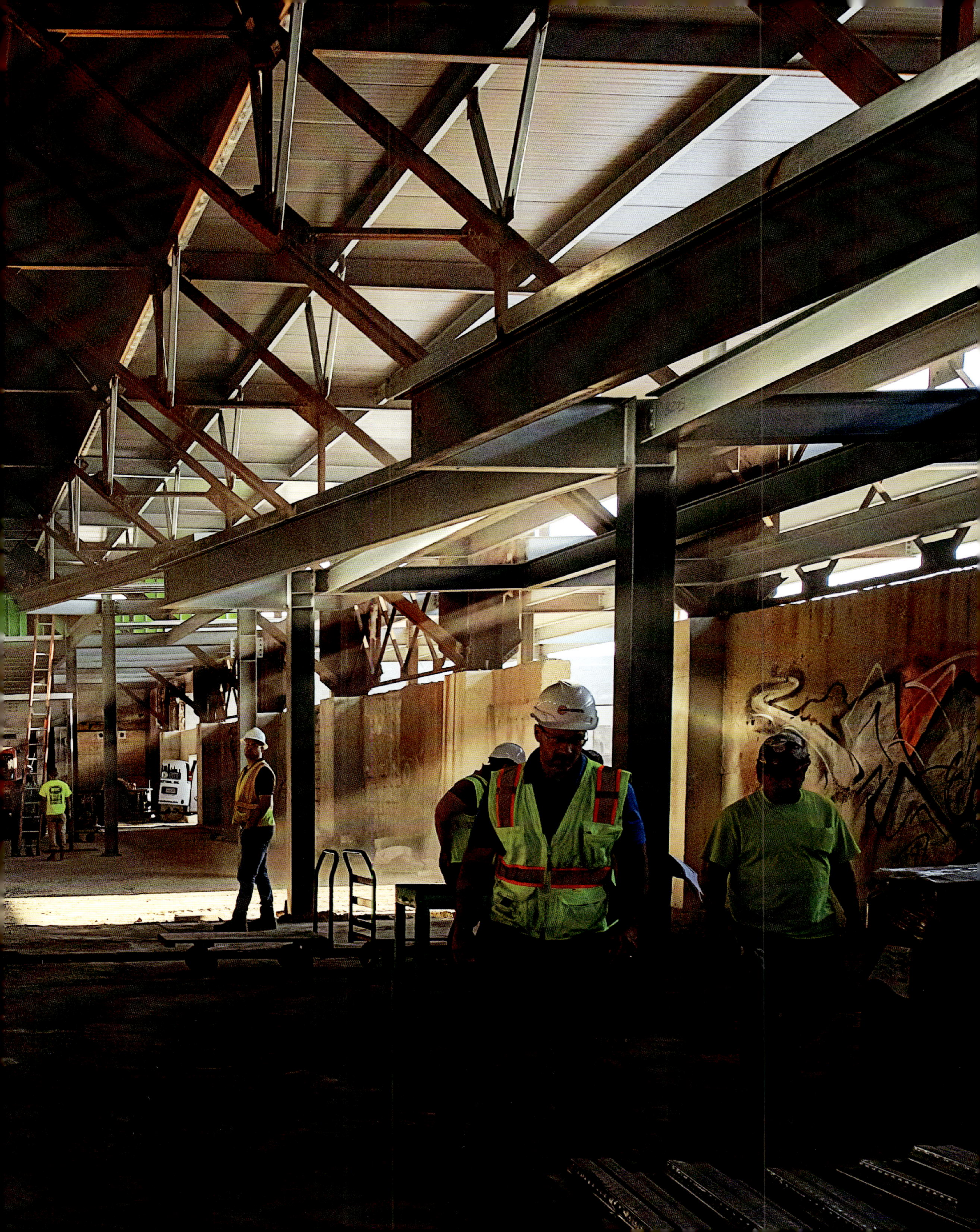

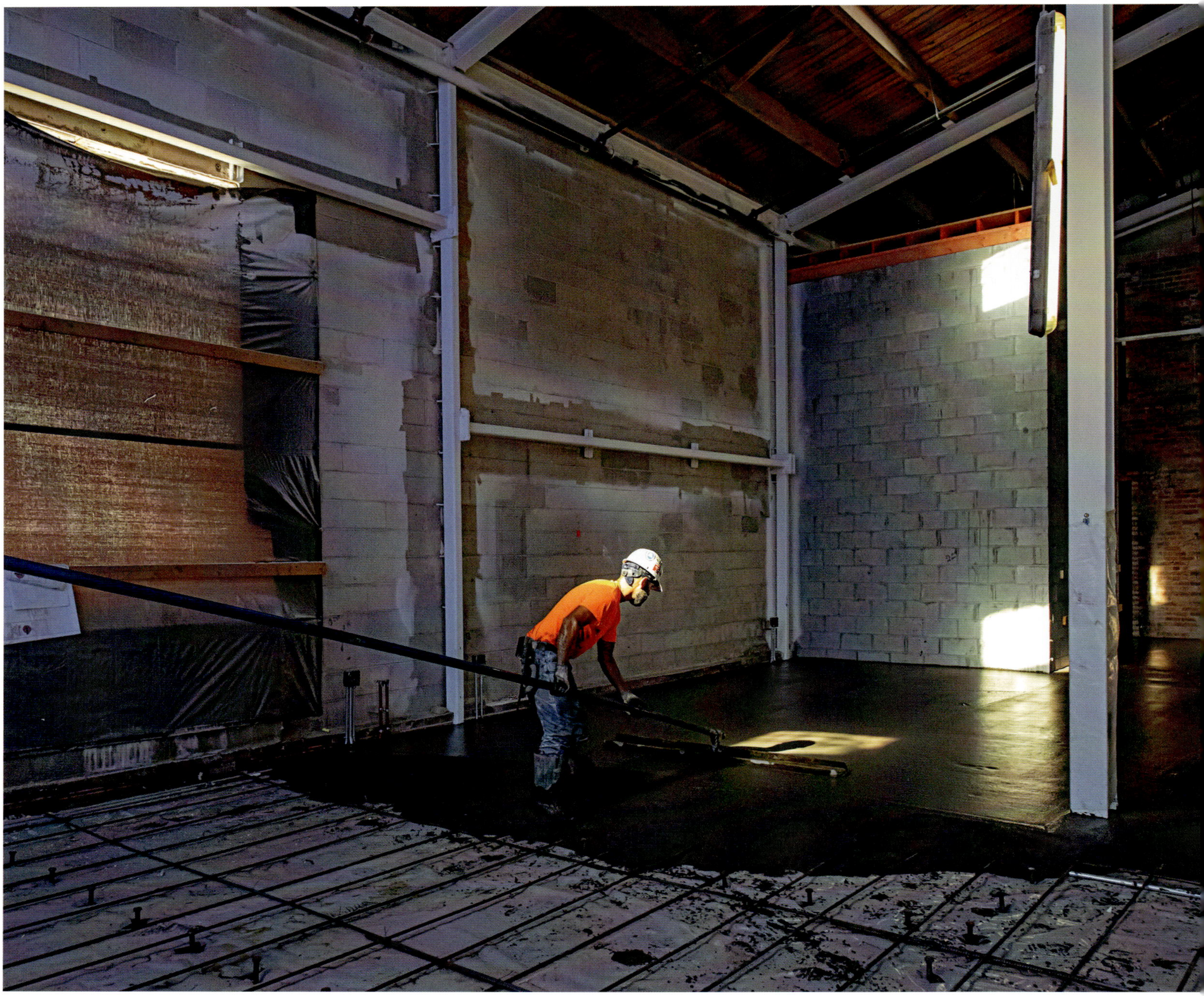

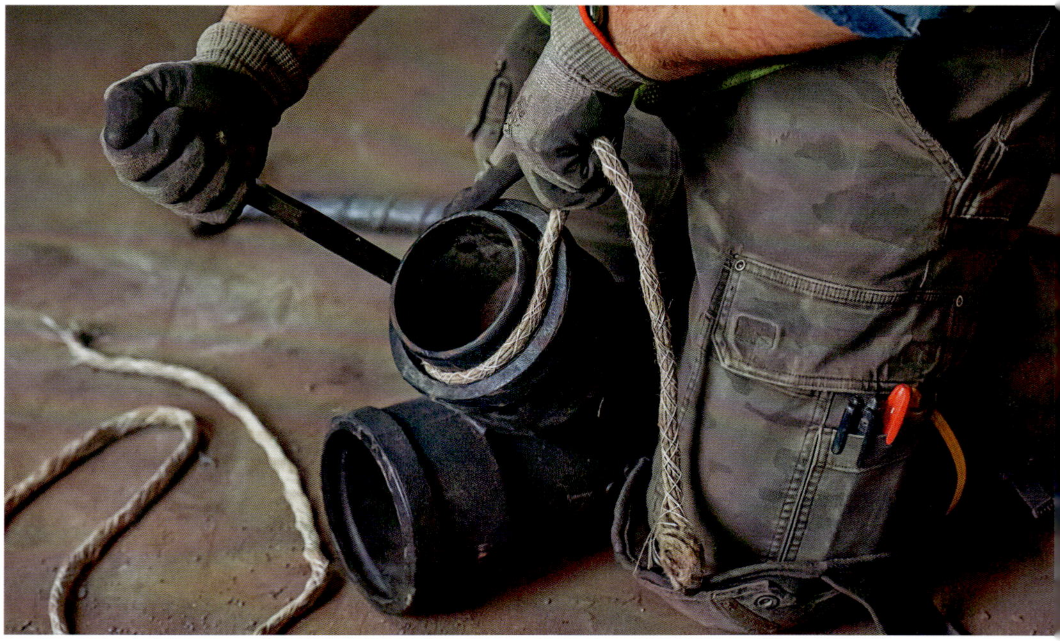

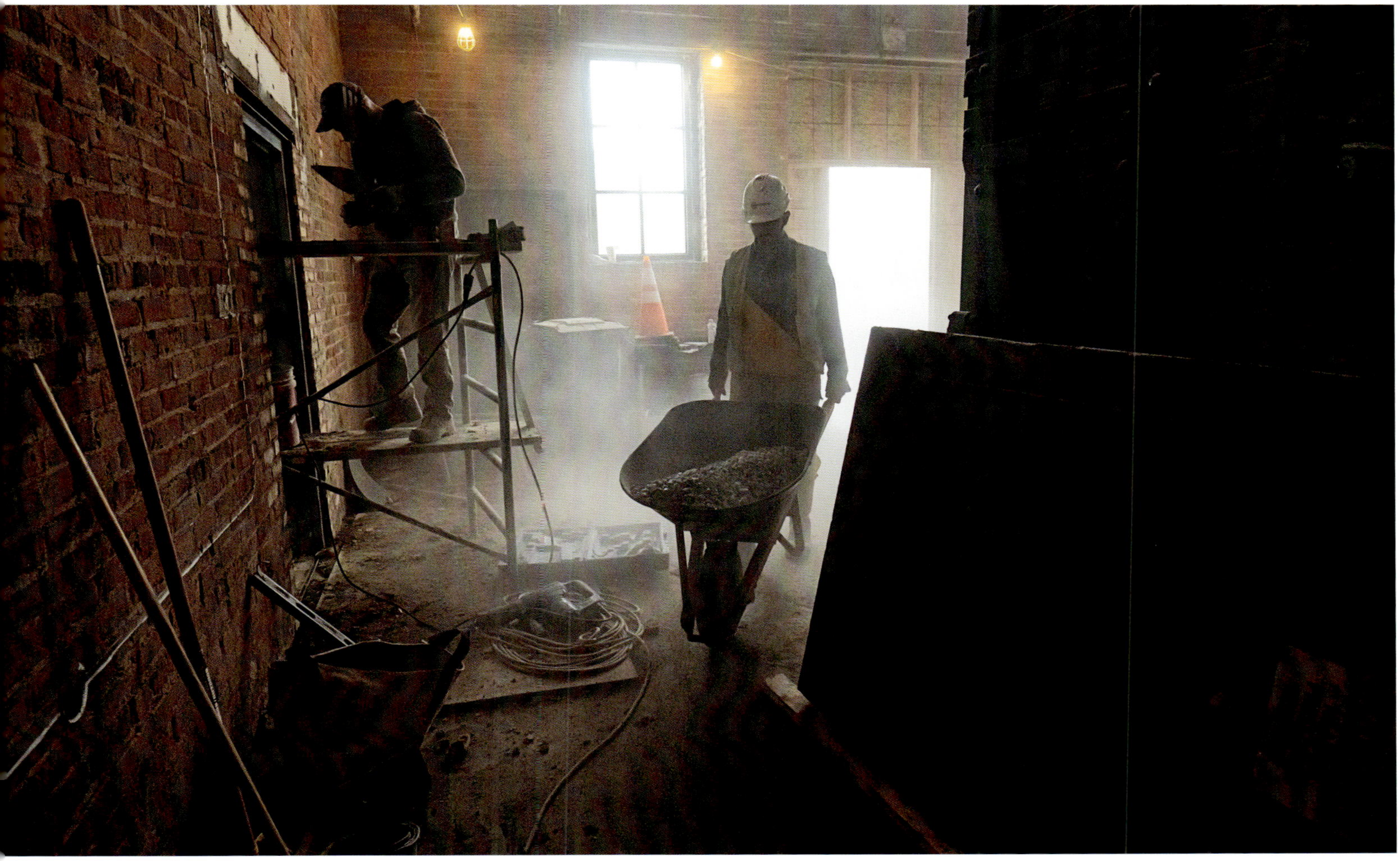

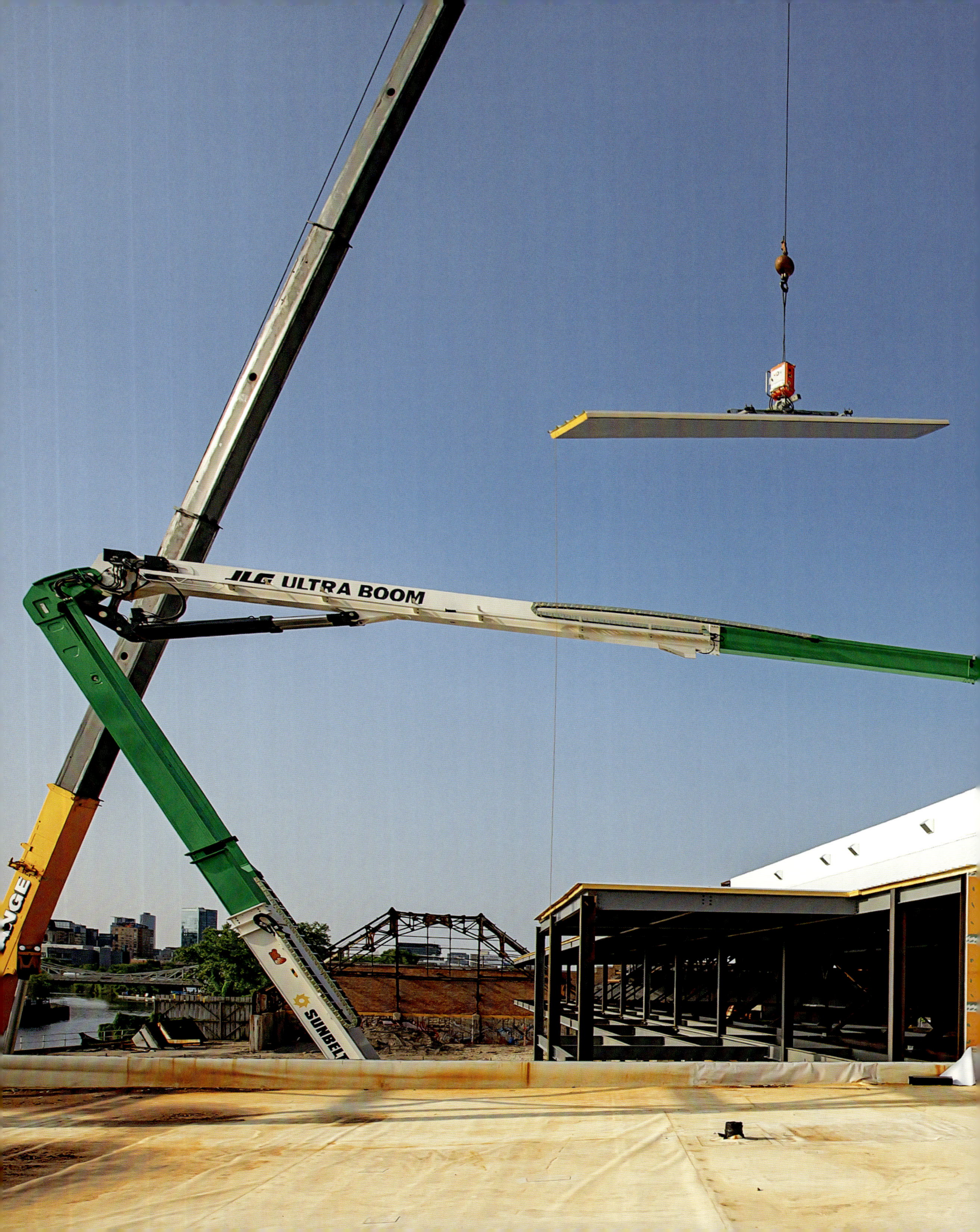
JLG ULTRA BOOM
SUNBELT

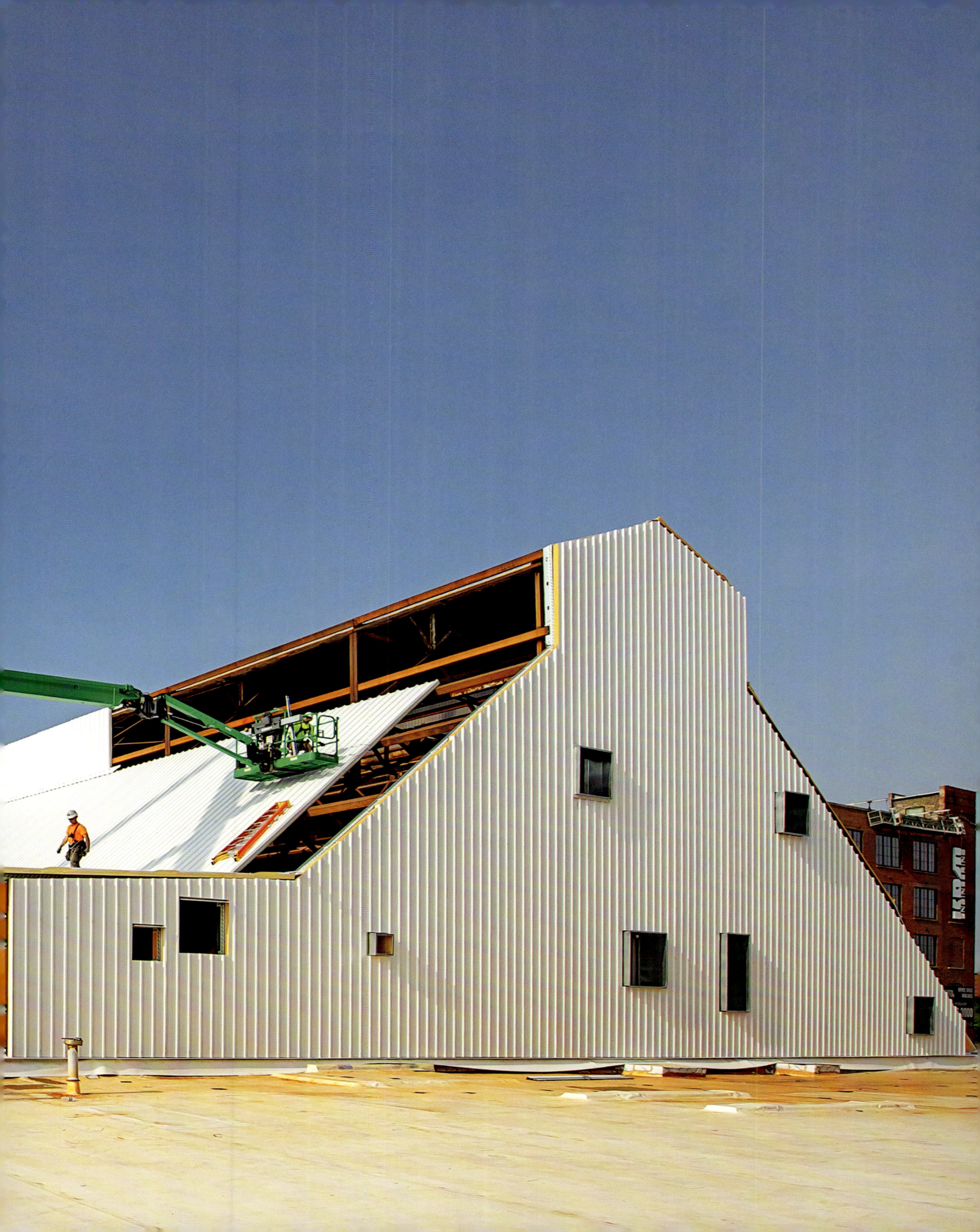

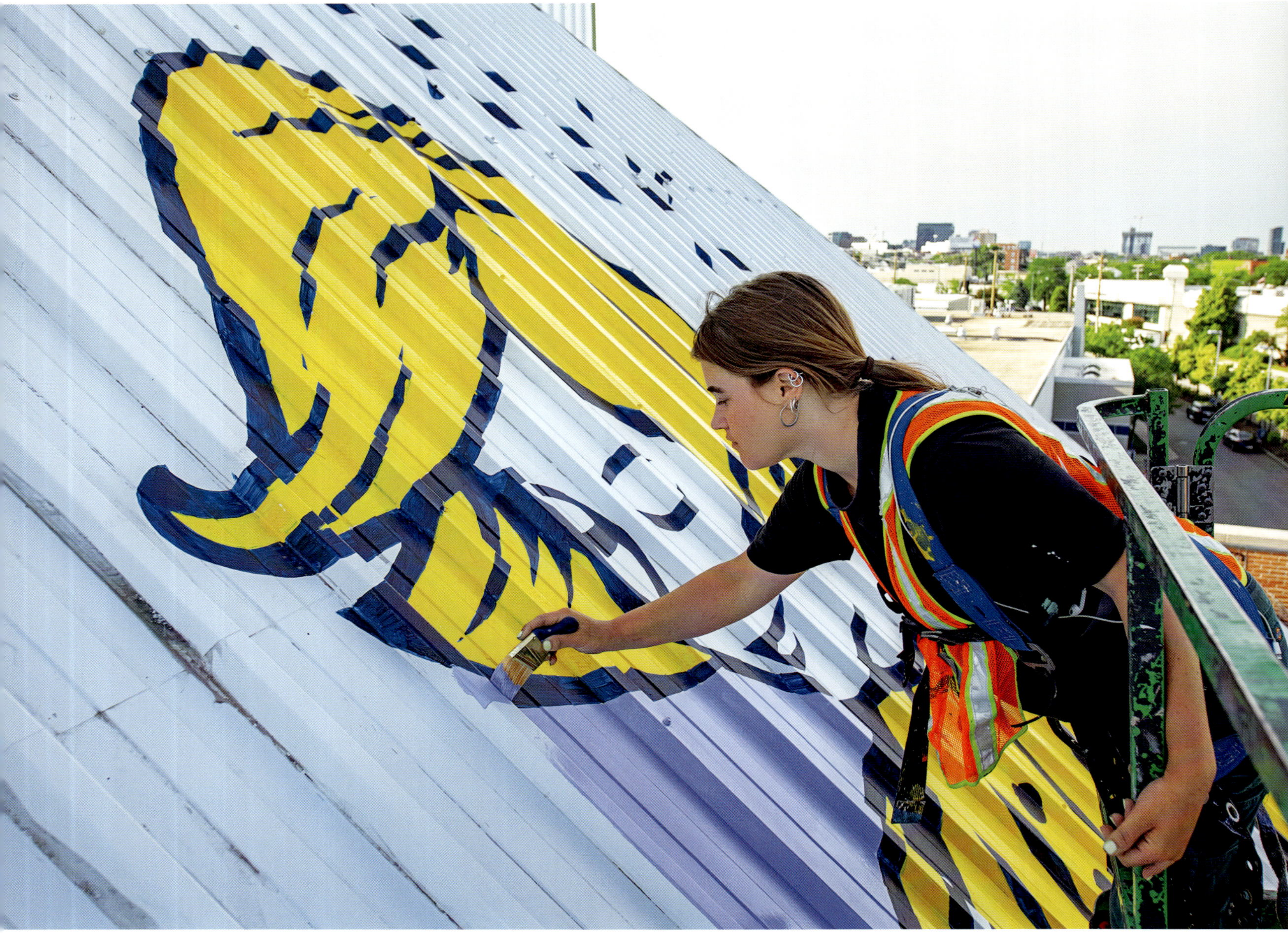

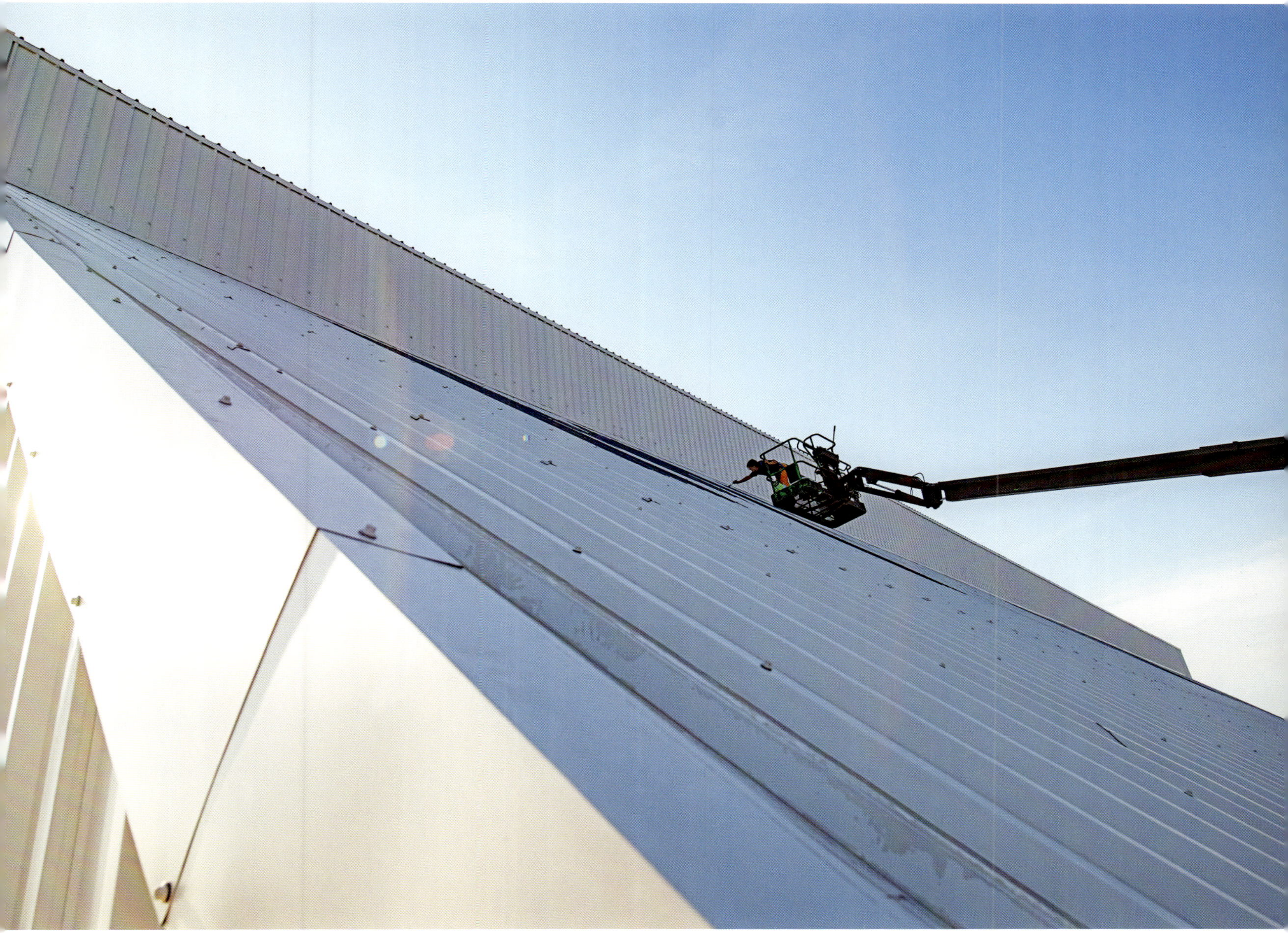

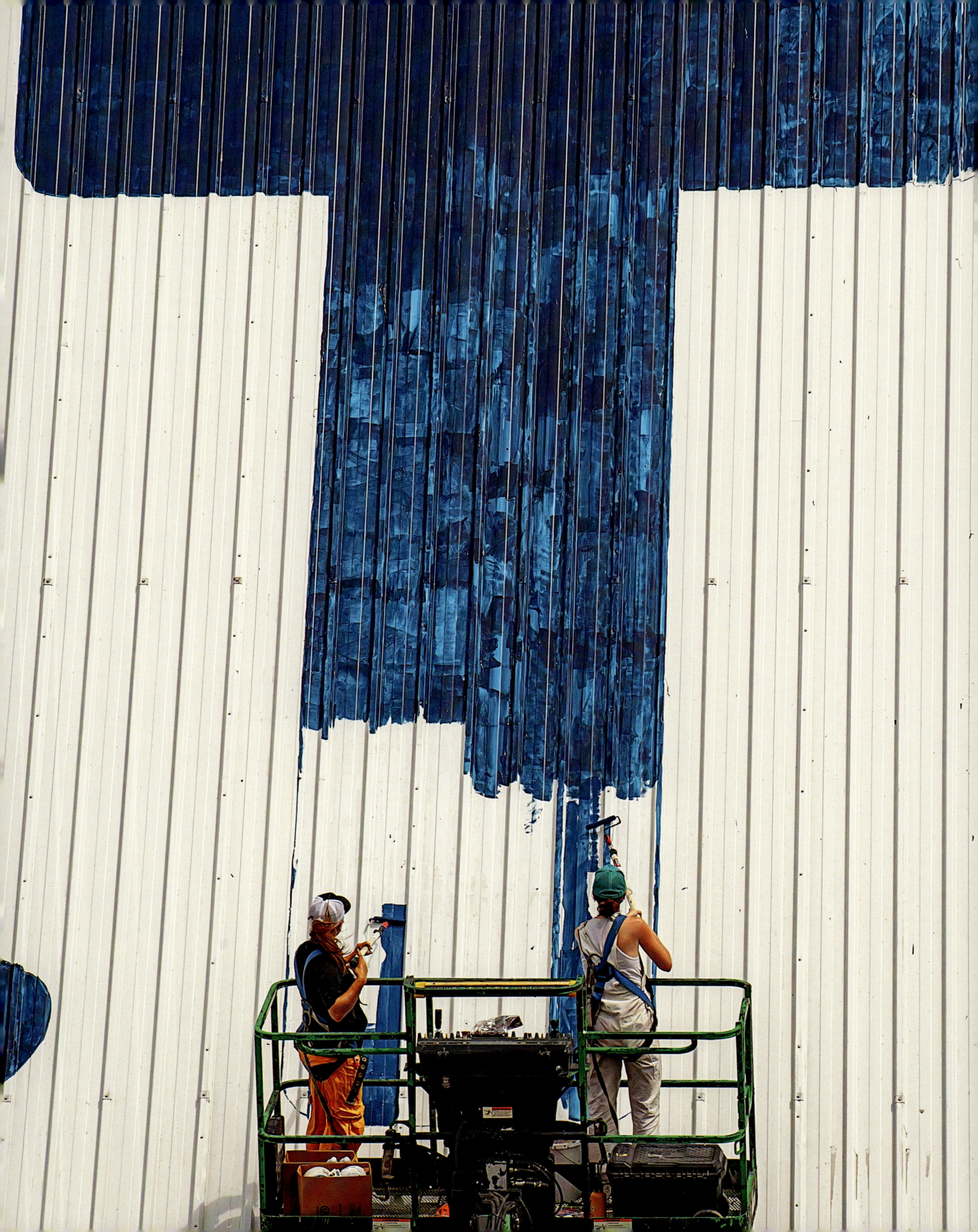

Many of us at Morton recognized the cultural significance of the building, particularly as it had become part of the landscape of Chicago. When Morton sold the complex, we wanted it to become a destination in the city of Chicago and to establish a new legacy for the future. But how do we reinvent that space and attach new meaning to it? There's no playbook for how to take an iconic industrial site, ensure that we preserve the structure and history, and reimagine it for the future. This journey took many months that stretched into years. We had to—and we did—find the right partners who shared that same vision and passion.

~ Denise Lauer, former chief marketing officer at Morton Salt, Inc.

Nº 5

SITE

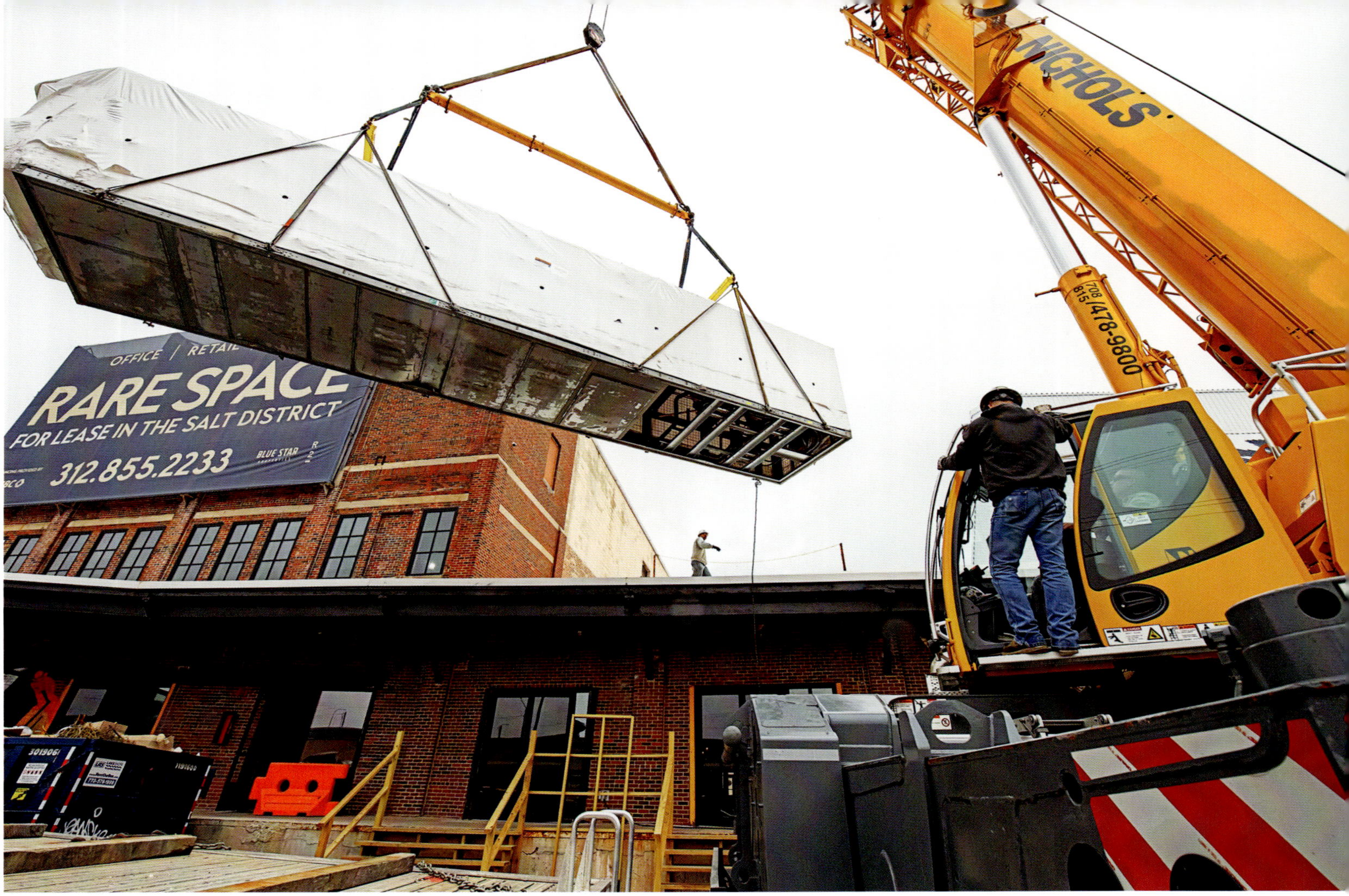
OFFICE | RETAIL
RARE SPACE
FOR LEASE IN THE SALT DISTRICT
312.855.2233
NICHOLS

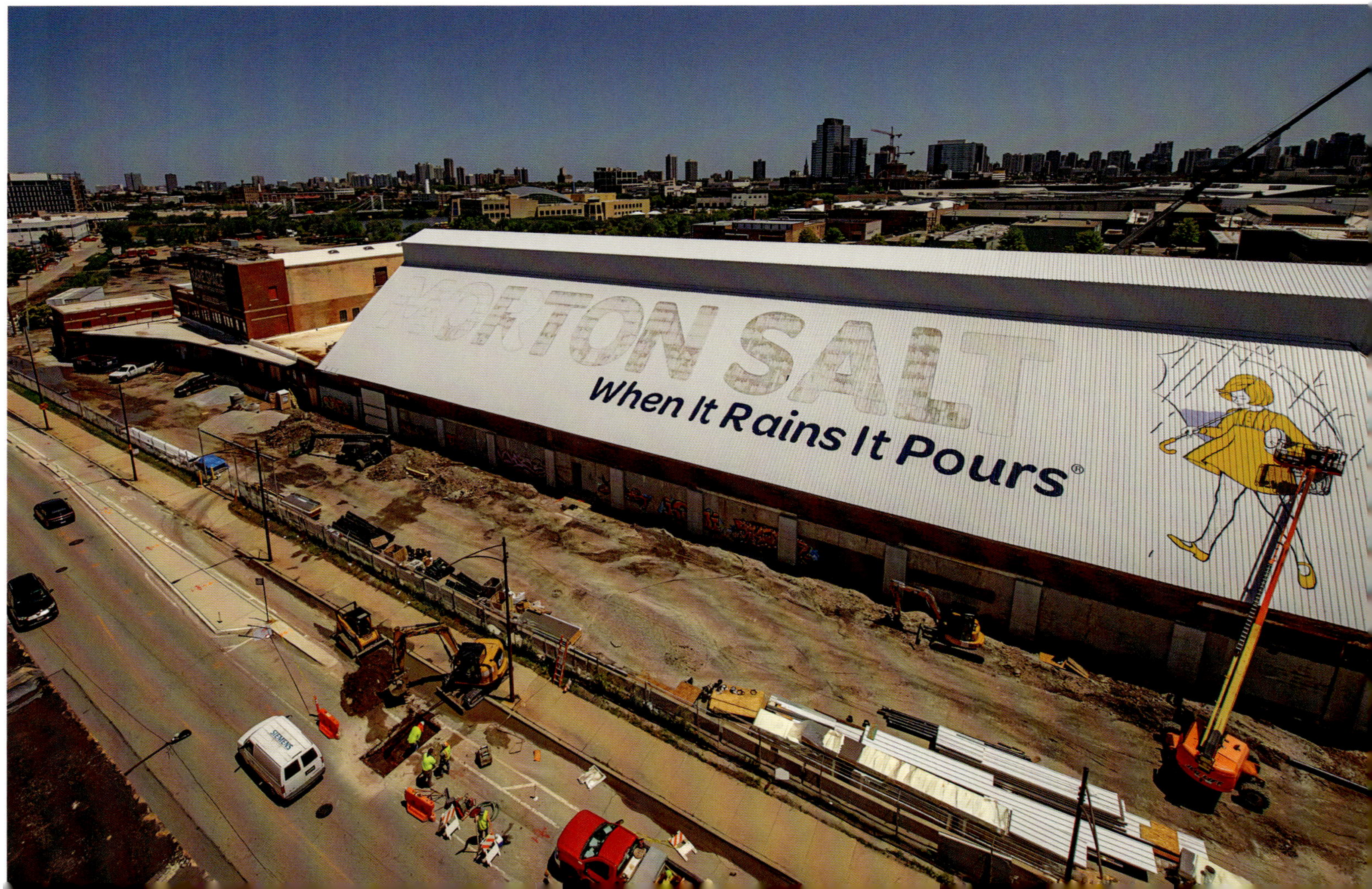
When It Rains It Pours®

Site

A Place to Celebrate History and Community

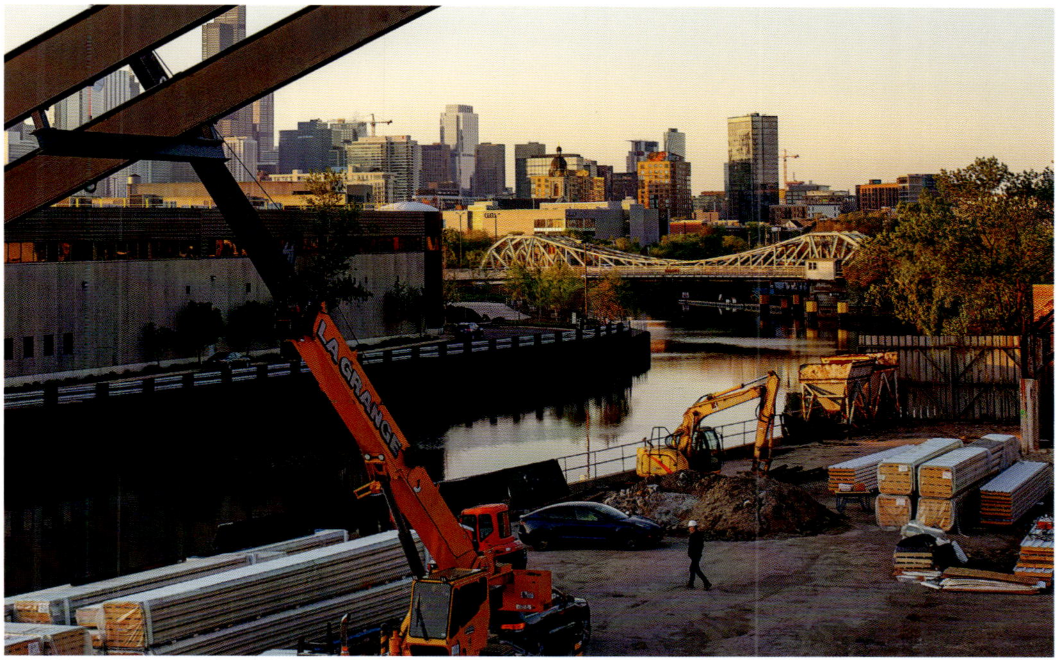

Situated along the North Branch of the Chicago River, the Salt Shed's site was a perfect spot for an industry like salt processing that used the river for transport and cargo a hundred years ago. When the Morton Salt Company left this plant after eighty-five years, the buildings were in various states of disrepair. Developers were interested in acquiring the property. For most of them, its size provided a temptation to tear everything down, scrape the site, and build something new and tall for the greatest financial gain.

One group did not want to demolish; these developers wanted to save the shed and the sign but faced complex challenges. They had to determine if the buildings could be saved and repurposed. If so, a viable and sustainable use had to be found. Ideas such as offices, markets and schools were explored. Saving the shed and keeping the sign intact required a complicated financial arrangement if Morton Salt's business was no longer physically present. There were major hurdles to overcome with the city, such as laws, codes, and zoning for the buildings and the oversized billboard.

Eventually a music and entertainment venue made the most sense. The team worked steadily with Morton Salt and the city to clear each hurdle. A creative investor came on board. Finally, they found their visionary partner—an independent local group specializing in the meticulous restoration of historic buildings and known for curating distinctive, beautiful spaces for music and food. The new collaborators could now take on the challenge of keeping the shed alive and restoring its beauty and structural integrity.

The transformation of the Morton Salt shed also aligned with a greater vision for Chicago by the city government and a decades-long effort to clean up the river and to return much more of it to public use. This has occurred along the Main Stem downtown, with the popular 1.5-mile Riverwalk. Yet there are a combined 156 miles of river on the Main, North, and South Branches, much more of which could become accessible for recreation. Repurposing a riverfront site like the Salt Shed supports that vision. Preservation of buildings is not only a sustainable choice within the building industry but can encourage preservation of natural resources. It provides more care and attention to the whole environment. It adds to the quality of life in a city.

So much had to align for the Salt Shed project to happen. It took two years of countless meetings, brainstorming sessions, and phone calls to buy the property and structure a deal with a guarantee that the sign would remain in place, plus another two years to find the venue partners. More than three years after that, the Salt Shed team, along with hundreds of workers, finished the extensive restoration, and opened its doors as a stunning venue for music and the arts: a place to celebrate history, culture, and community.

Site

A Place to Celebrate History and Community

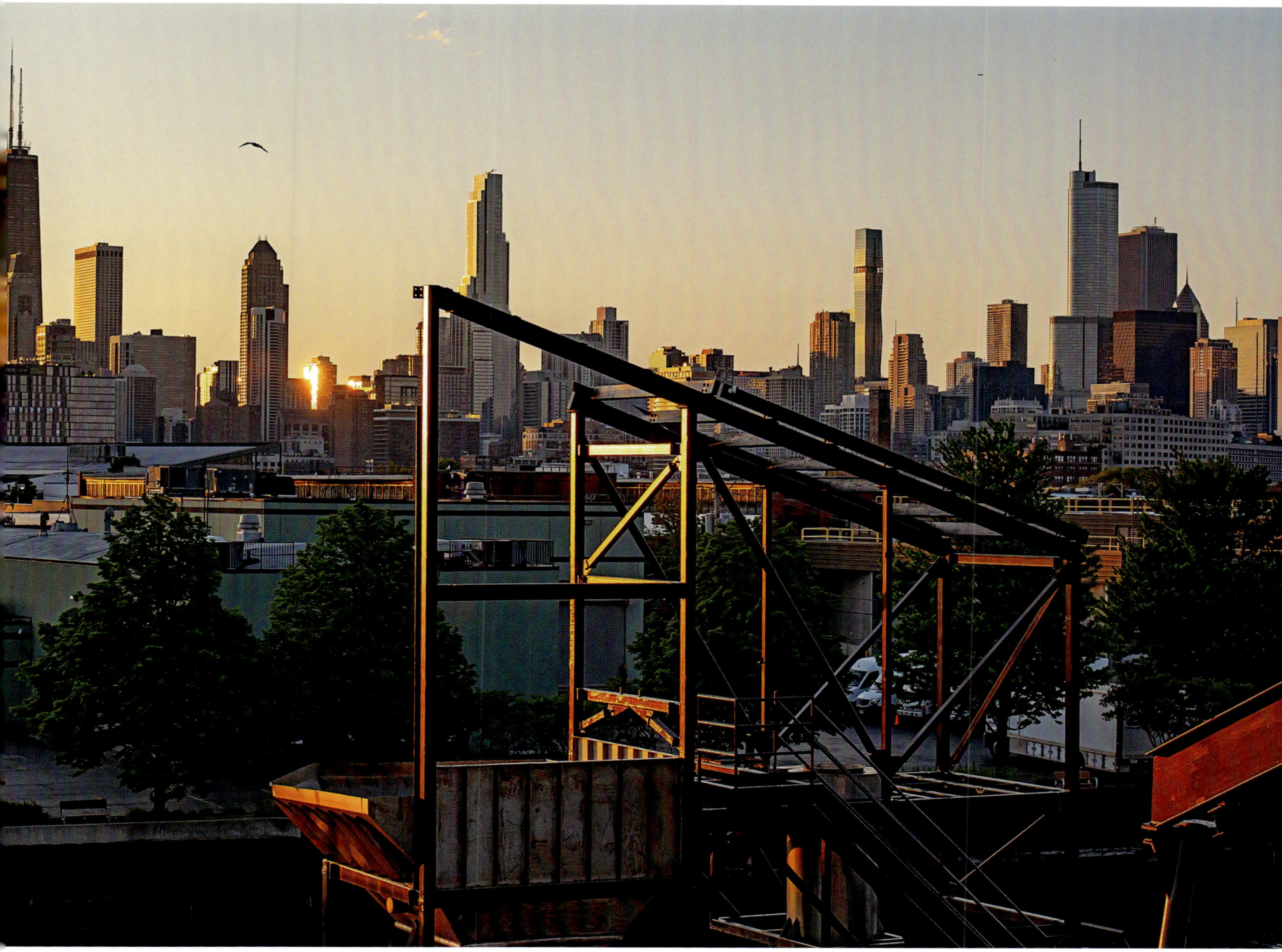

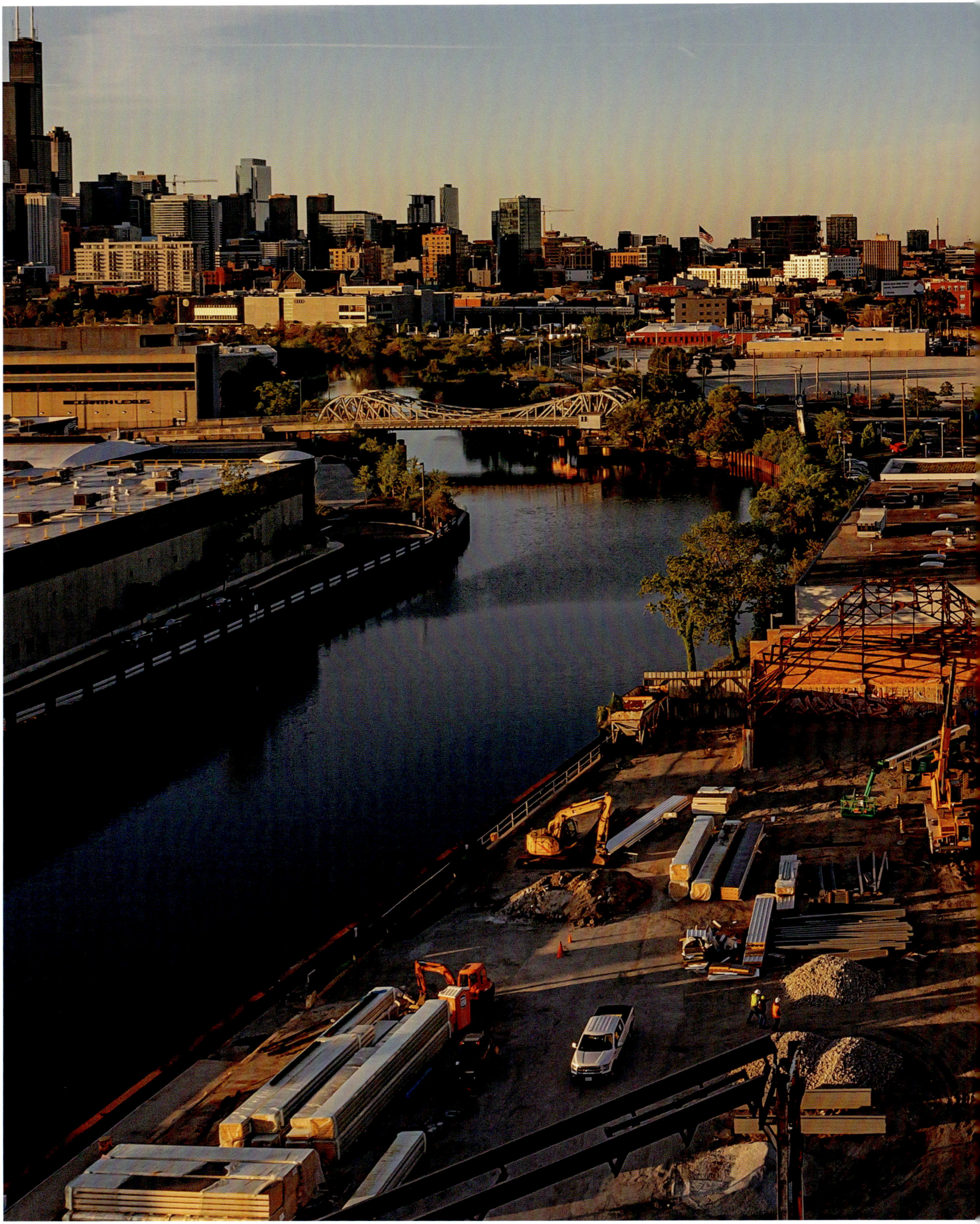

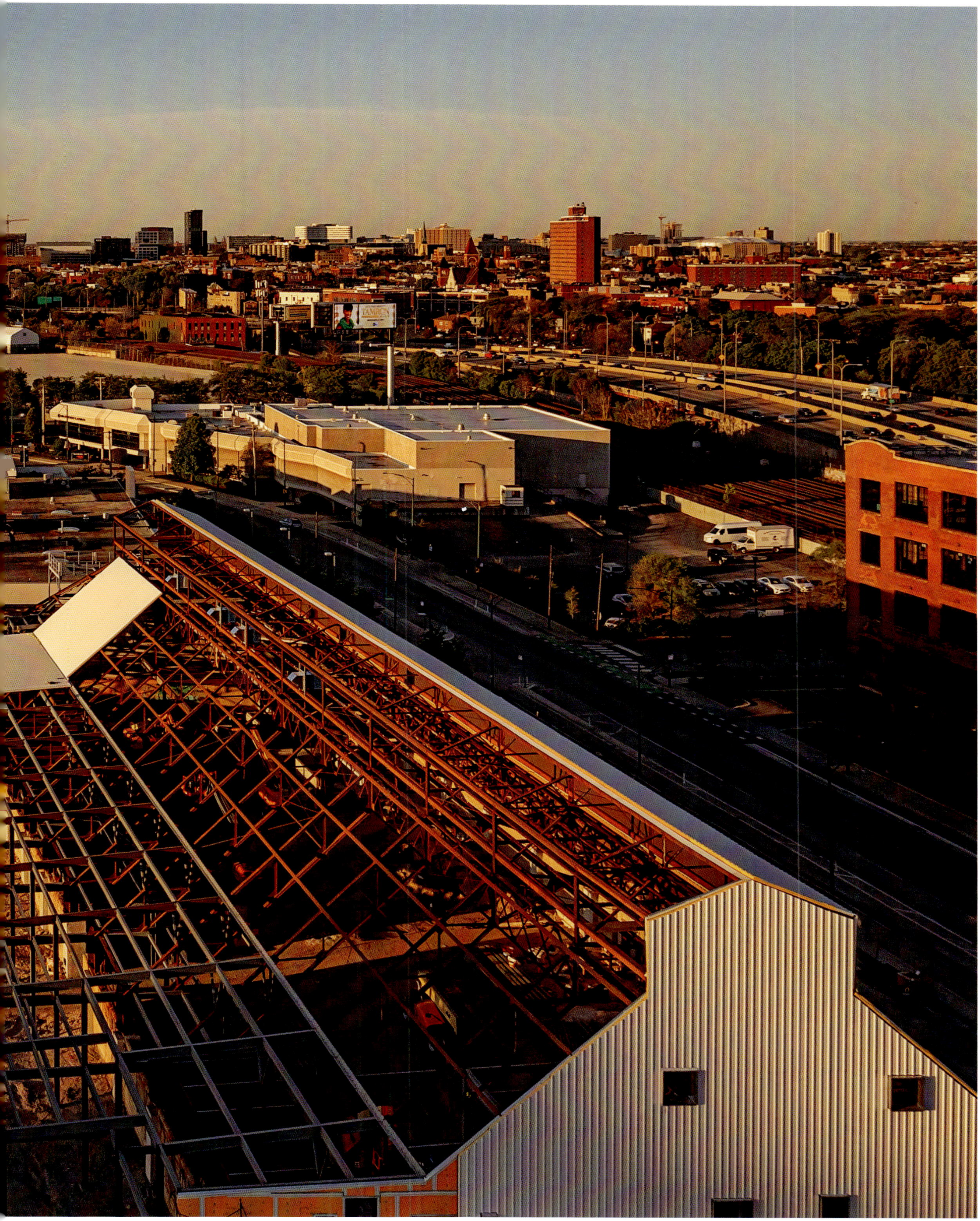

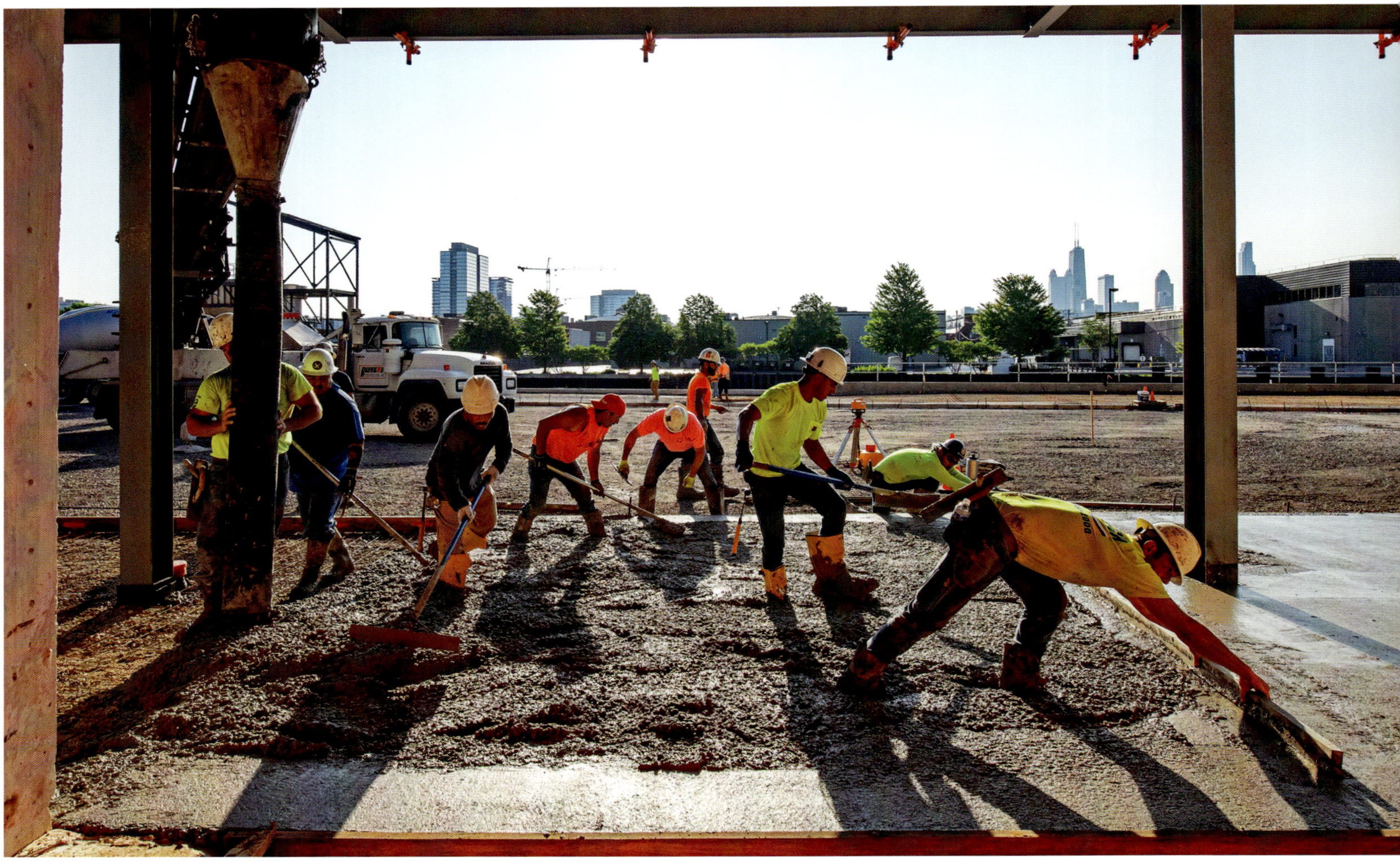

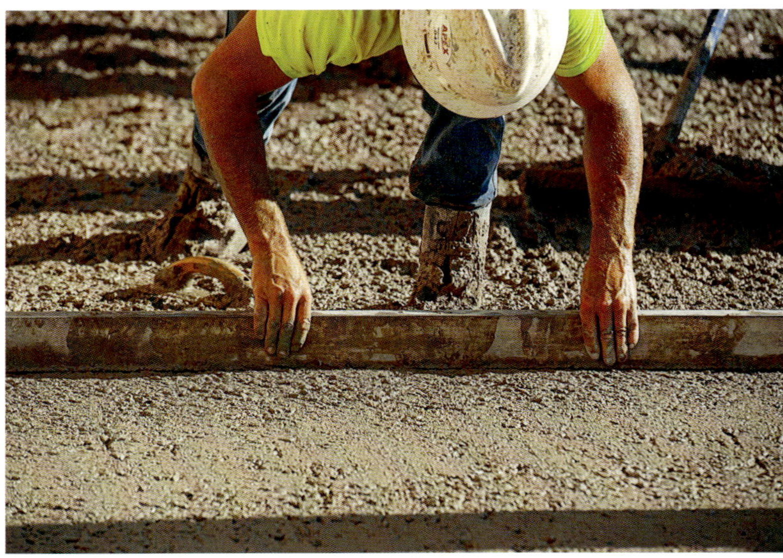

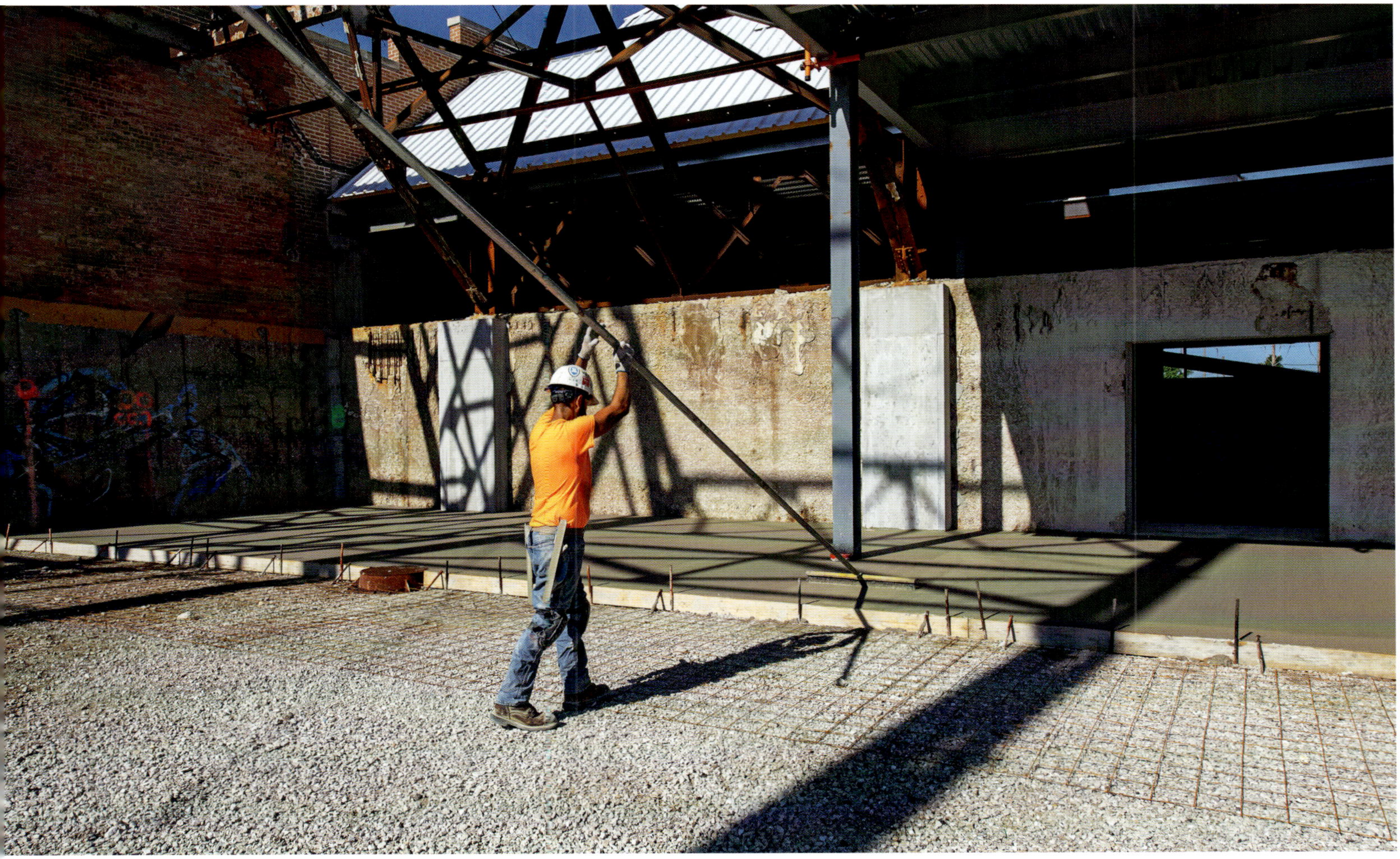

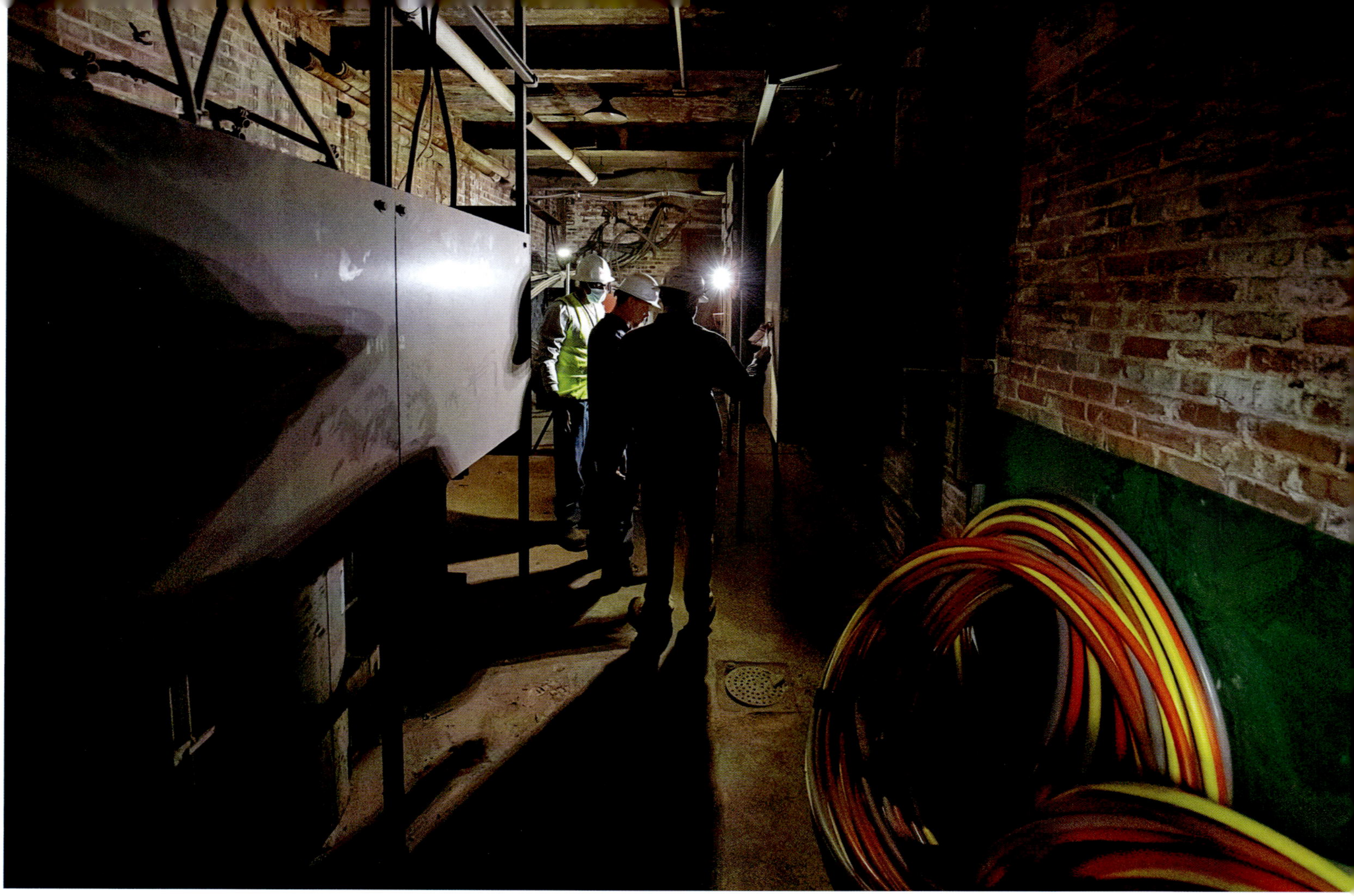

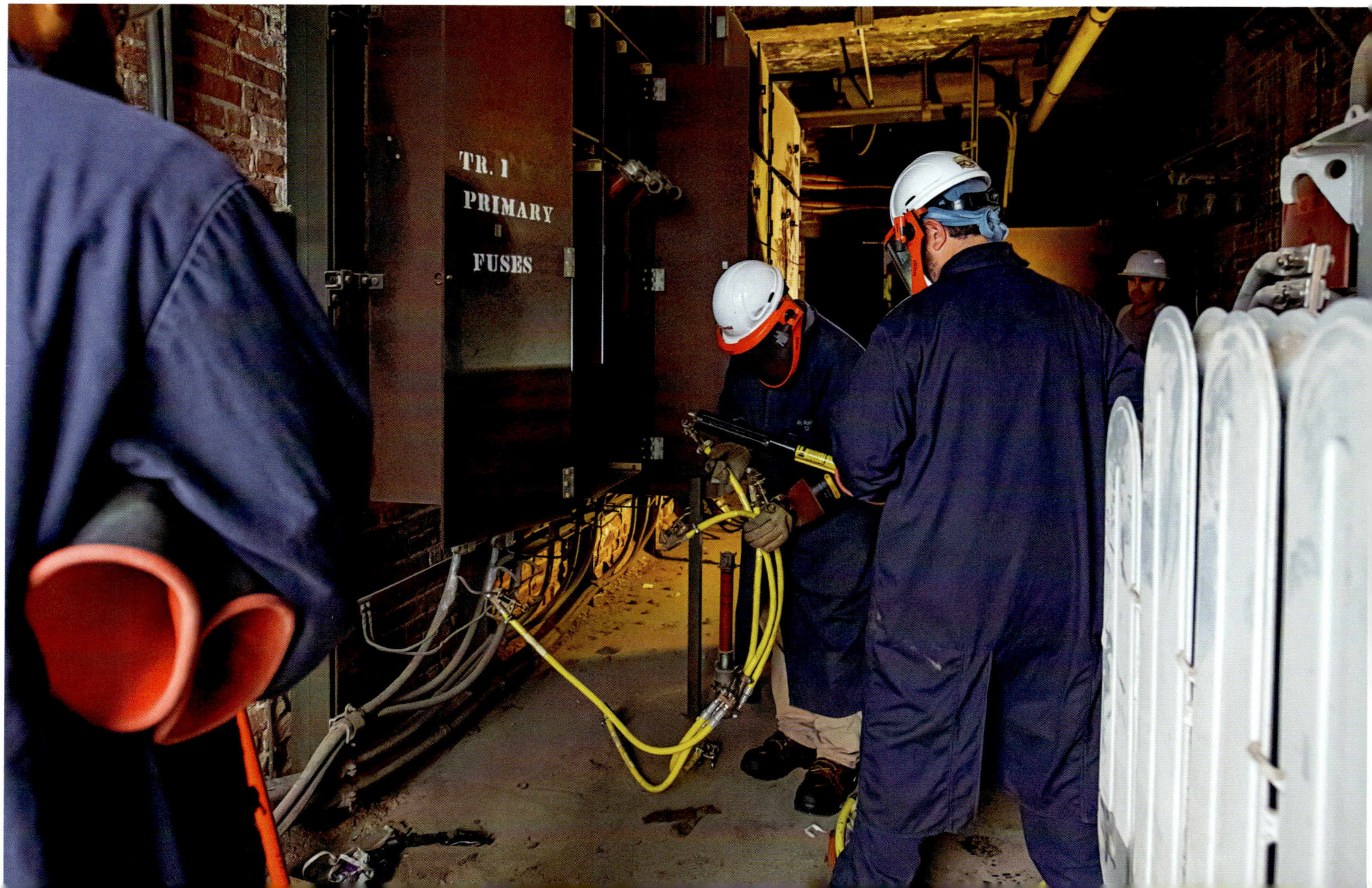
TR. 1
PRIMARY
FUSES

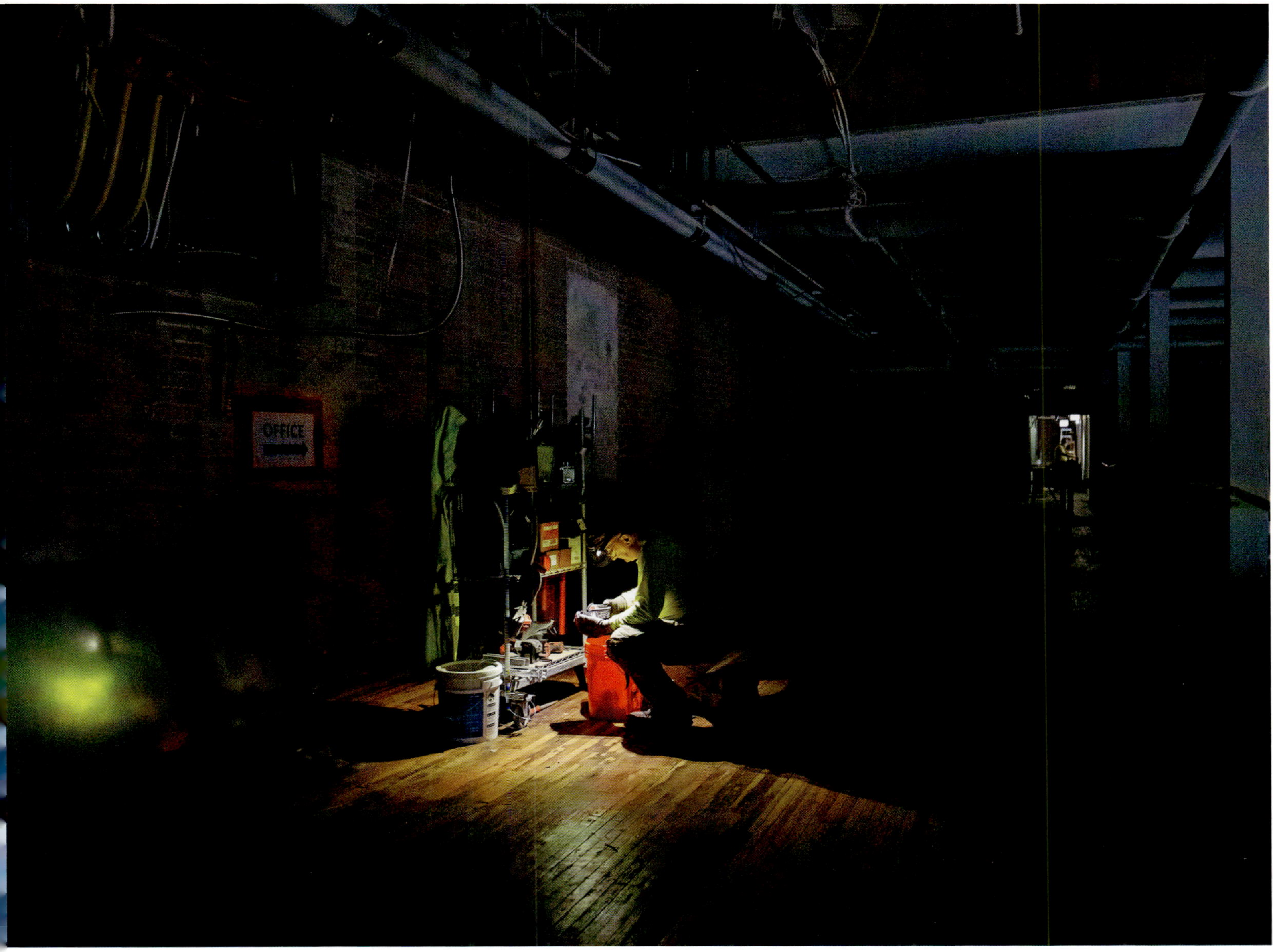
OFFICE

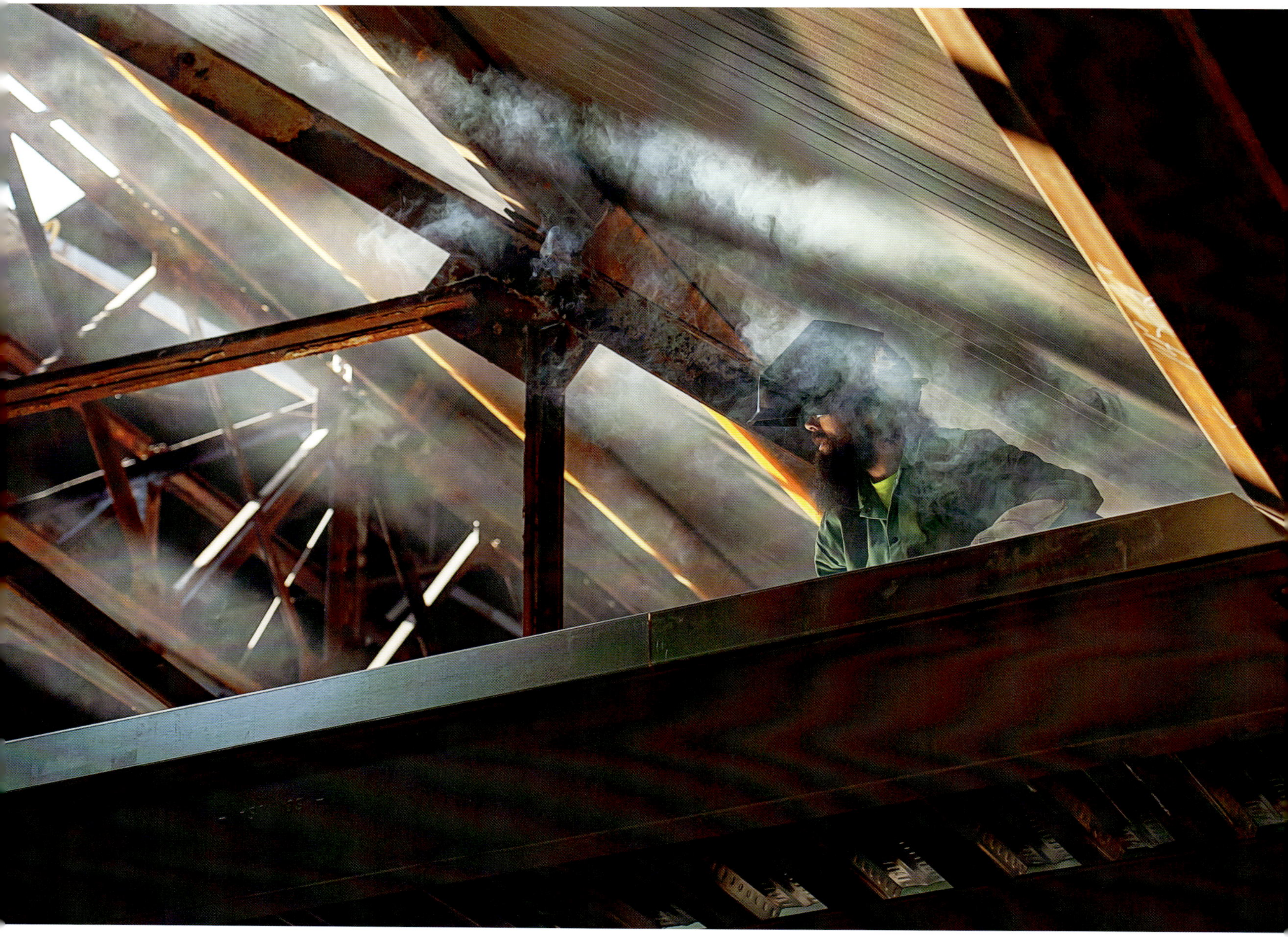

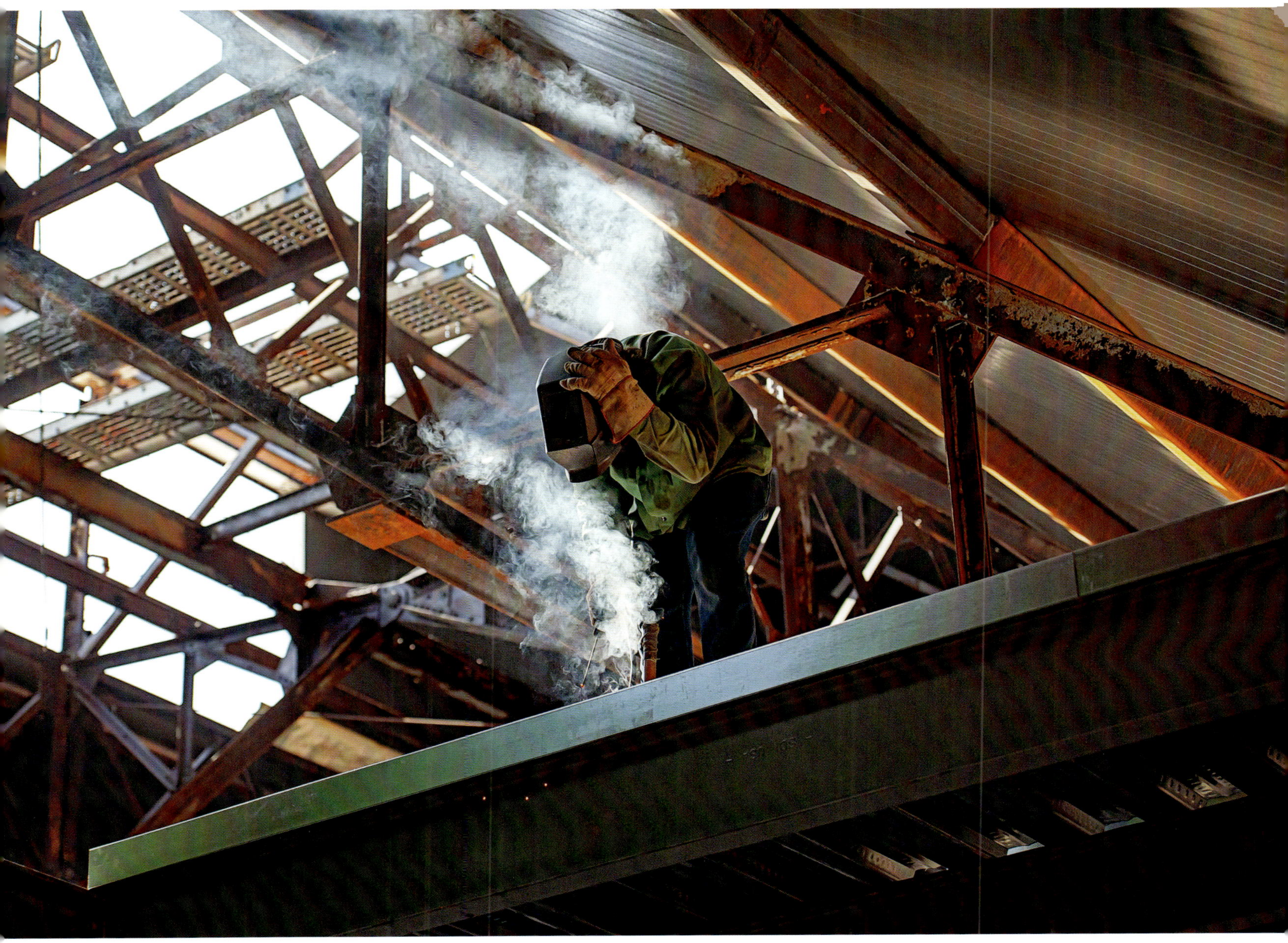

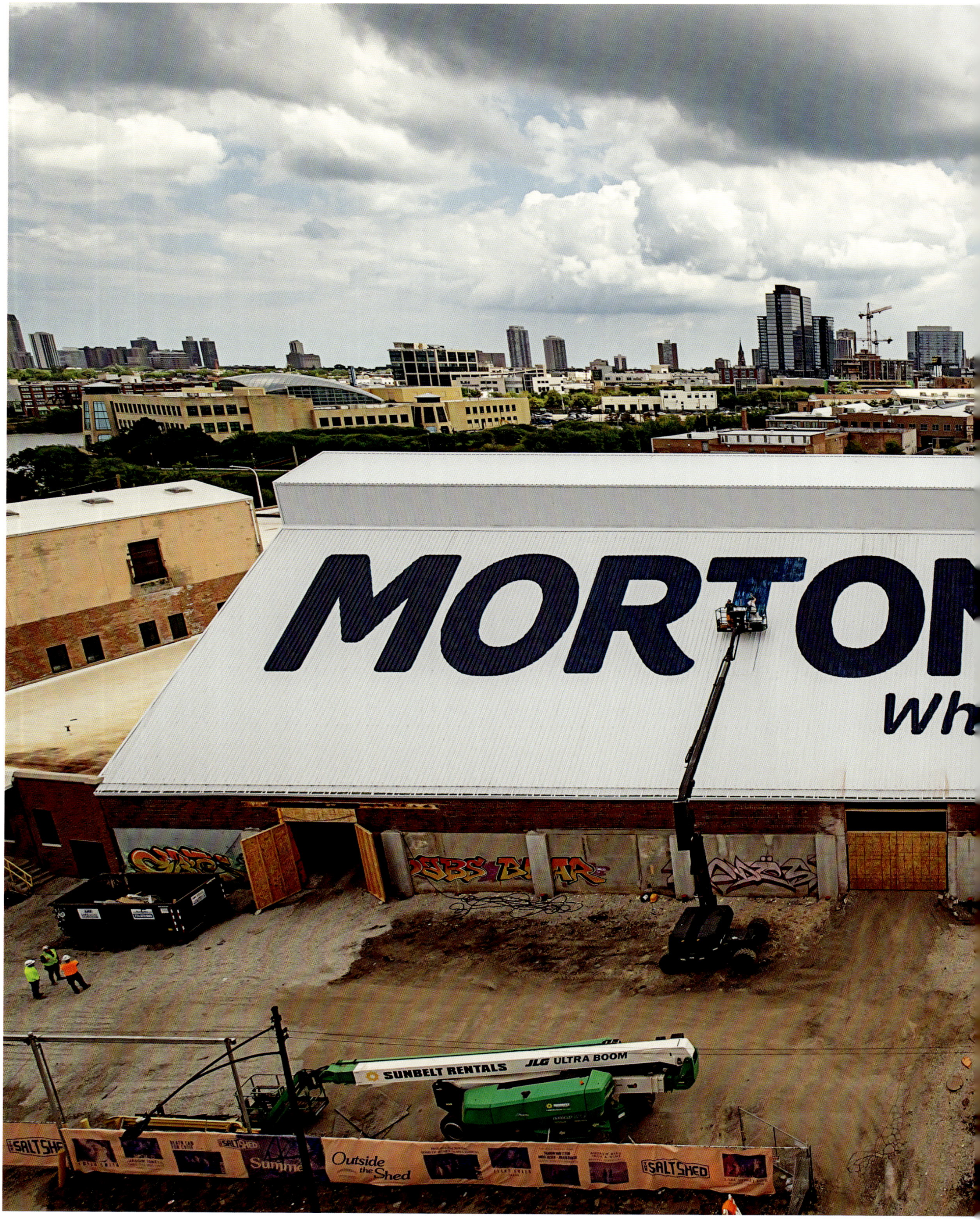

MORTON
Wh
SUNBELT RENTALS
JLG ULTRA BOOM
SALTSHED
Outside the Shed

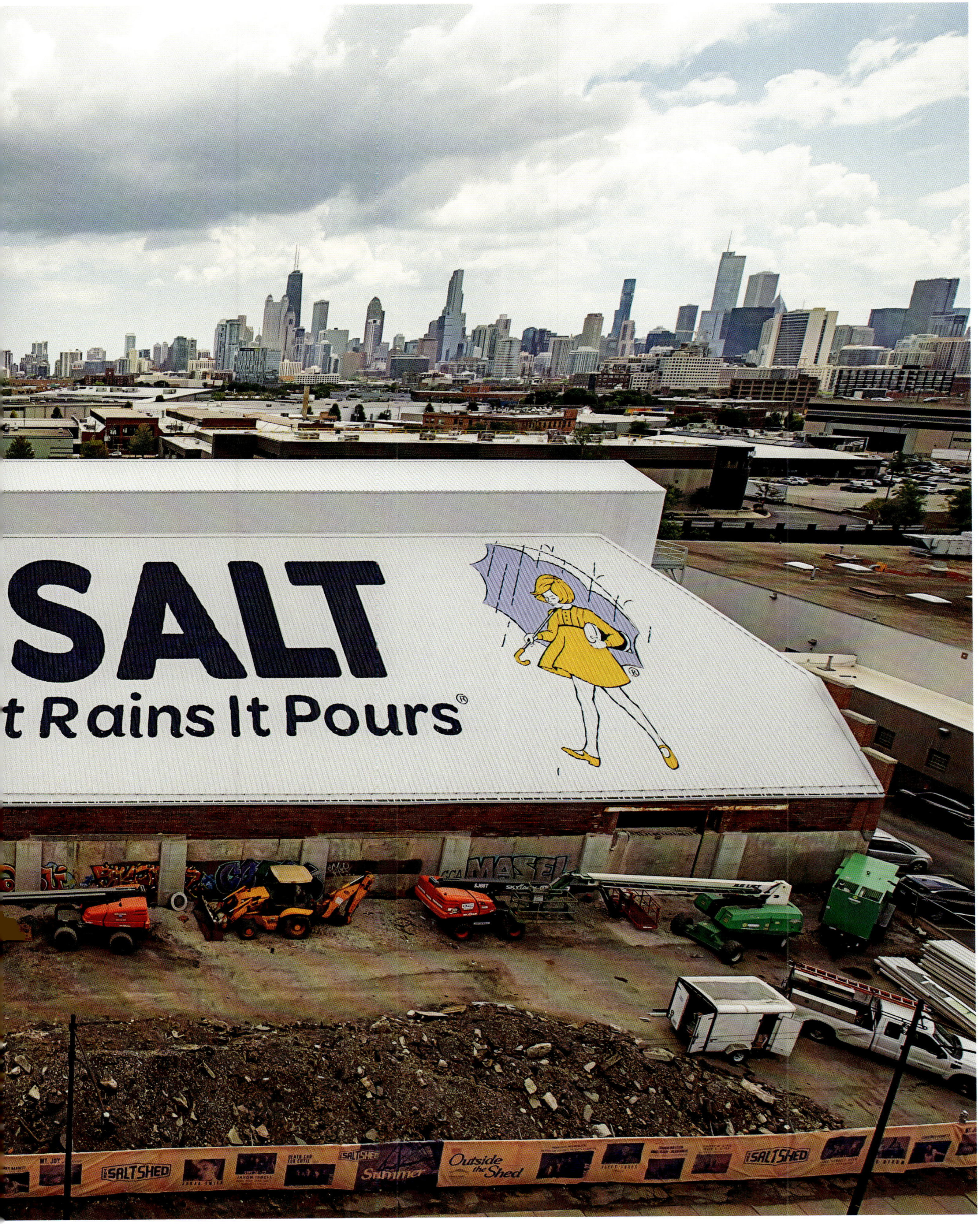
SALT
t Rains It Pours®
SALTSHED
Outside the Shed
SALTSHED

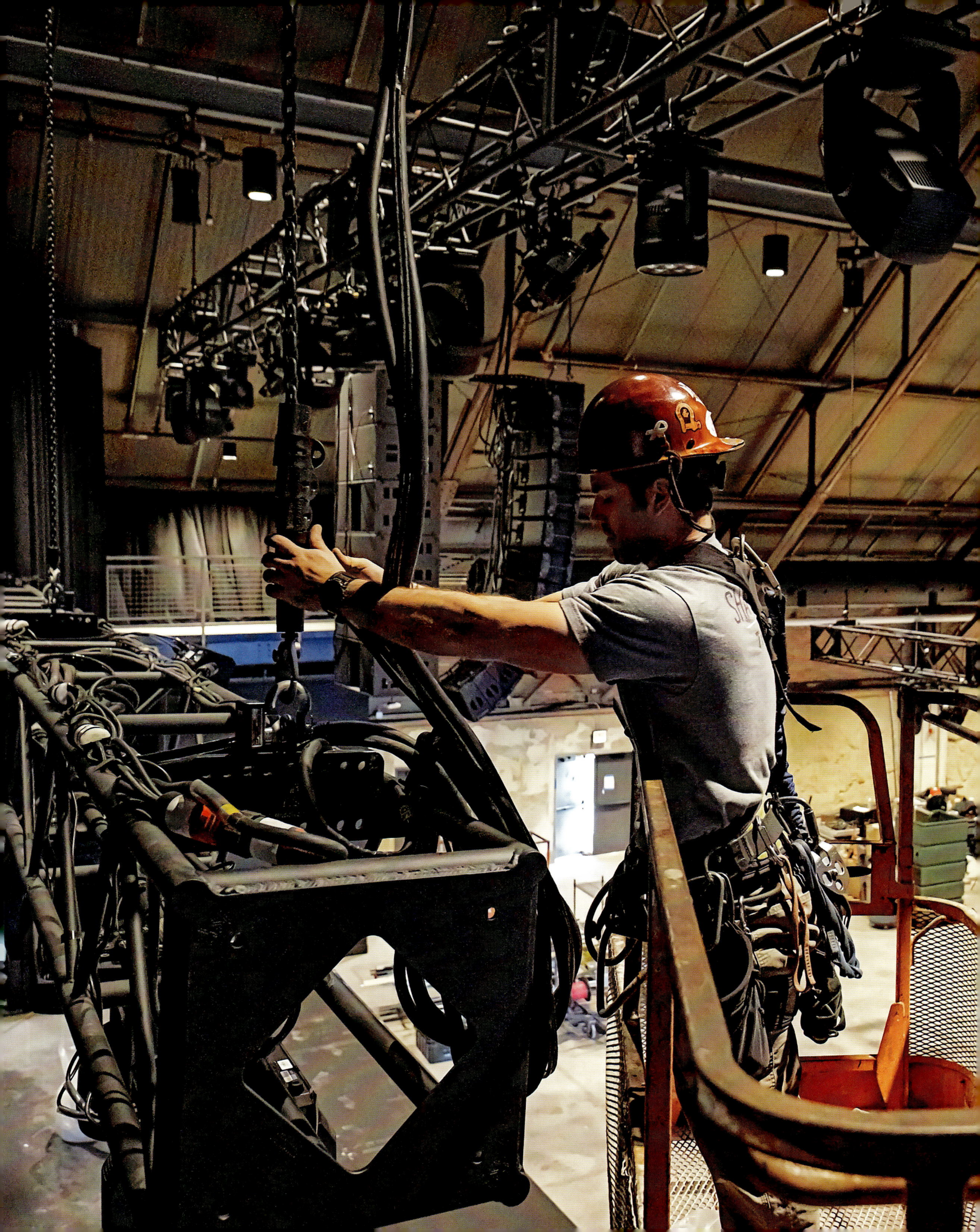

The Morton Salt building with the Umbrella Girl on the roof was a landmark to me as I traveled across the city. If a high-rise replaced it, without walkable or green spaces, it would erode the character and the human scale of the community. When a building like that is kept from demolition, it can help save an entire neighborhood. Now the restored Salt Shed brings indoor-outdoor space to be enjoyed by thousands and reaffirms that Chicago continues to be a city of neighborhoods.

~ Ron Gordon, architectural photographer + preservationist

Nº 6

SHED

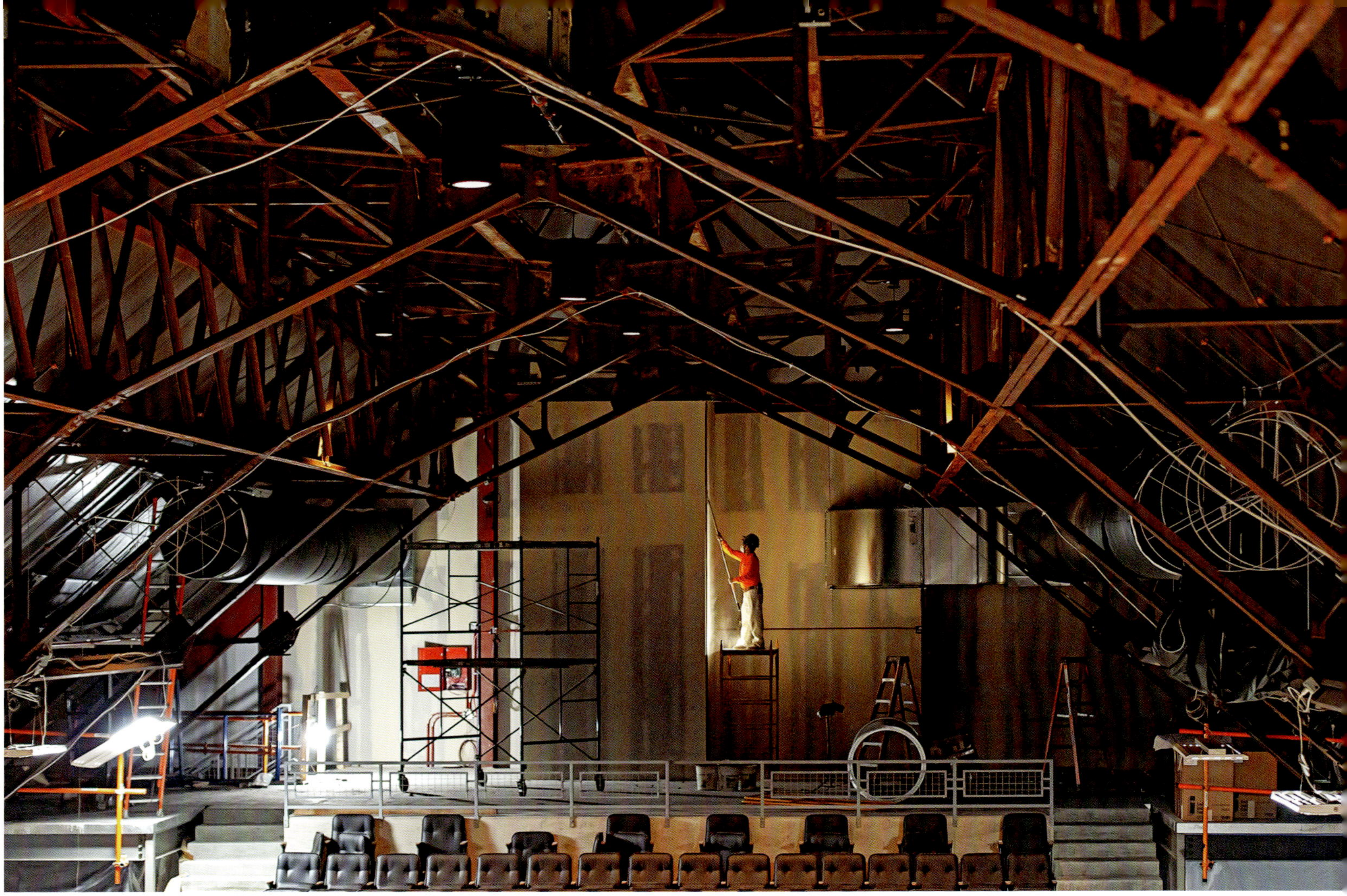

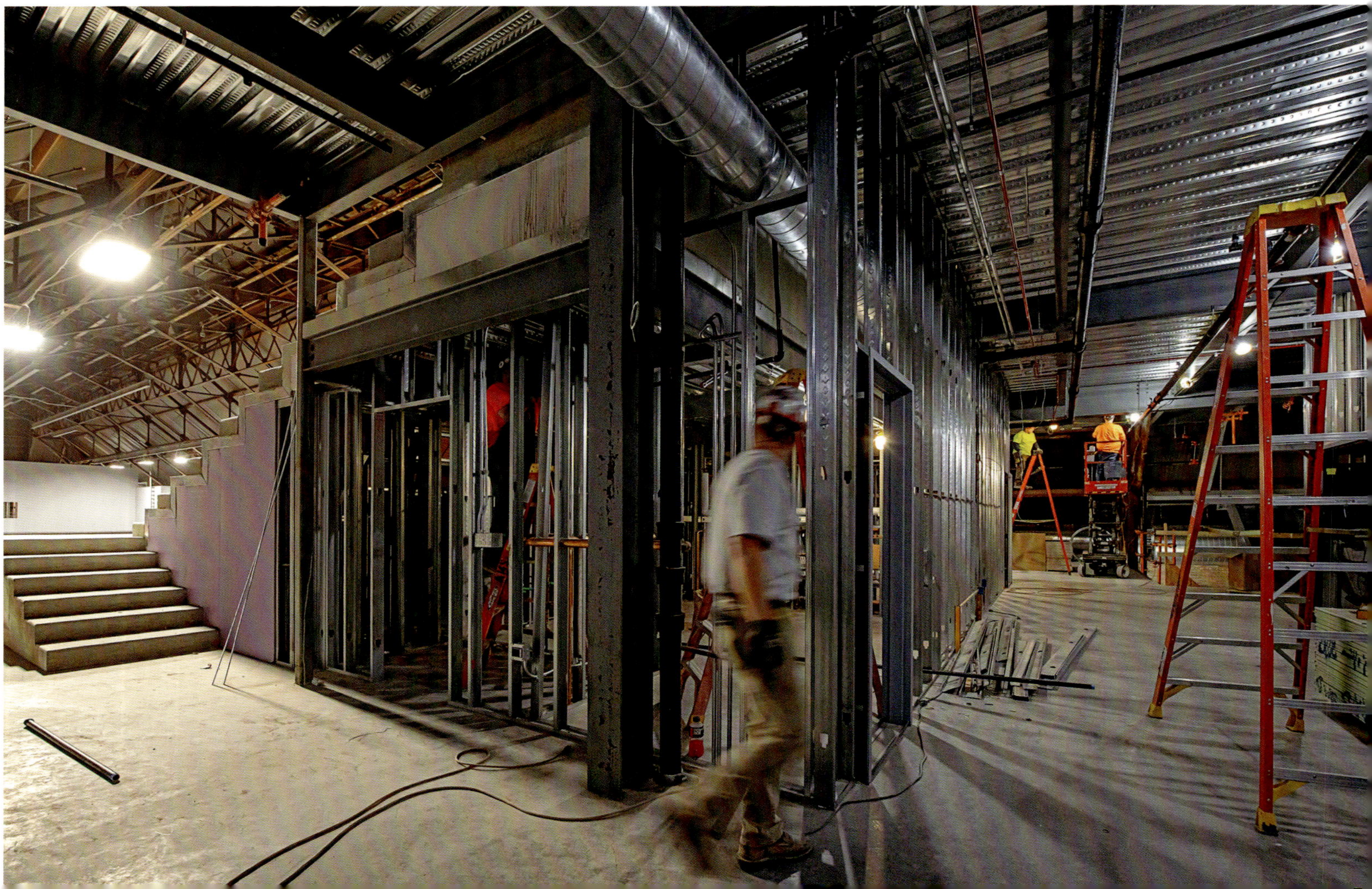

Shed

A Race to the Finish

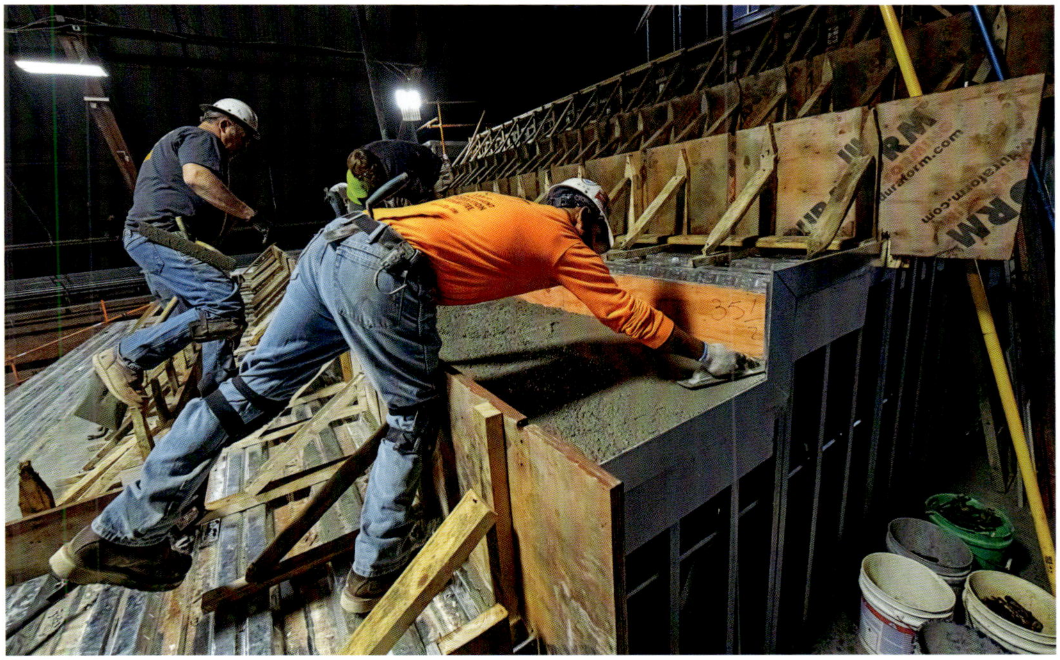

Once the Salt Shed had been a space that was safe for a few workers in hardhats to come and go. Now it would be a place that could welcome 3,500 music fans indoors and 5,000 people celebrating out on the fairgrounds.

The opening date seemed a long way off, but as it approached, the energy and sense of urgency began to ramp up. The number of workers was growing each day, with more and more people busy in every area of the shed. Many of the trades seemed to be pulling ten- and twelve-hour shifts. Sound, light, stage production, and venue workers began their own race to the finish, staying late at night and on weekends. Final Inspections of every kind were looming, just days and hours before the very first show.

That final winter, I traded the frozen, muddy terrain for the warmth of the shed's giant heaters and its nearly nonstop activity inside. There were people everywhere, moving within a cacophony of saws, hammers and drills, to the beeping of lifts moving around the shed.

Electricians worked throughout; their giant four-foot spools of electrical wire draped across the shed floor. They installed over fifty thousand feet–around ten miles of conduit. Carpenters built out the stadium seating, and cement masons created the levels and the stairs, hammering in hundreds of wood forms, before pouring and finishing the concrete. Tile setters cut, placed, and grouted thousands of small blue tiles in vast bathrooms. Large aluminum ducts for the heating and cooling systems snaked around ceiling areas. The operations staff devised systems for managing the space and the flow of people, all while wearing safety gear, dodging lifts, and avoiding wet concrete. Out on the street, excavators resumed work to bring water service to the building, finally wrapping up a few days before the opening.

The back of house above the stage began to take shape, a maze of metal studs that would soon become green rooms, hallways, bathrooms, showers, offices, and a kitchen. At the stage area and all around the shed, the highly detailed, highly technical process of creating a world-class sound and lighting system took place daily after nearly four years of planning and design.

A few weeks before opening night, massive speakers and imposing lighting rigs were placed high up in the air, as the production crew began installing equipment, testing programs, refining the systems, seeking perfection. The work went practically around the clock.

A sense of camaraderie prevailed over the exhaustion. People pitched in, understanding the significance and the role of the building's past in its new capacity. The indoor venue had its first concert put on the calendar. Artists were booked, tickets were sold. The show really would go on.

Shed

A Race to the Finish

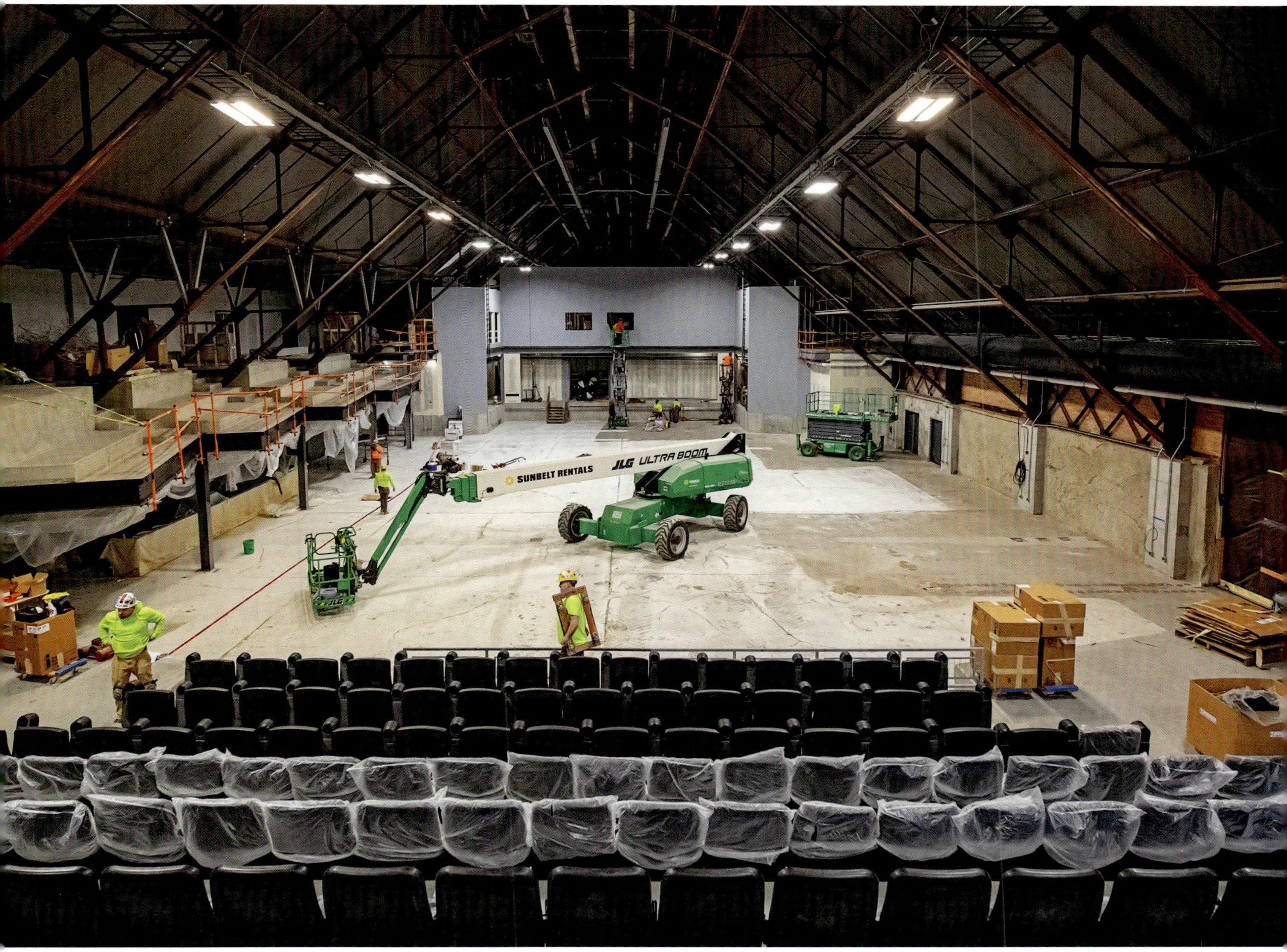

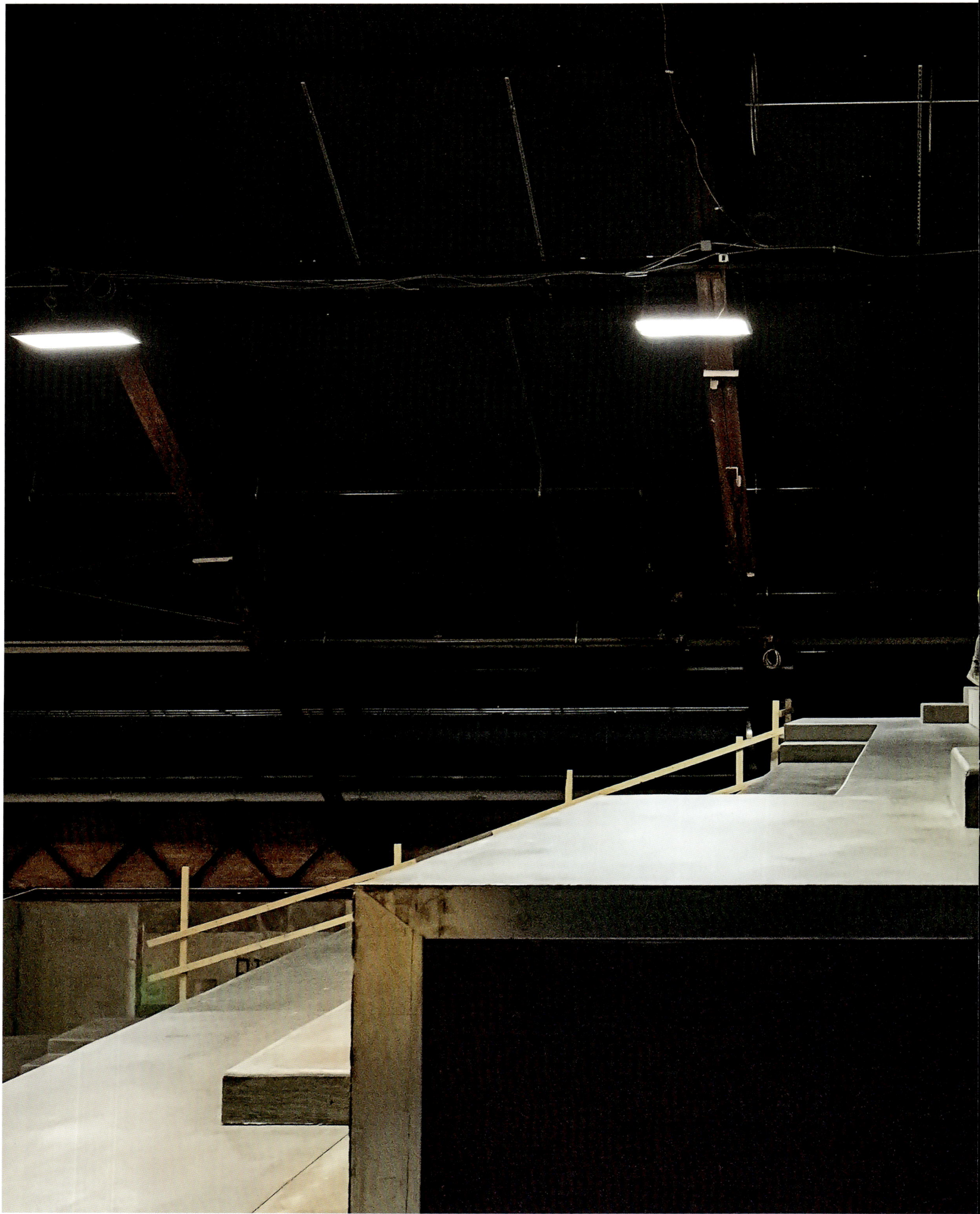

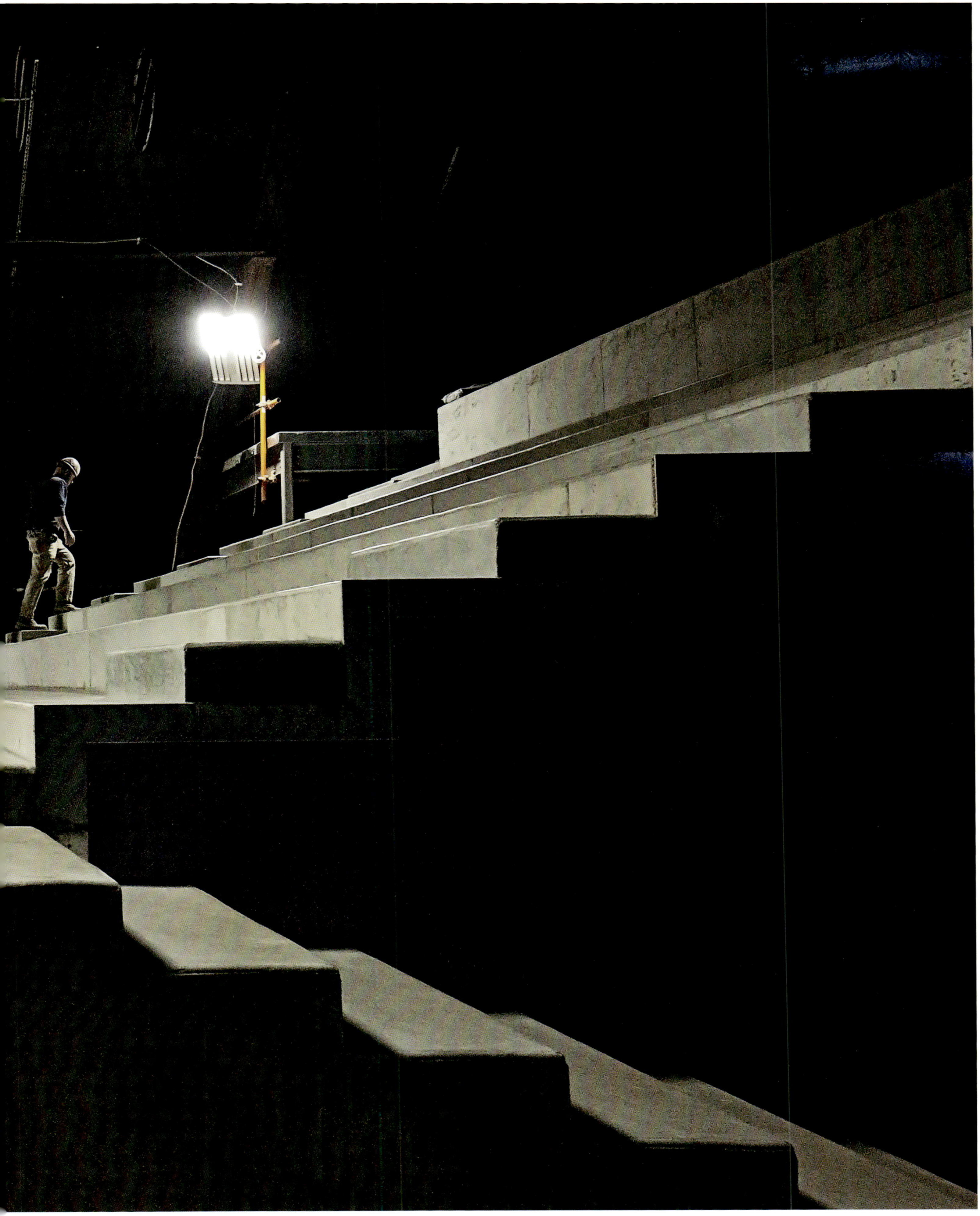

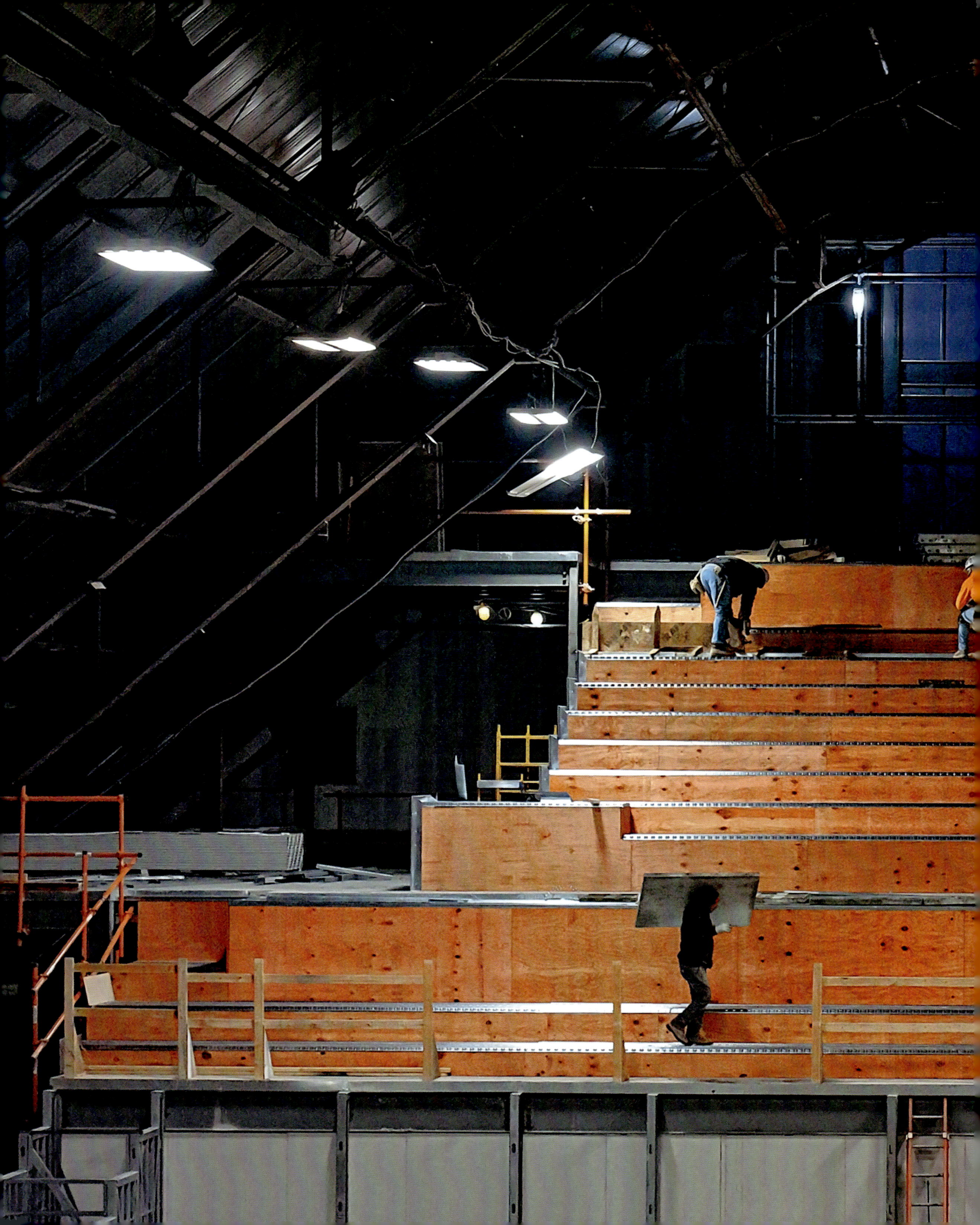

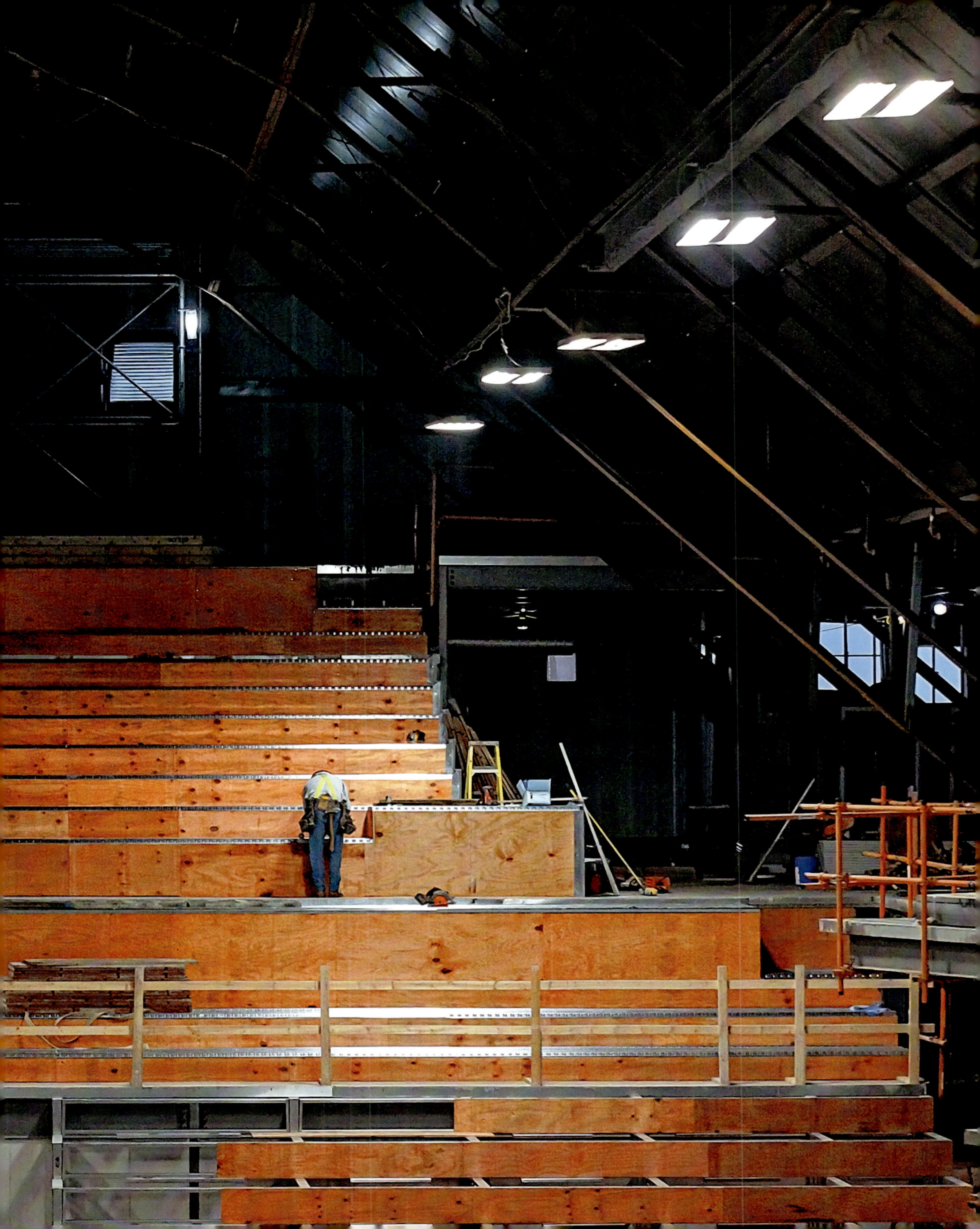

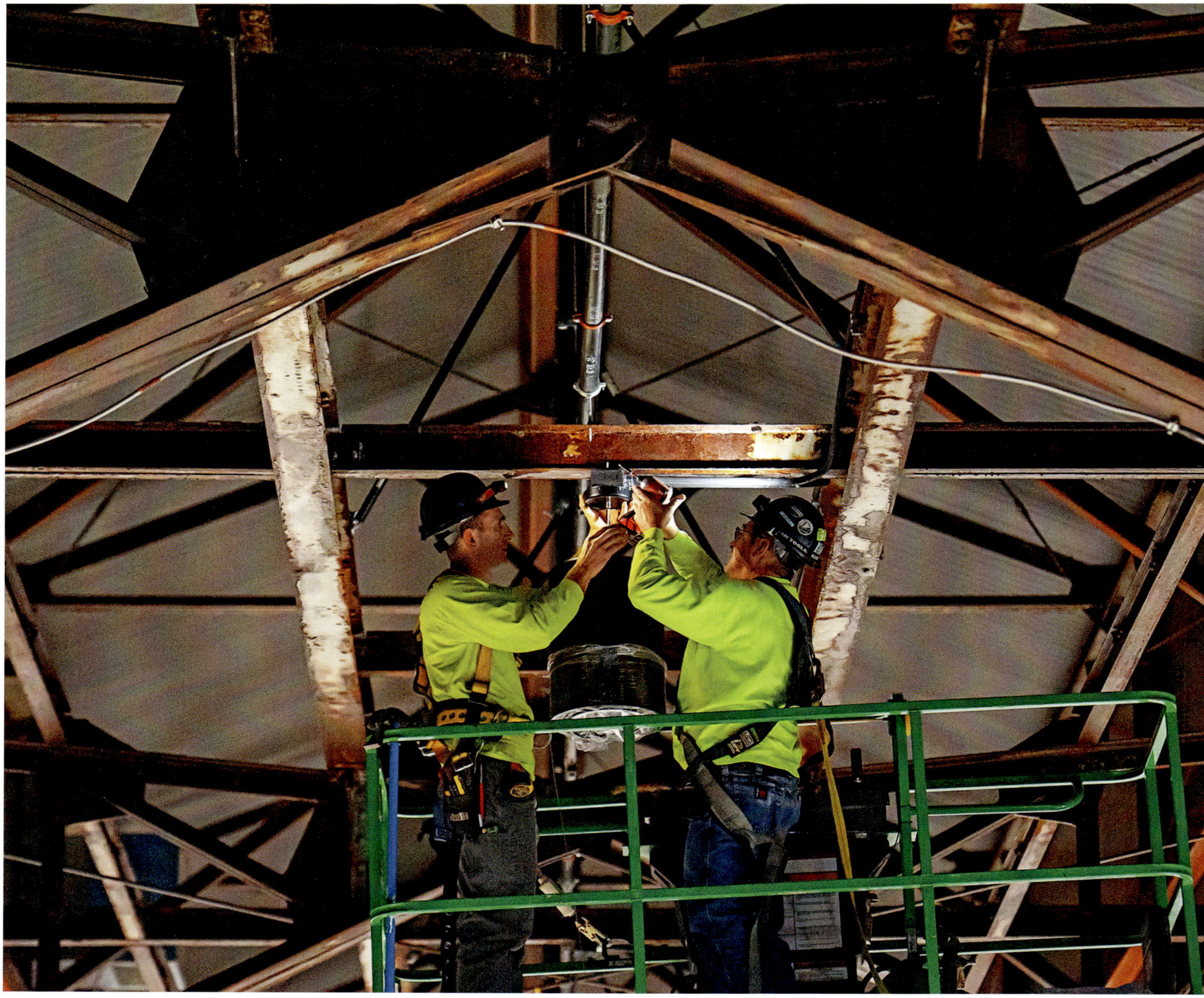

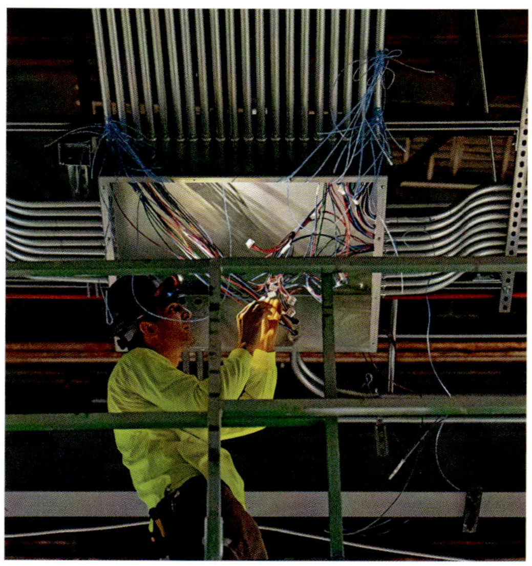

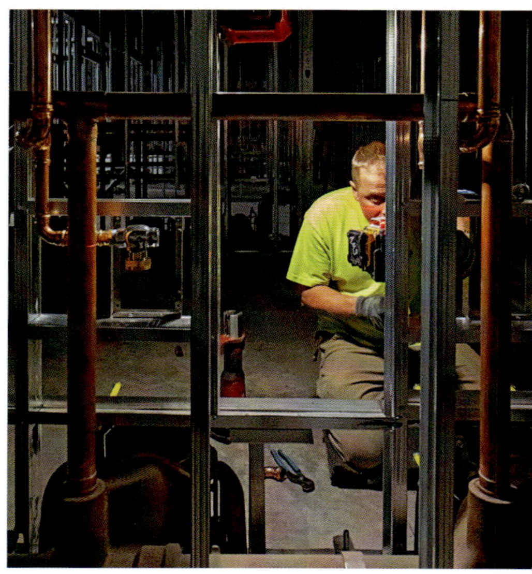

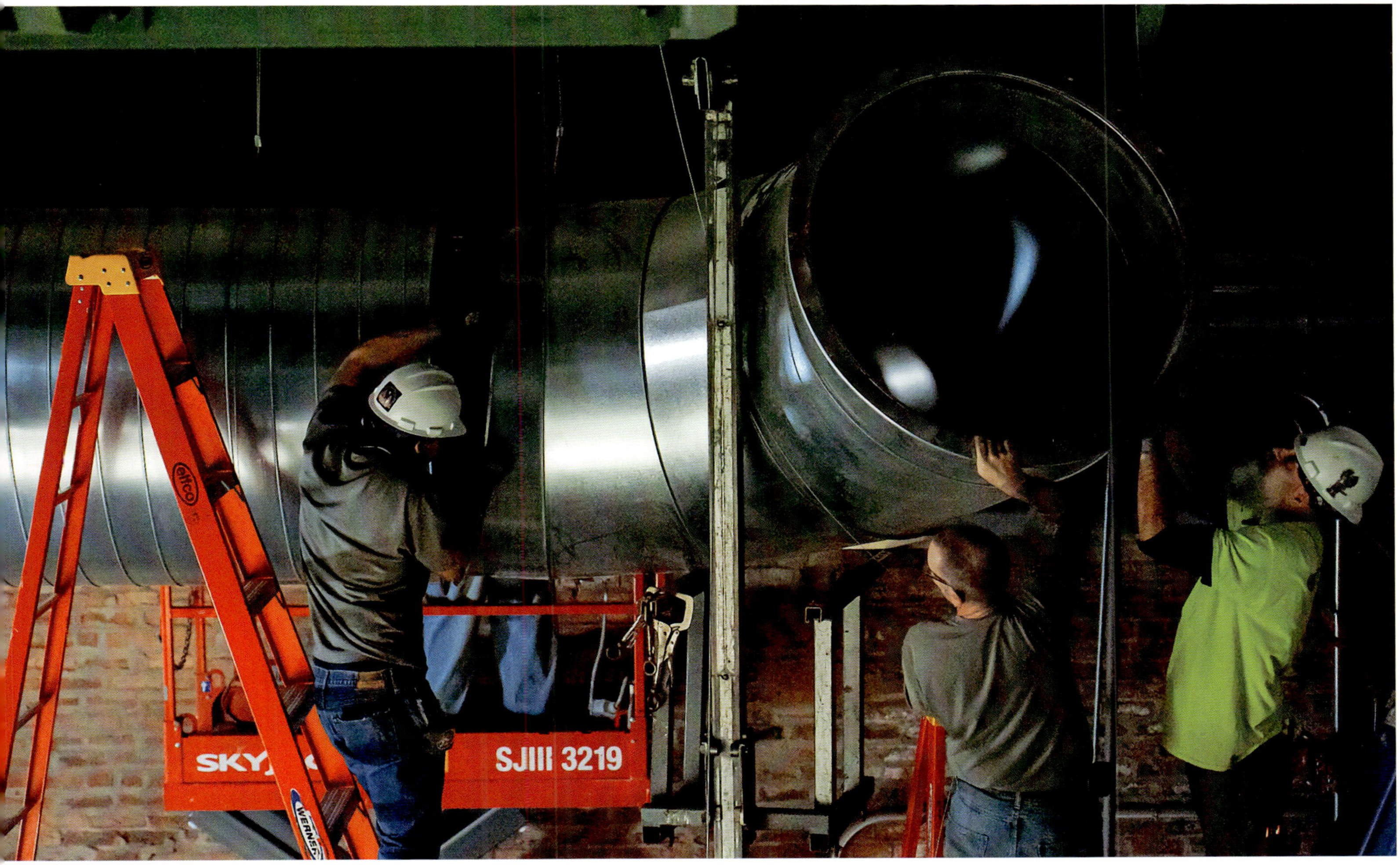
SJIII 3219

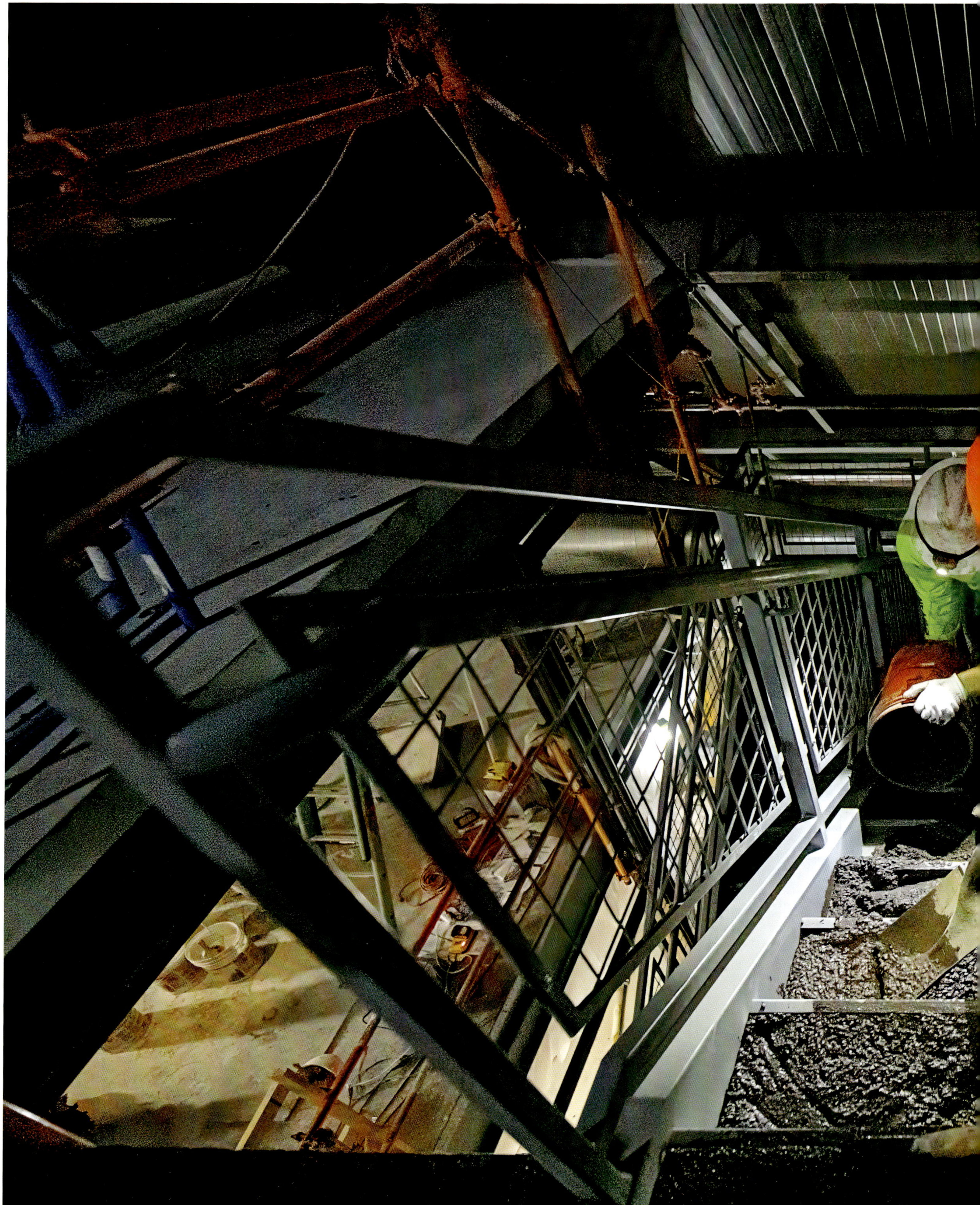

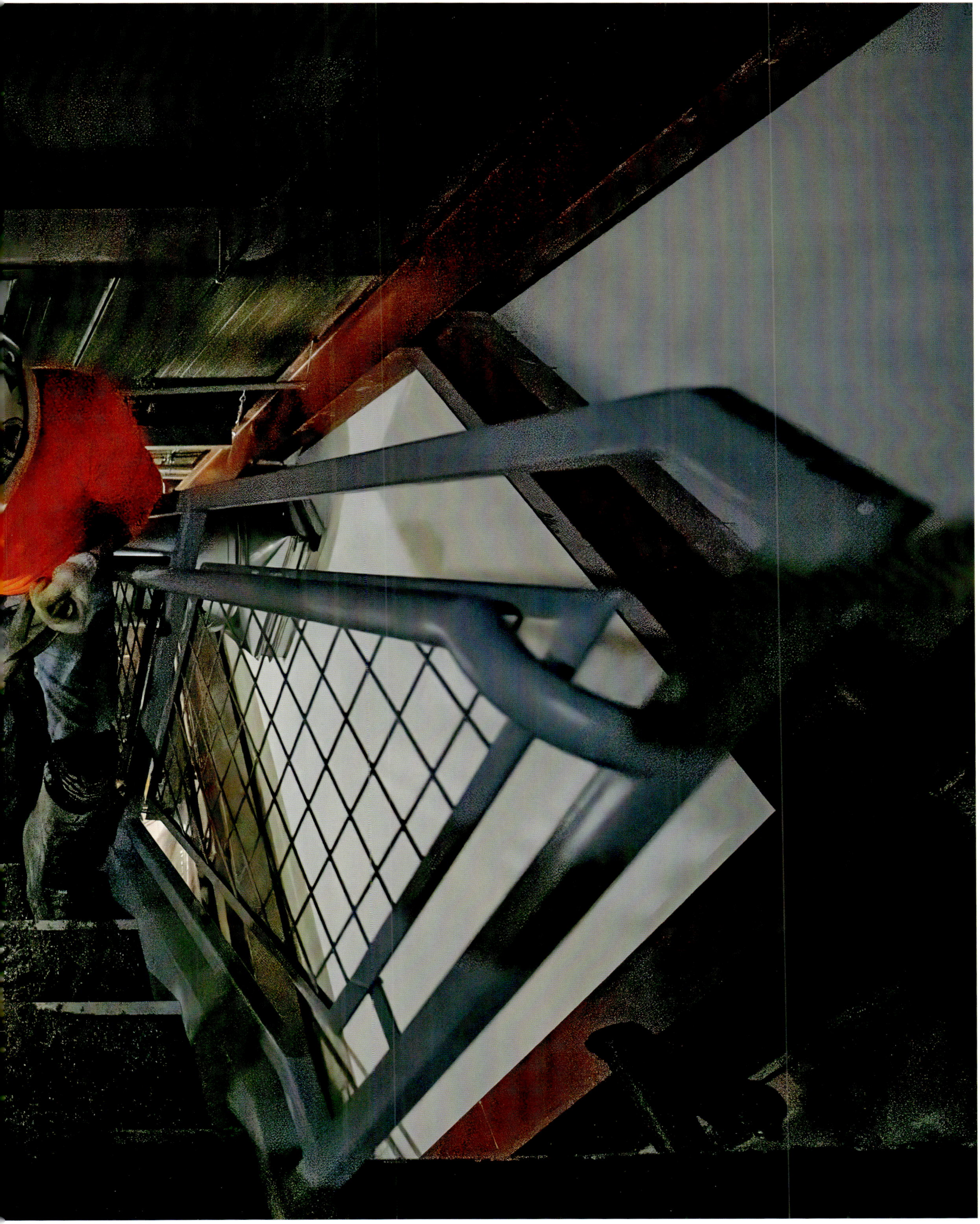

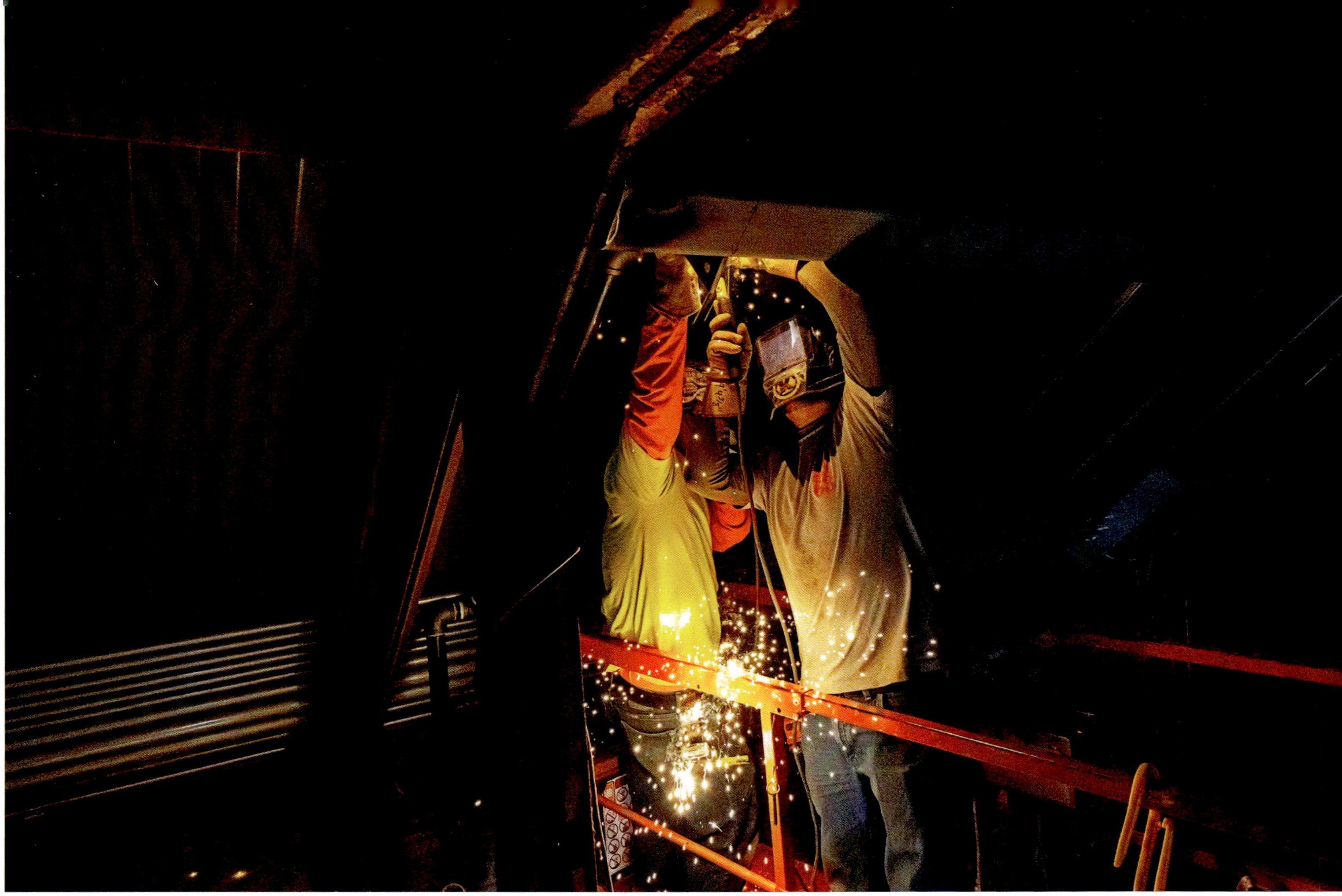

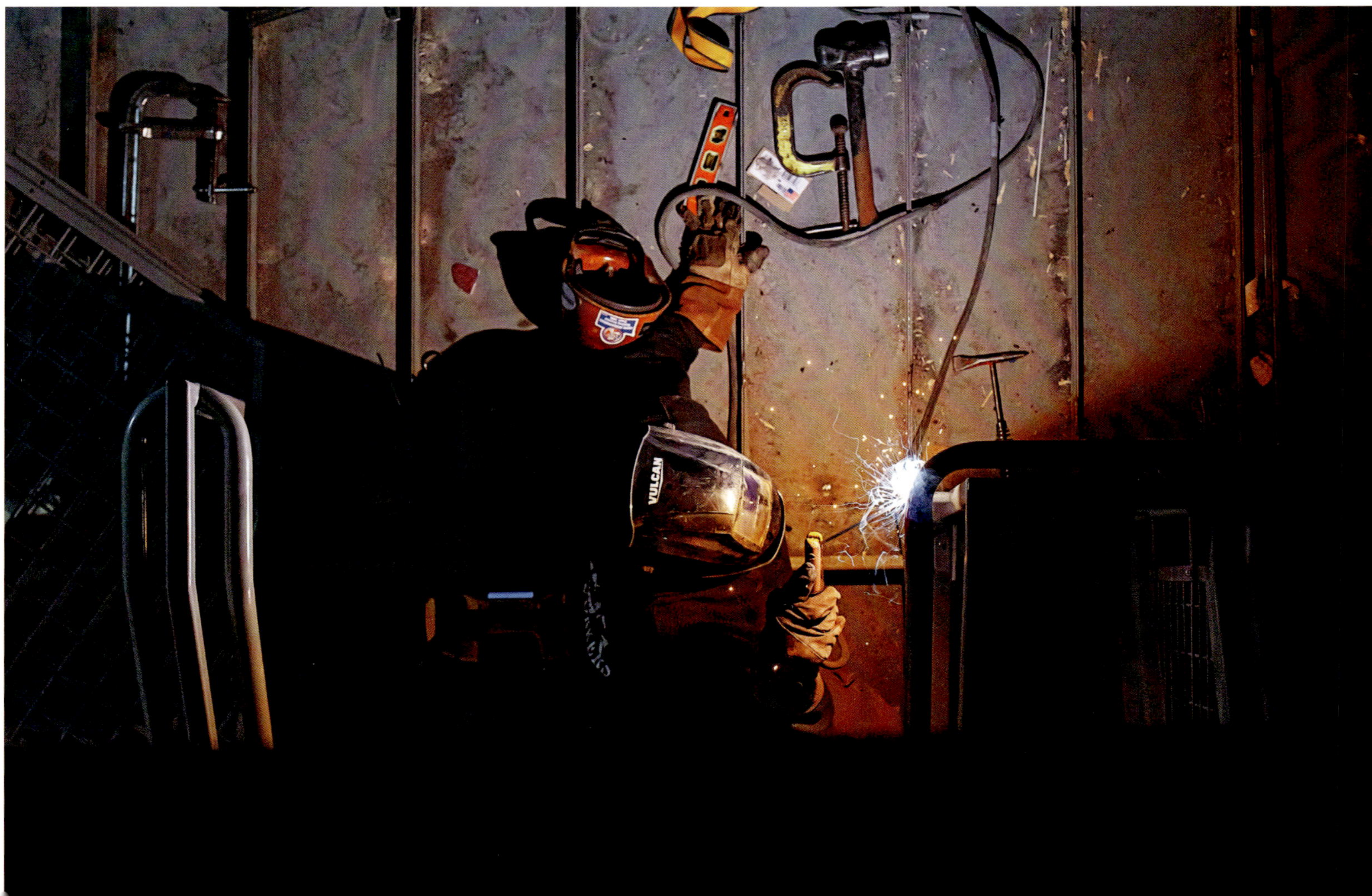
VULCAN

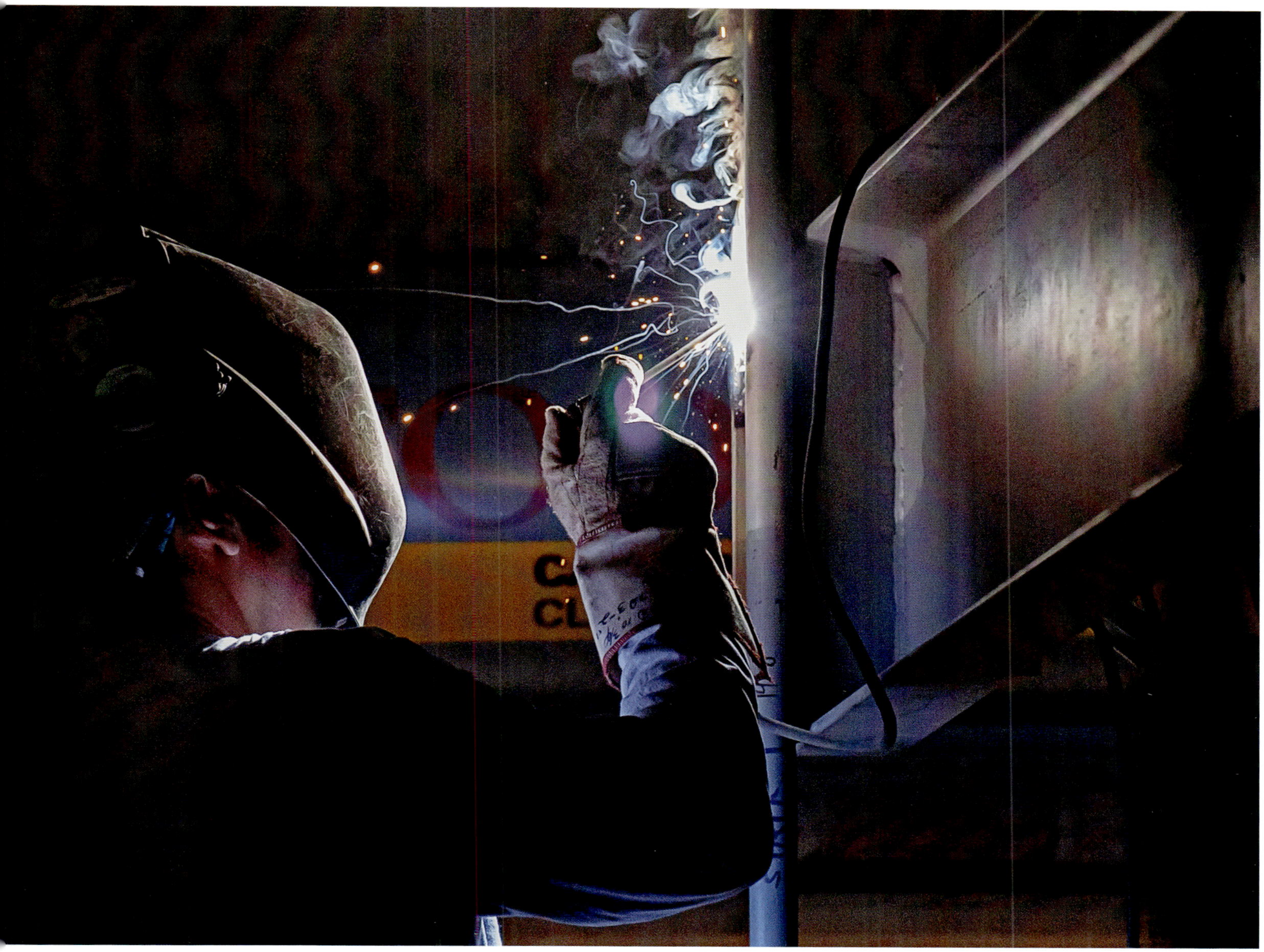

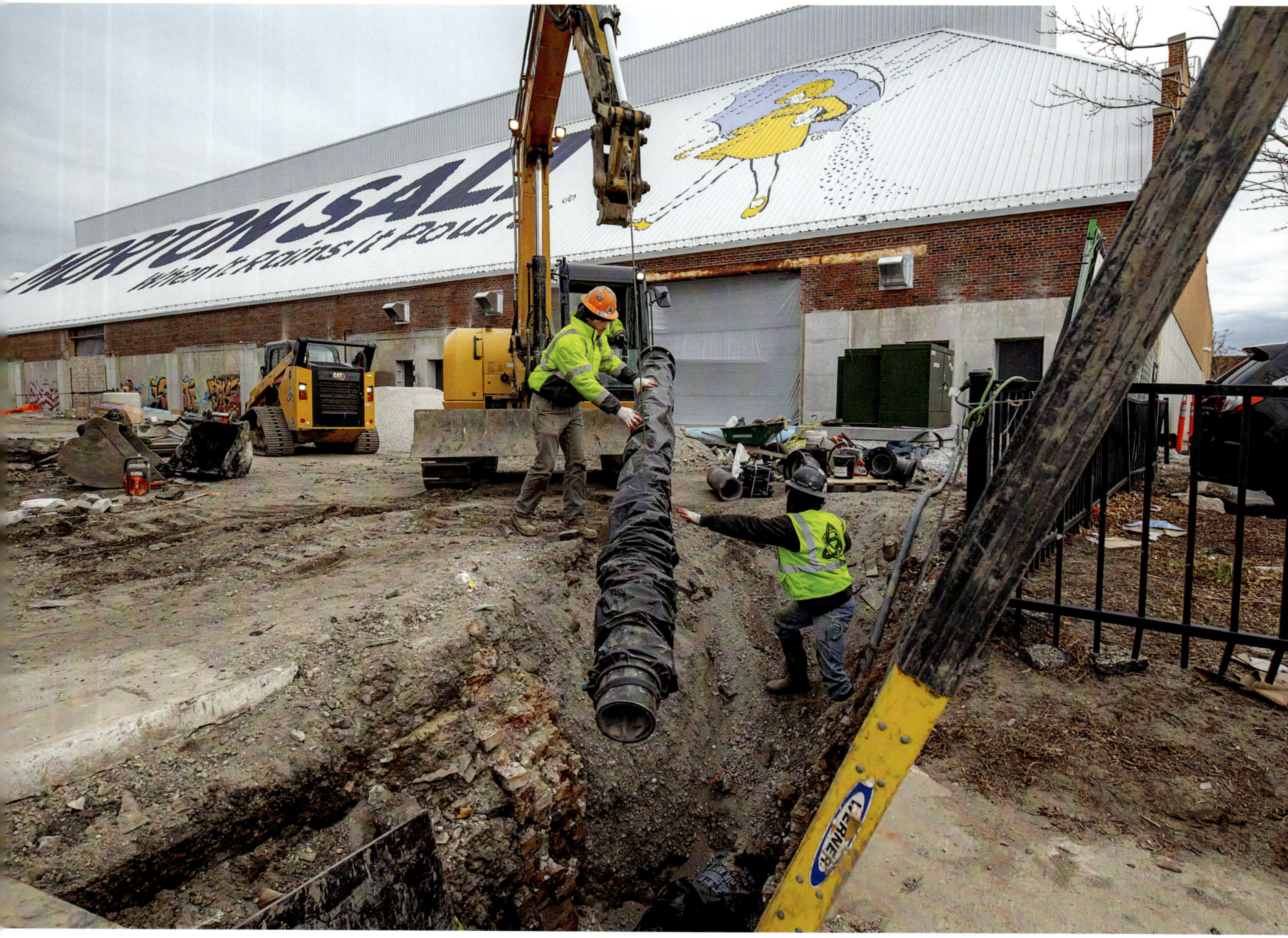

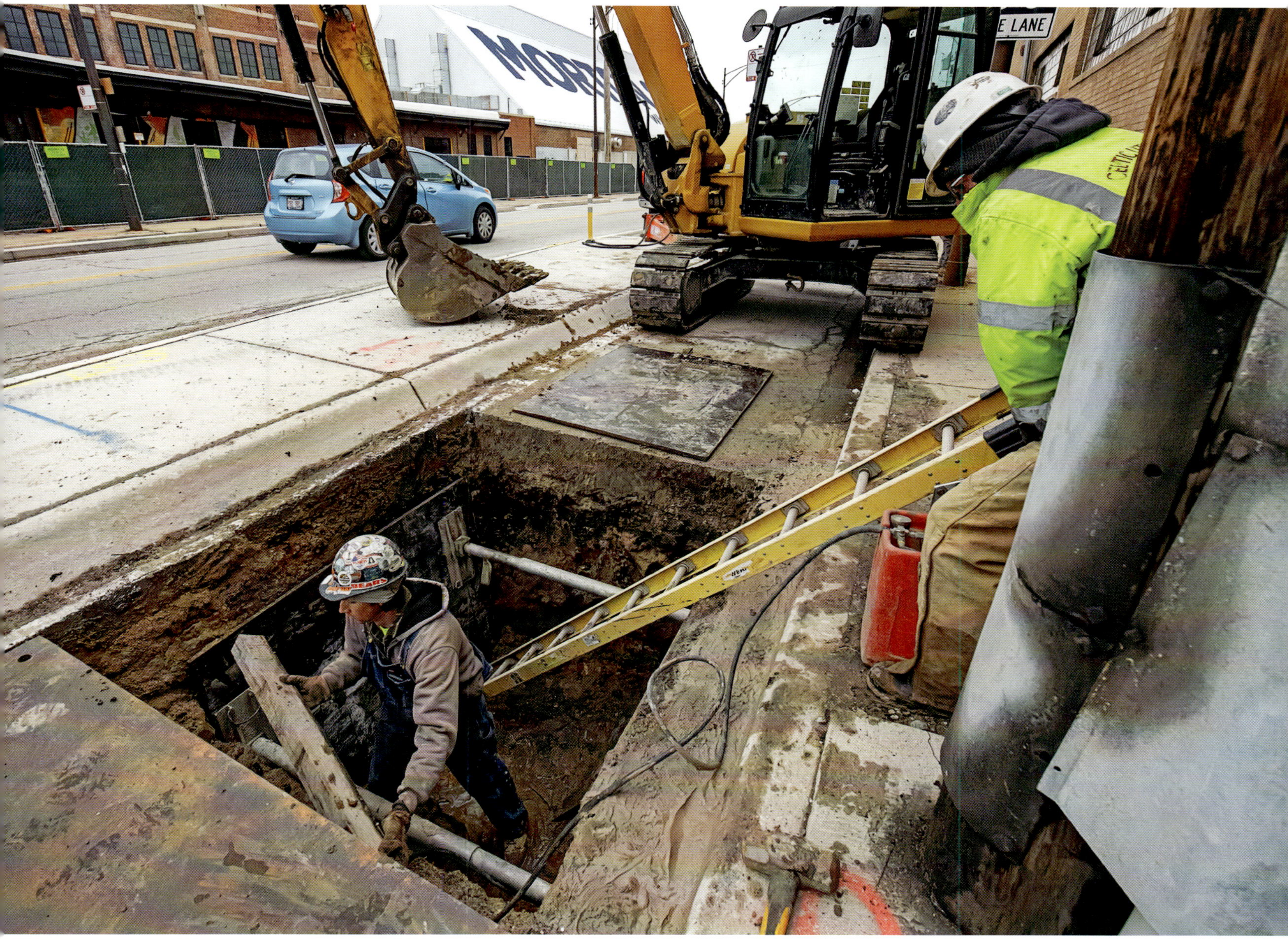

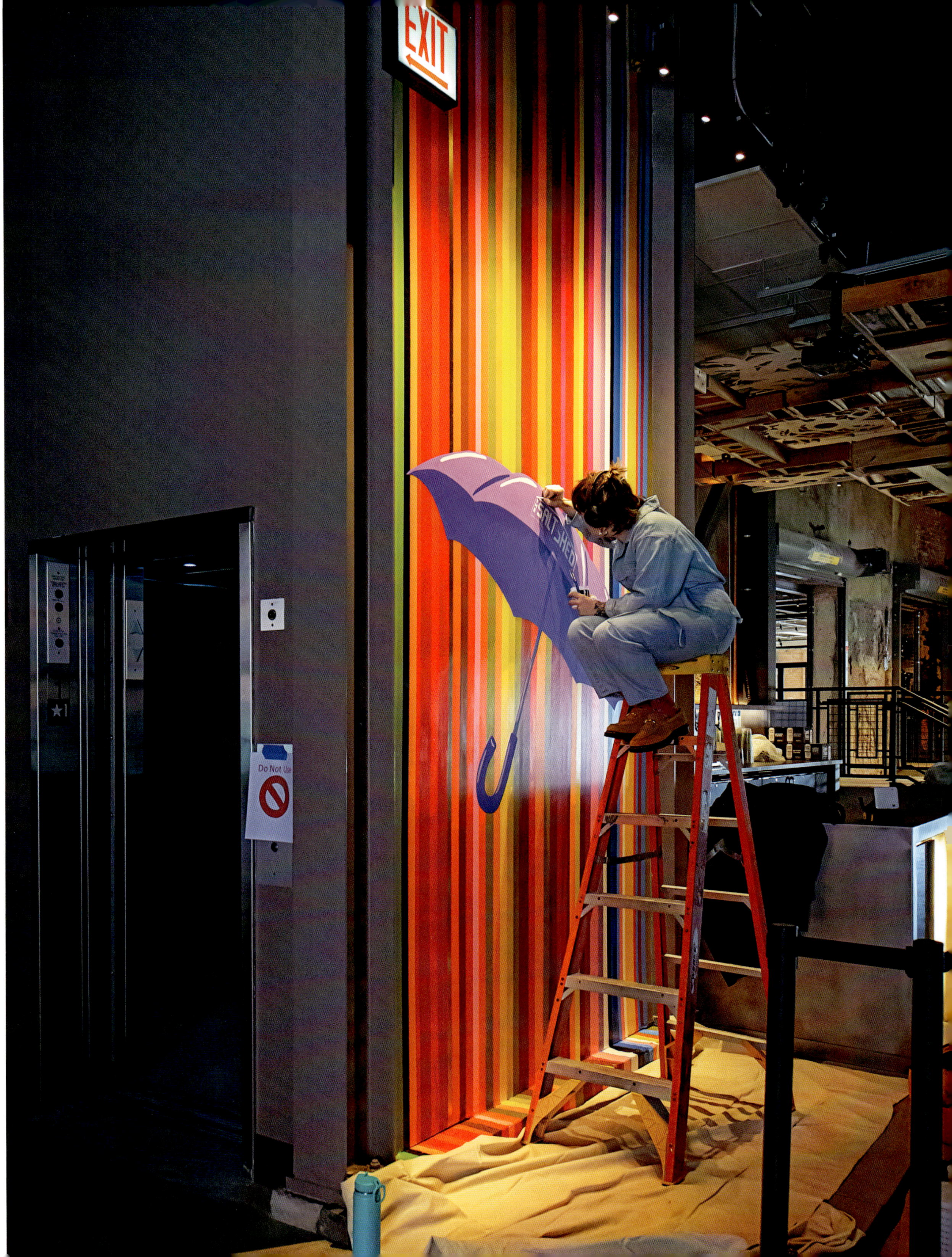
EXIT

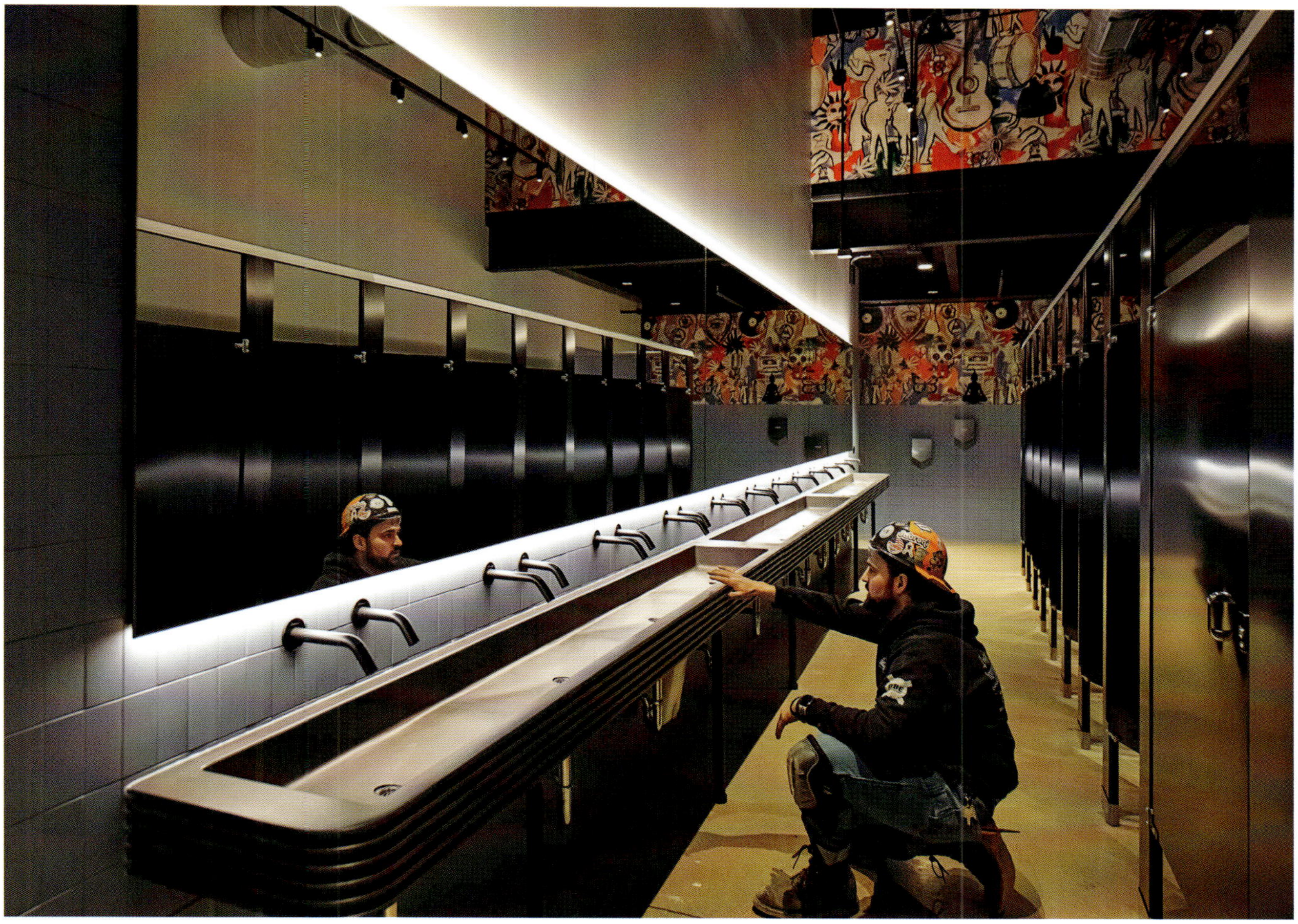

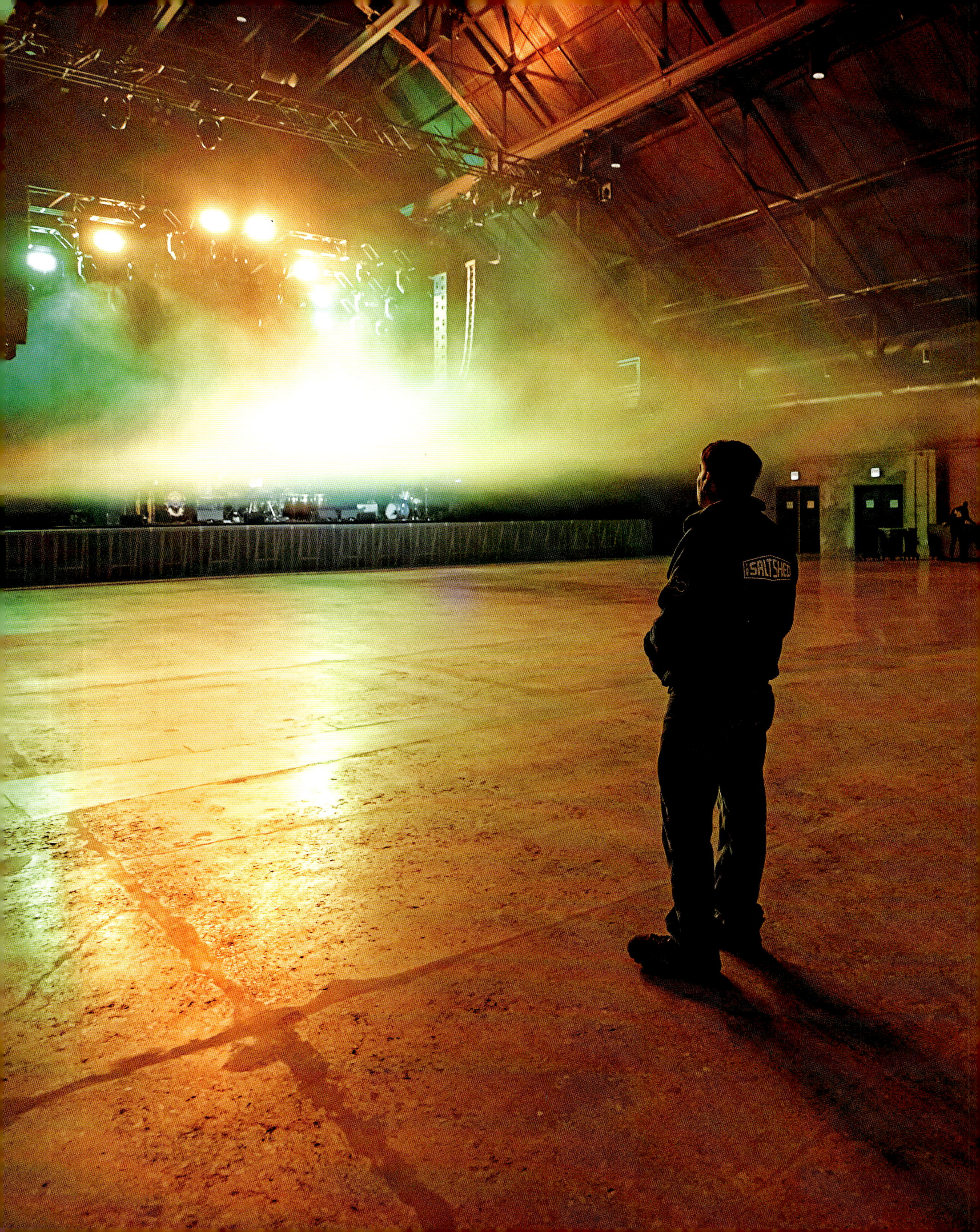
SALTSHED

It is remarkable how Chicago transforms and reinvents itself. Whether that is a result of the Great Chicago Fire or other disasters, we gave the world the first steel frame building, the Chicago School of architecture and the first skyscrapers.

We are a powerhouse of ideas, which is not always recognized as a Chicago characteristic, beyond the Midwest region or on a national scale.

Recognizing historic buildings and reusing them is also about creating strong, healthy communities and honoring that history and that structure, architecturally, culturally and historically. A building like the Salt Shed can be a living landmark, giving back to the community and celebrating its history and its new use.

~ Ward Miller, the Richard H. Driehaus executive director of Preservation Chicago

No 7

FUTURE

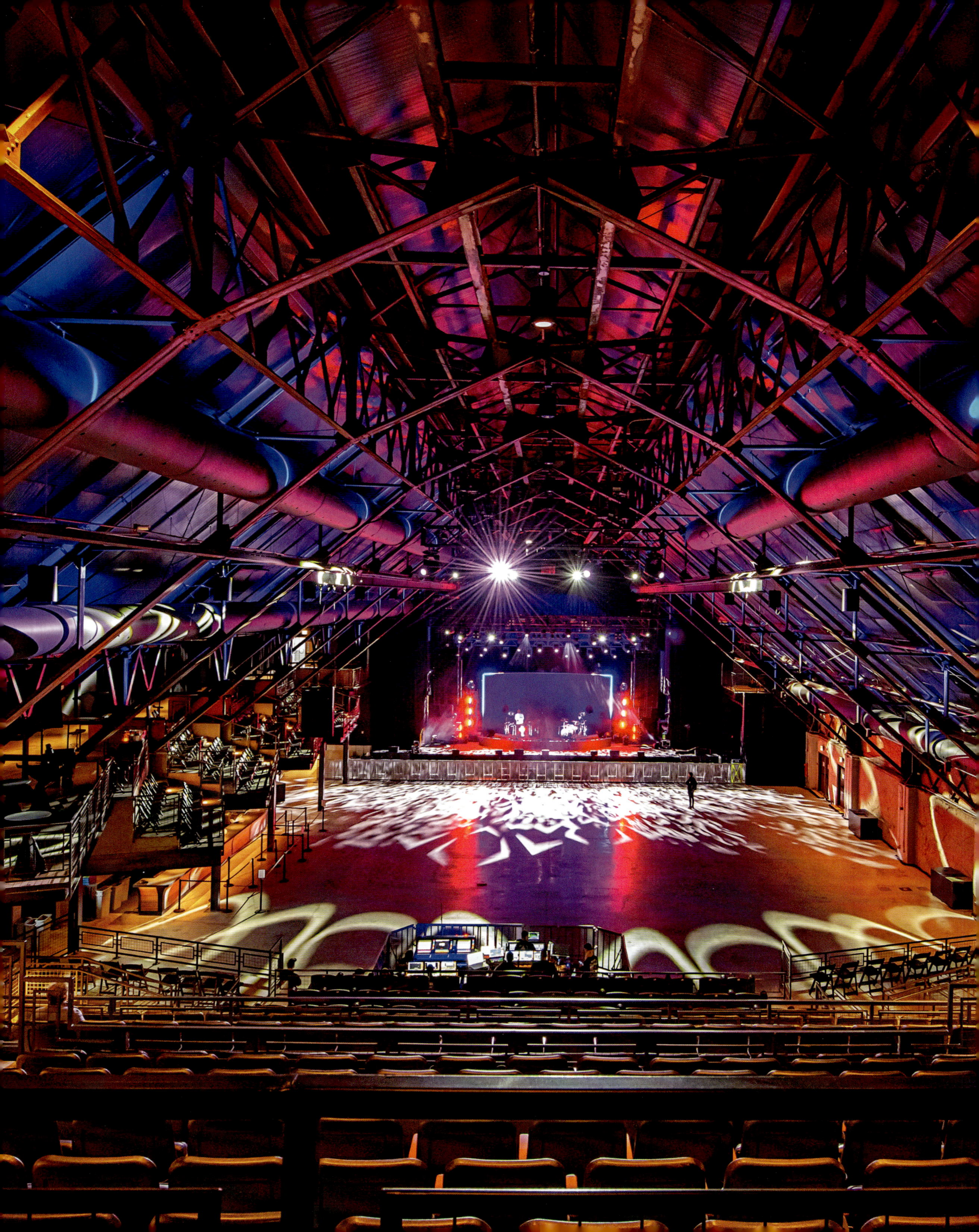

Future

A Second Life for an Historic Structure

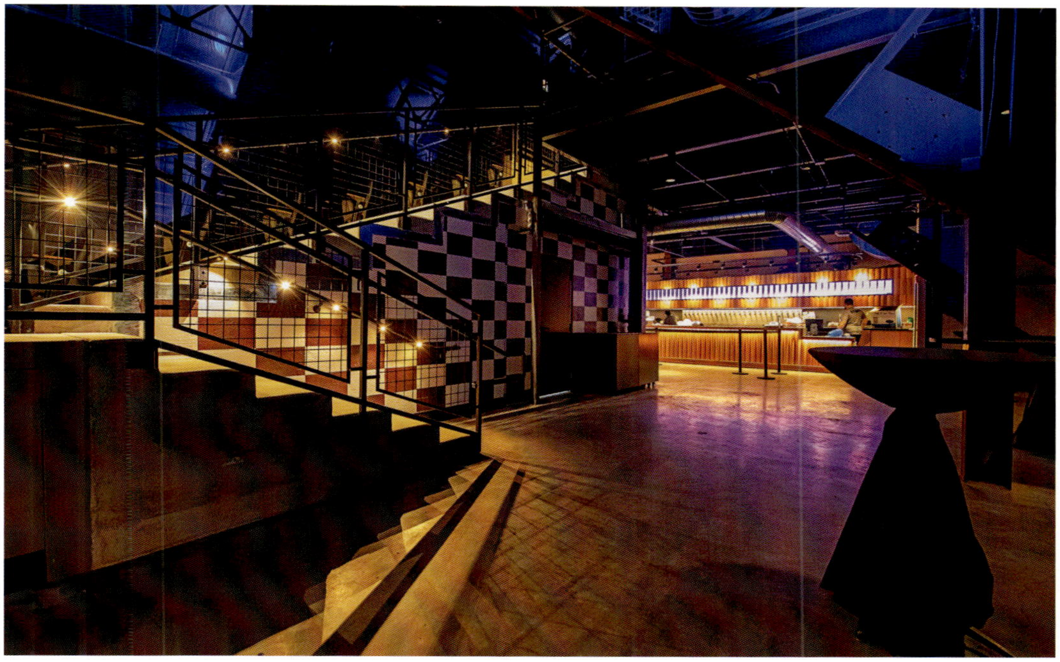

On a chilly evening just after Valentine's Day in 2023, a few thousand people streamed onto the grounds of the Salt Shed, through the same gate I'd first walked through on Blackhawk Street back when it sported barbed wire and a "no trespassing" sign. They walked ahead to enter through new sets of doors–once the old loading docks–and into the expansive lobby of the old packaging building. Friends and family, amazed, spilled into the towering space to celebrate at the first indoor show.

Years before, on another dark winter evening, the future stewards of the building had been impressed as they walked through the abandoned shed. Even in disrepair, the possibilities of this place were striking and exciting. Dreams were shared and ideas sketched out. Plans were drawn, and models created. Steel was tested, reinforced, and rebuilt; the ground excavated and filled back in. Pipes were placed, then buried, transformers installed, and conduits hidden behind drywall, then covered under coats of paint. Hot water flowed, floors were swept, and glass polished. The trades' crews dwindled and then began to disappear, replaced by stage production crews.

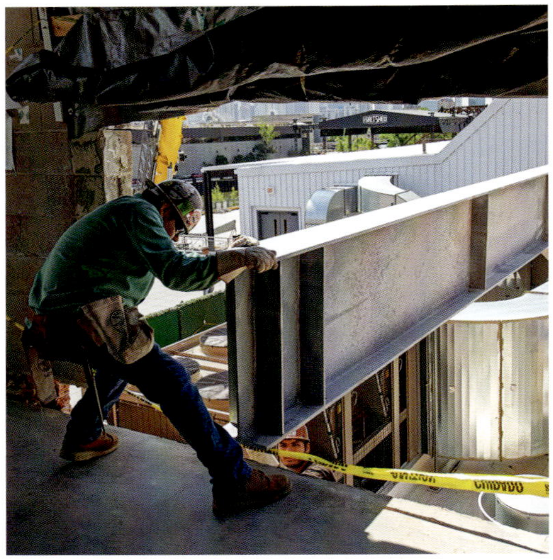 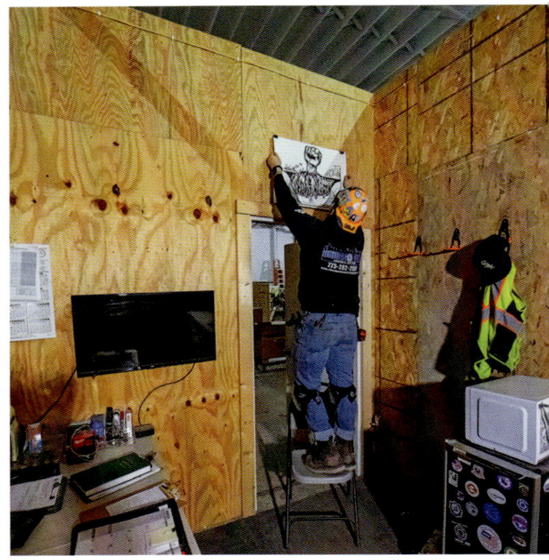

At last, construction workers packed up their tools and materials that they stored onsite in large metal boxes that were hoisted and deposited onto trucks to be taken away. Many had been there for months or even years. The plumbing foreman took down his union poster from the plywood wall of a makeshift office and took it to the next job.

Generations have danced at many moving and joyful performances by a dazzling group of artists. Although the shed maintains many elements and the feel of the original, the former Morton Salt complex has an entirely new reason for being. The era of salt is over. Its second life in the arts is well underway.

Ultimately, the goal of architecture is to shelter and create spaces that improve human life and foster a sense of belonging, which make better, stronger communities. Buildings and spaces come alive with people—working, playing, living. This landmark space is filled with new energy, revealing why preservation is essential for future generations. New structures add to the fabric of our town, and each building we save helps sustain the soul of our city.

Chicago's might is no longer rooted in the steel or meatpacking or salt industries. Our history helps us stay connected to each other and keeps the city grounded and sturdy. Like the sign with the Umbrella Girl, the new building is a marker of where we are and where we're going.

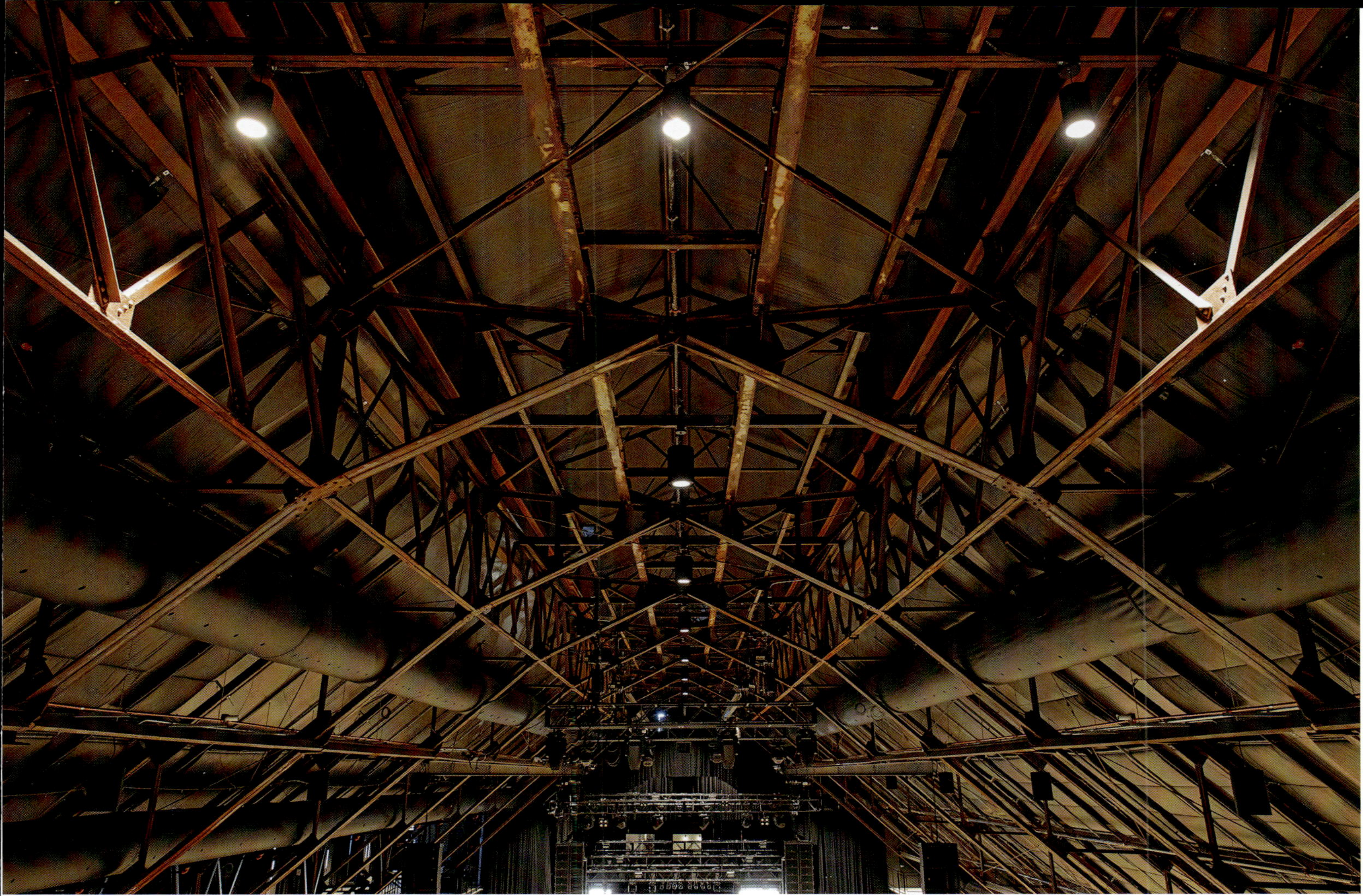

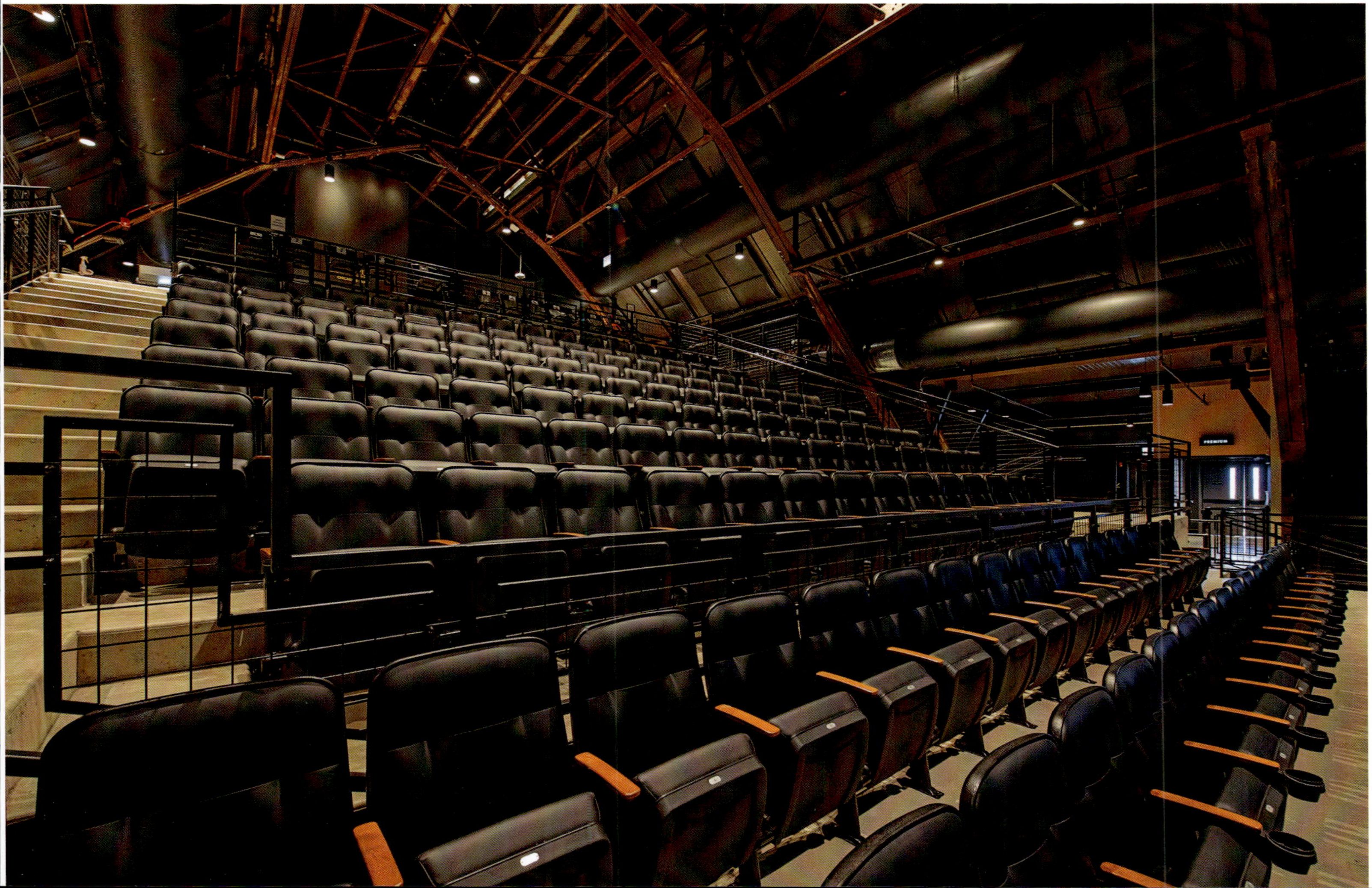

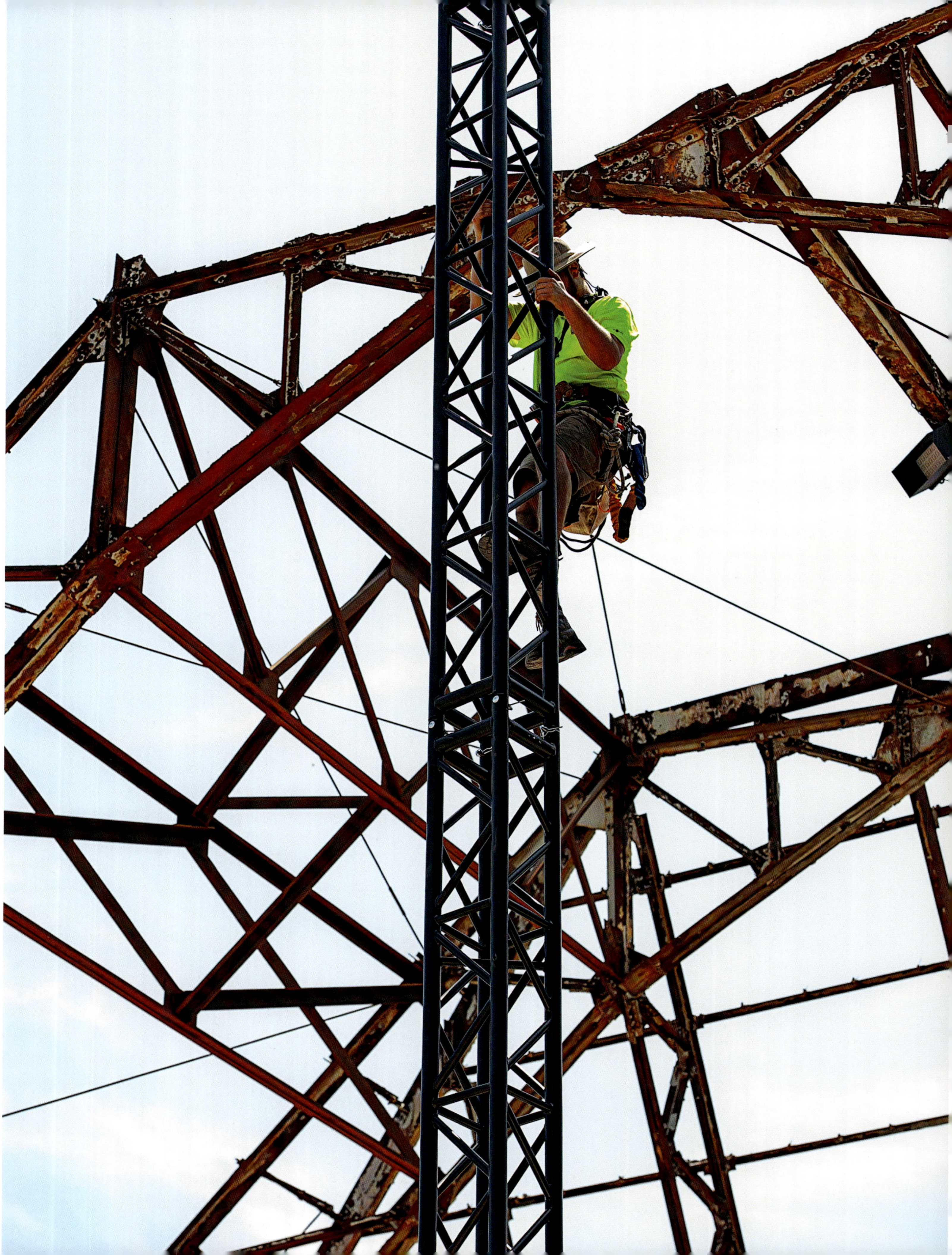

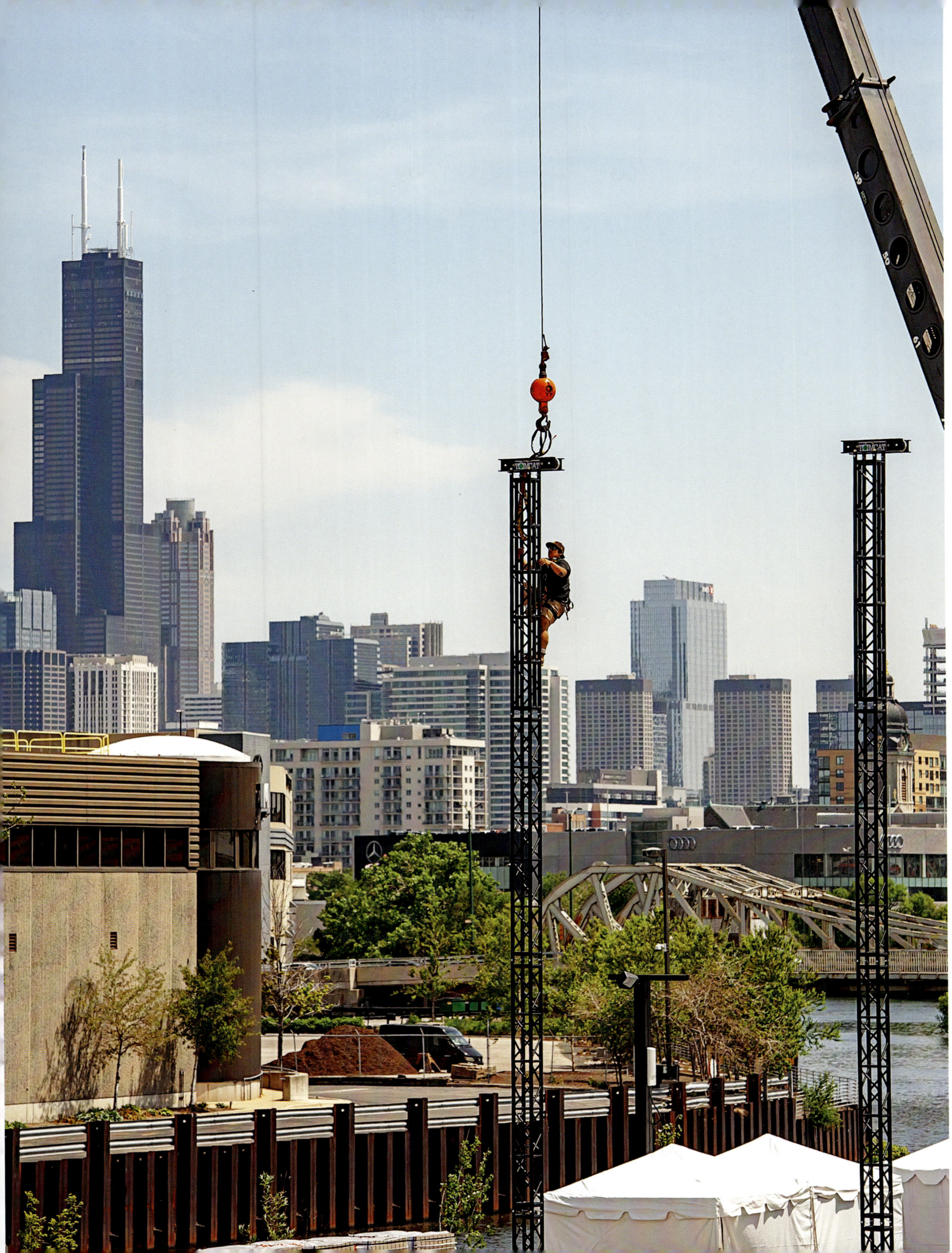

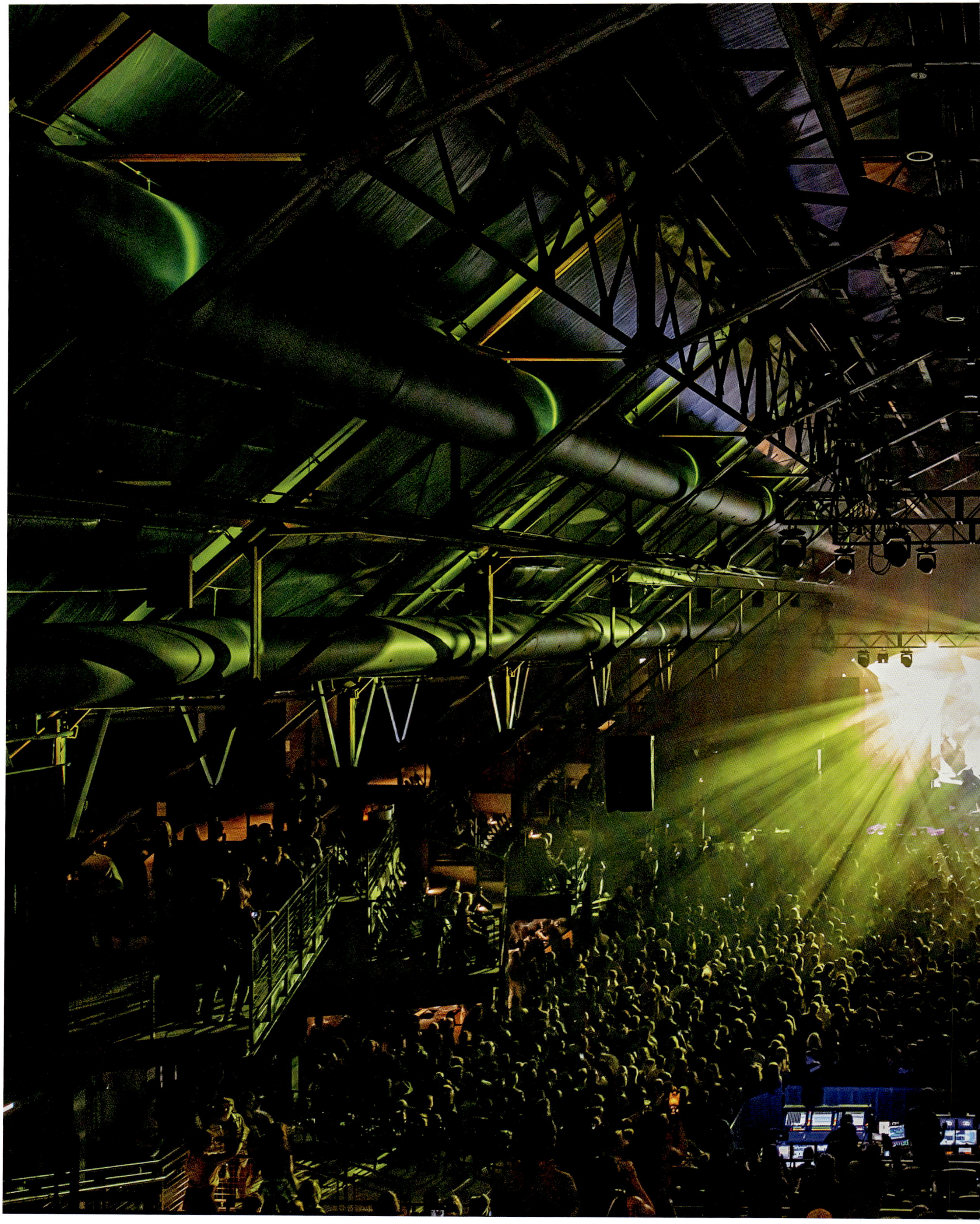

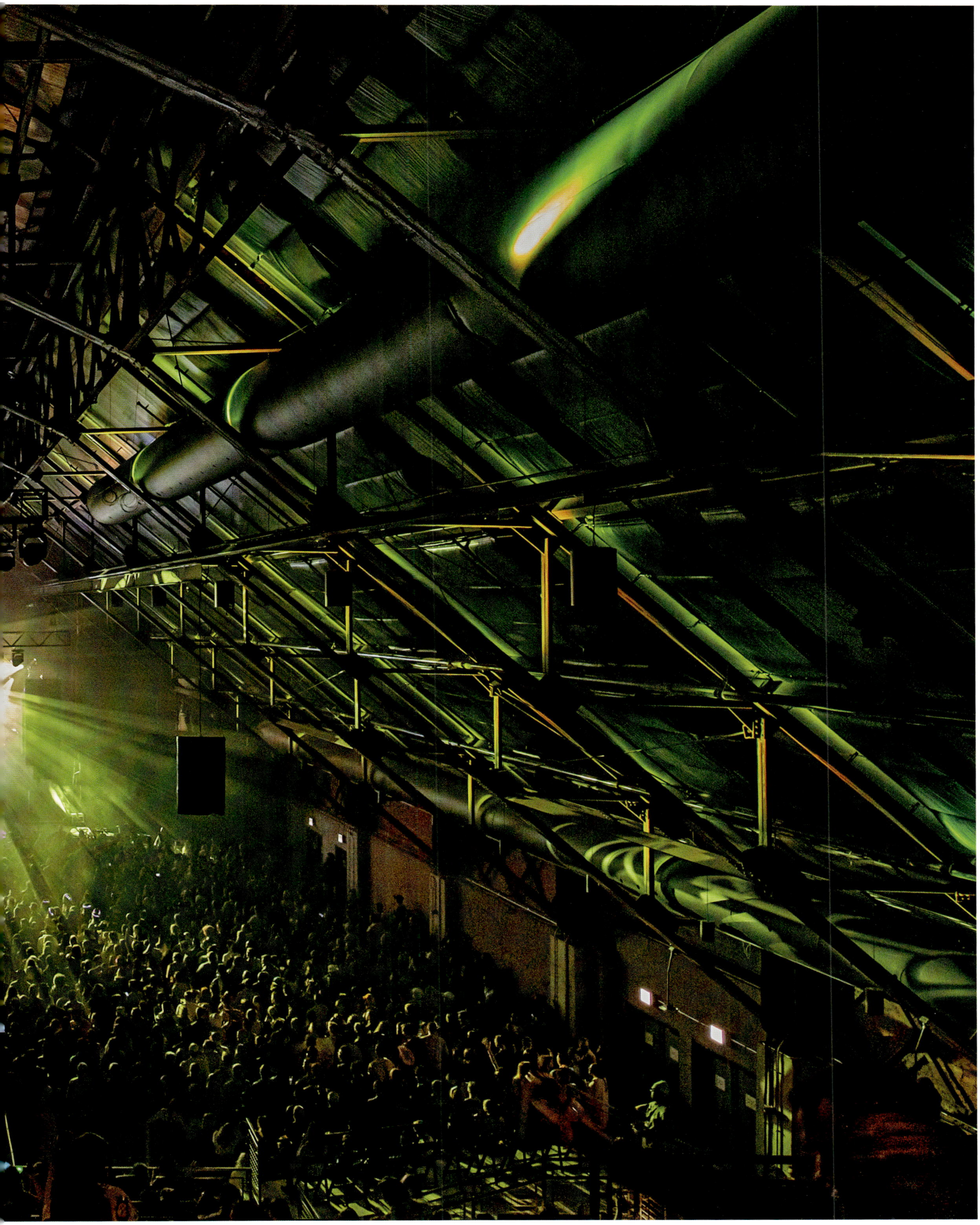

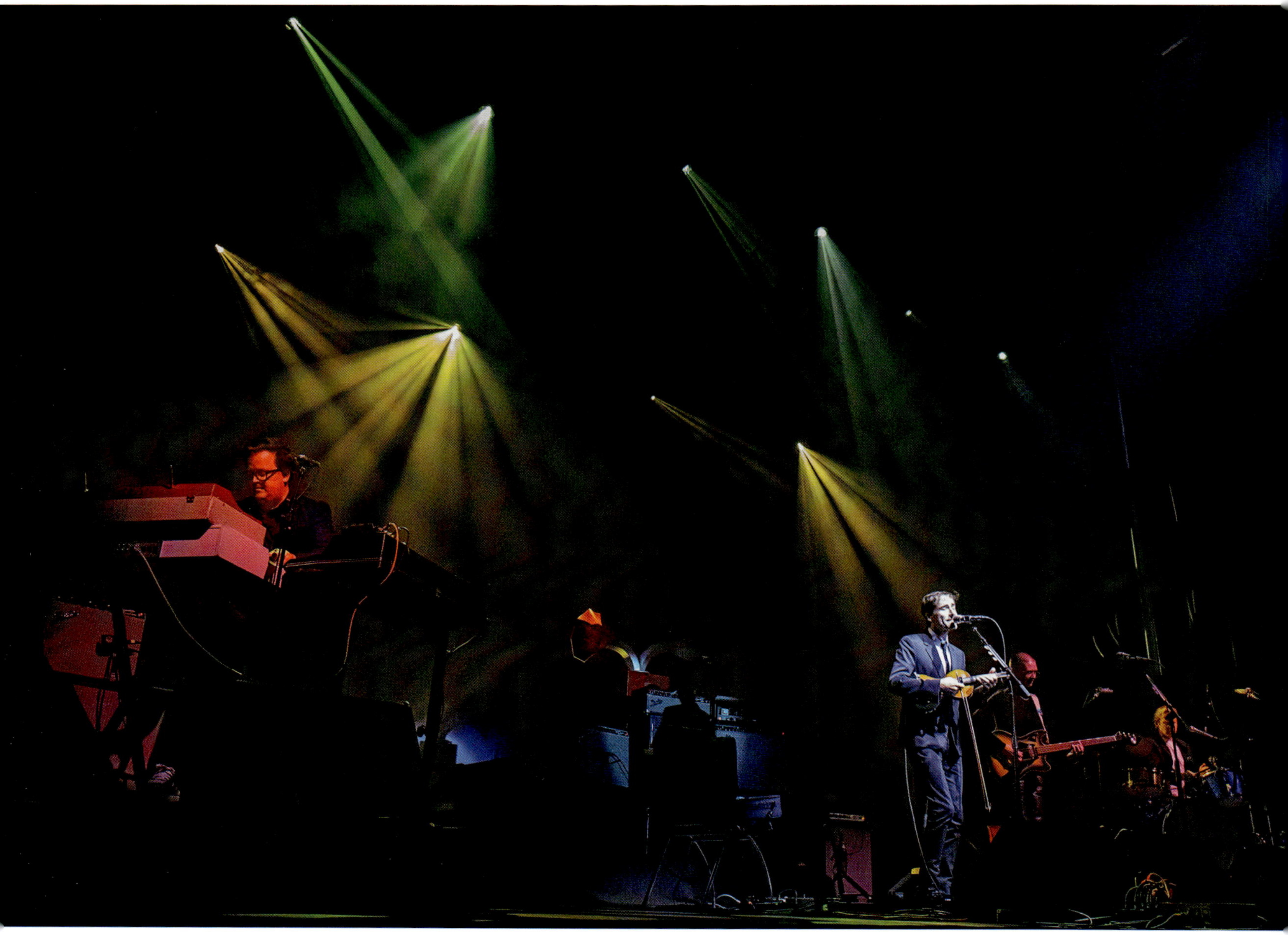

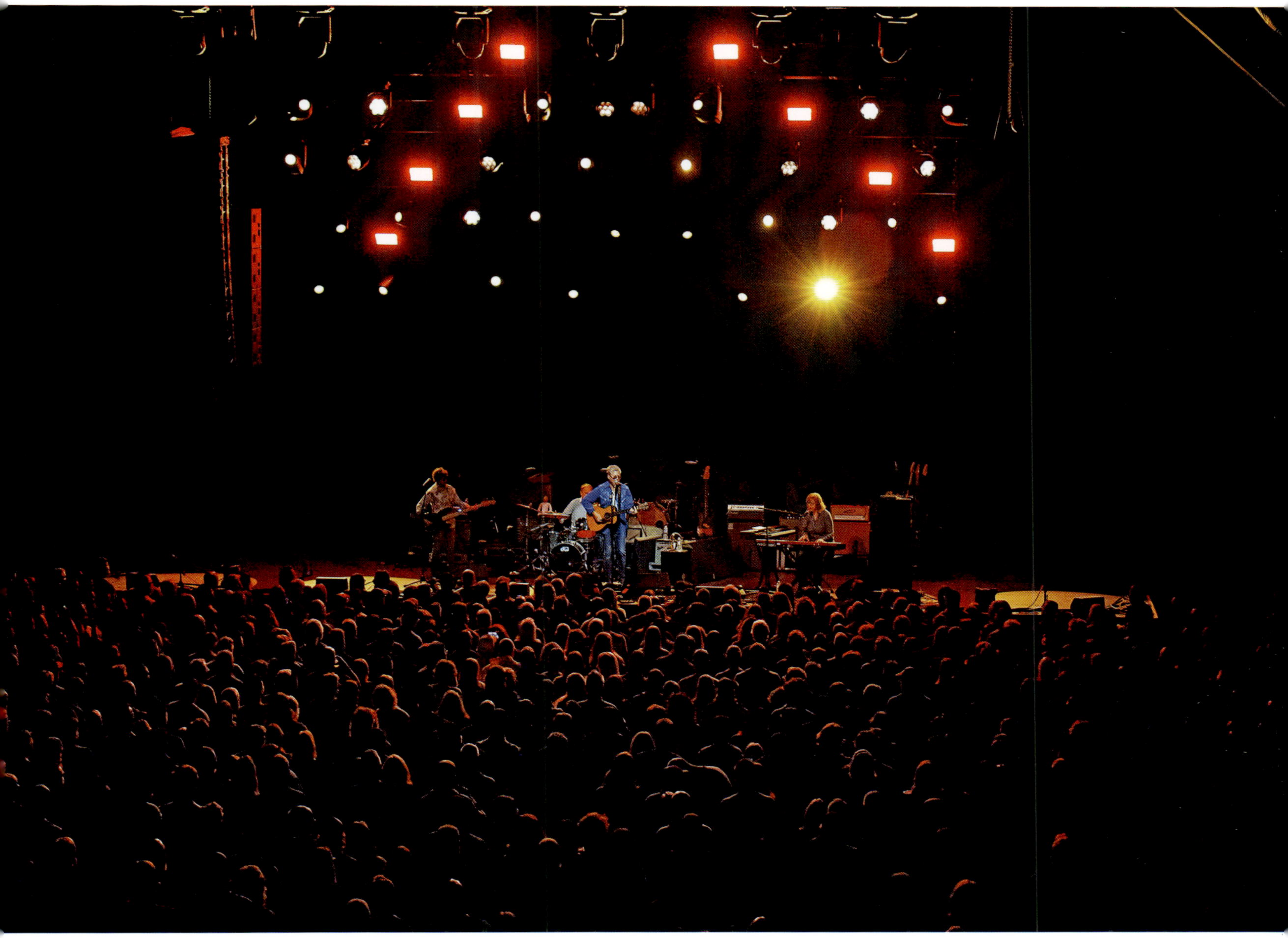

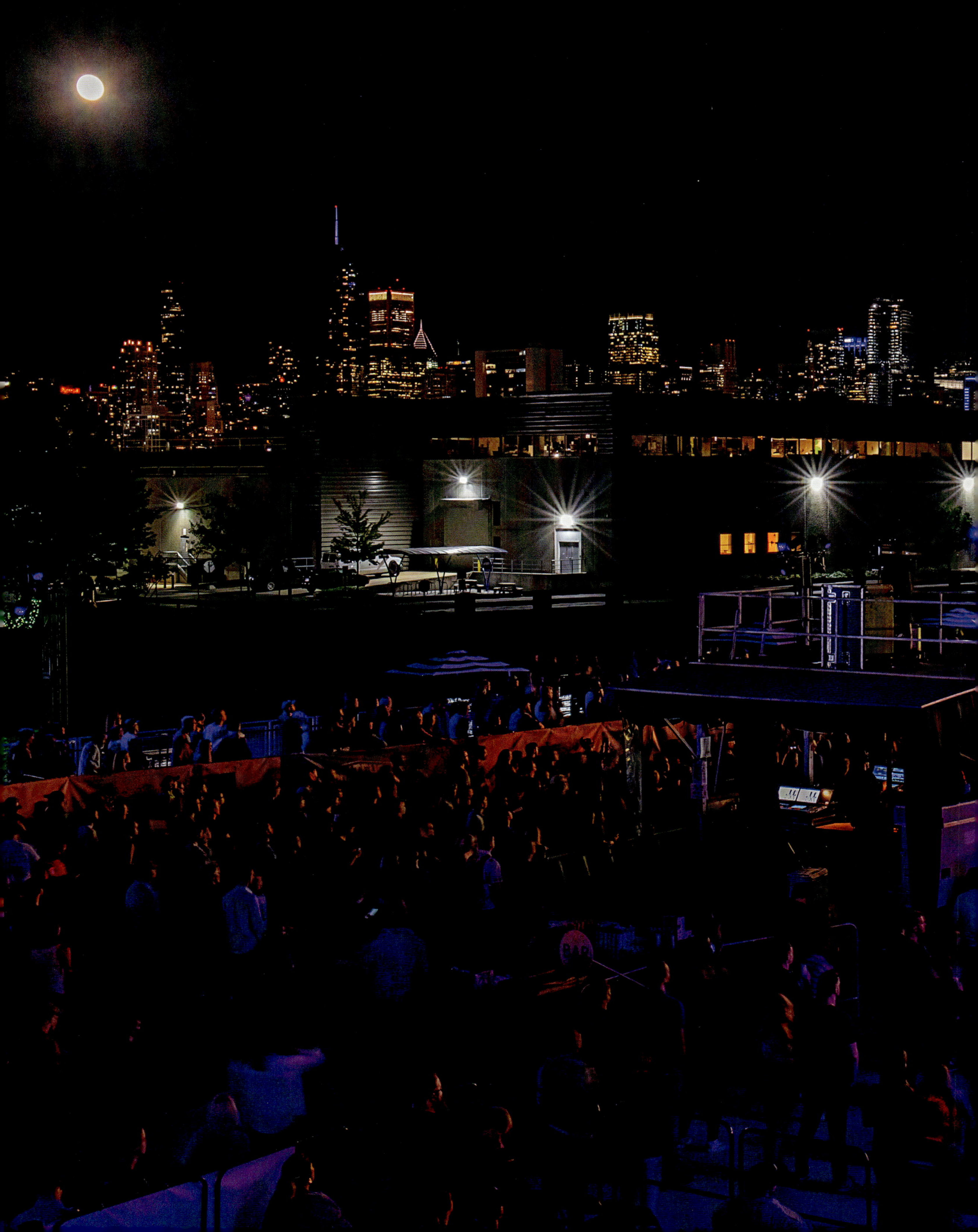

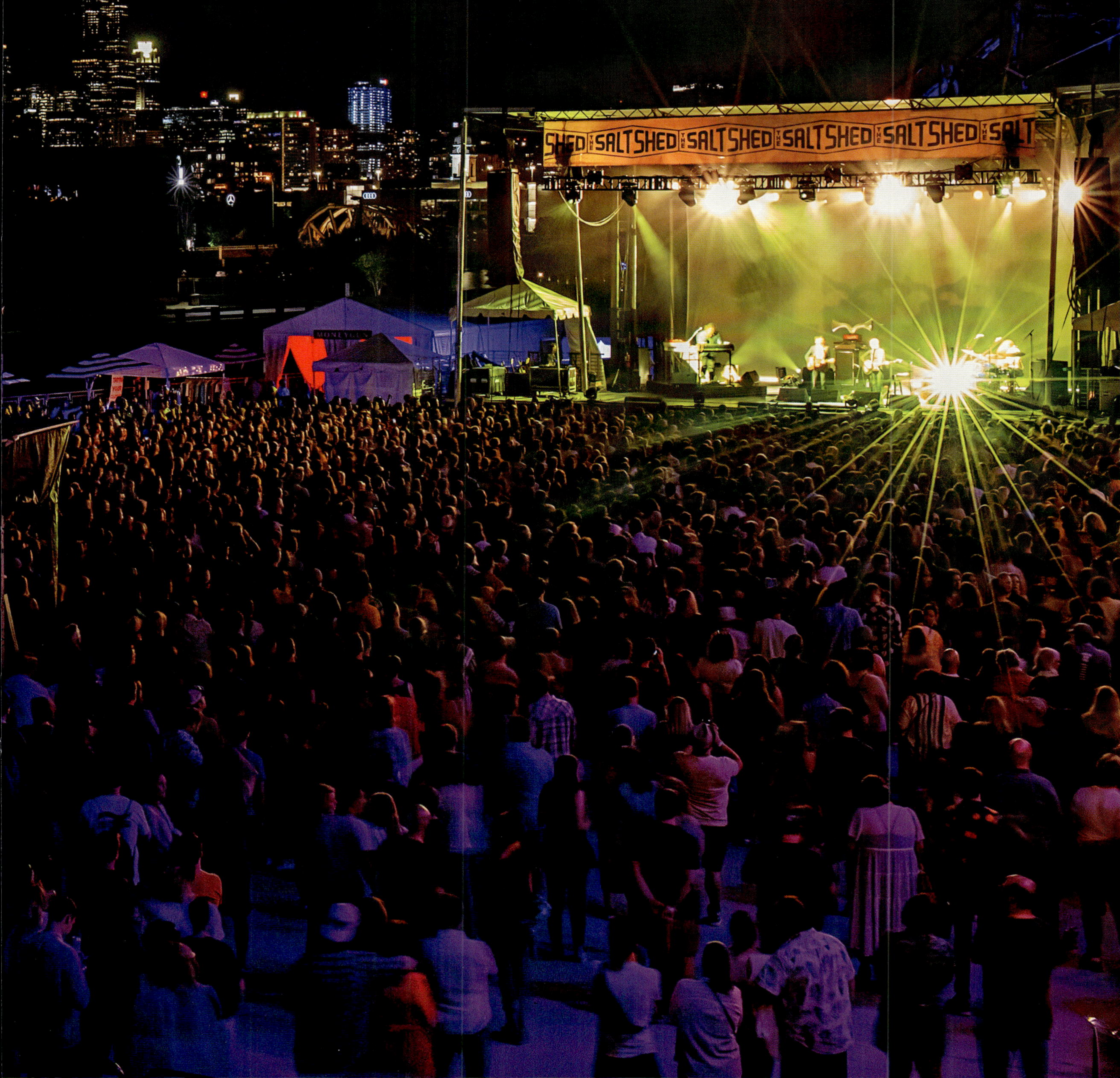
SHED SALT SHED SALT SHED SALT SHED SALT

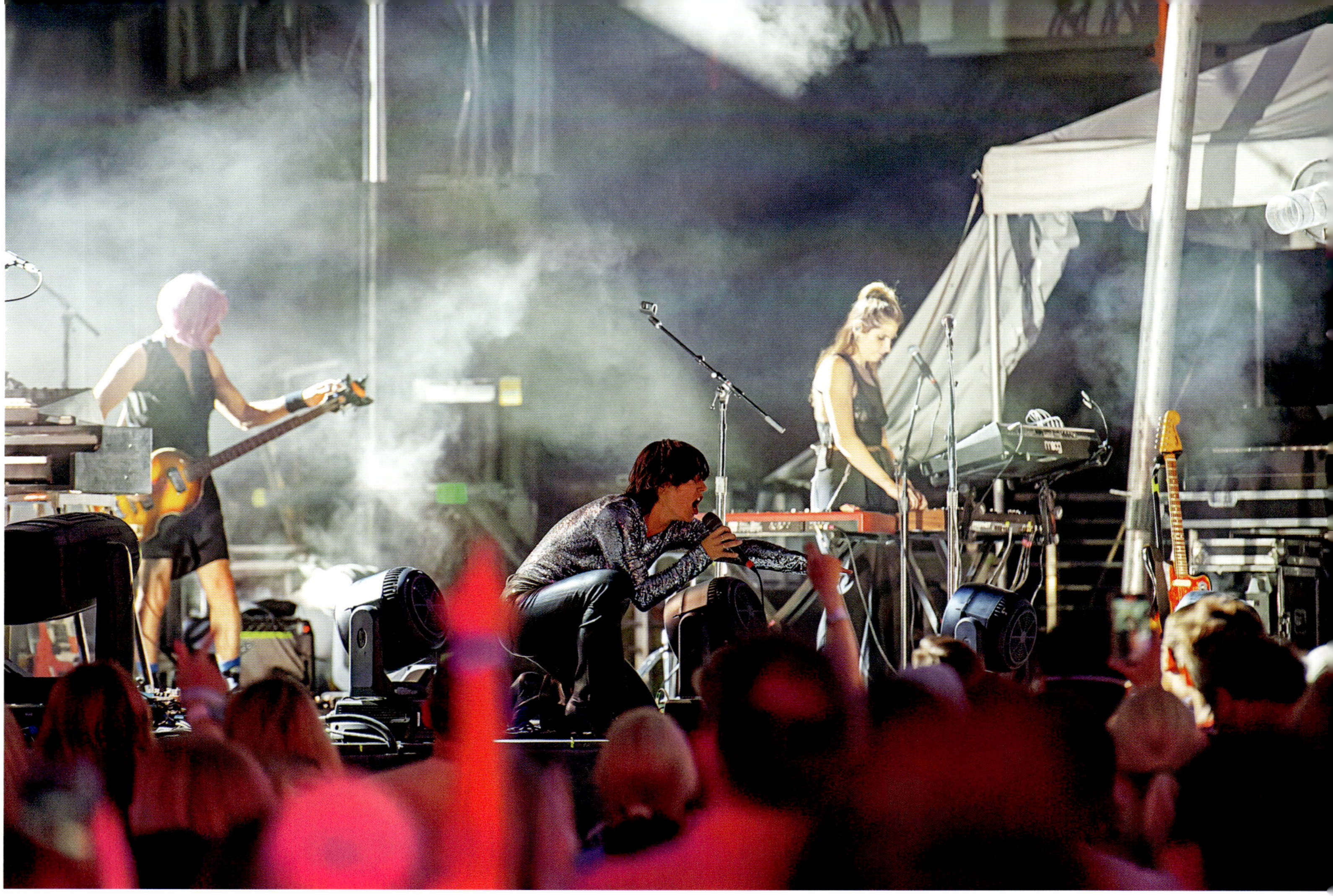

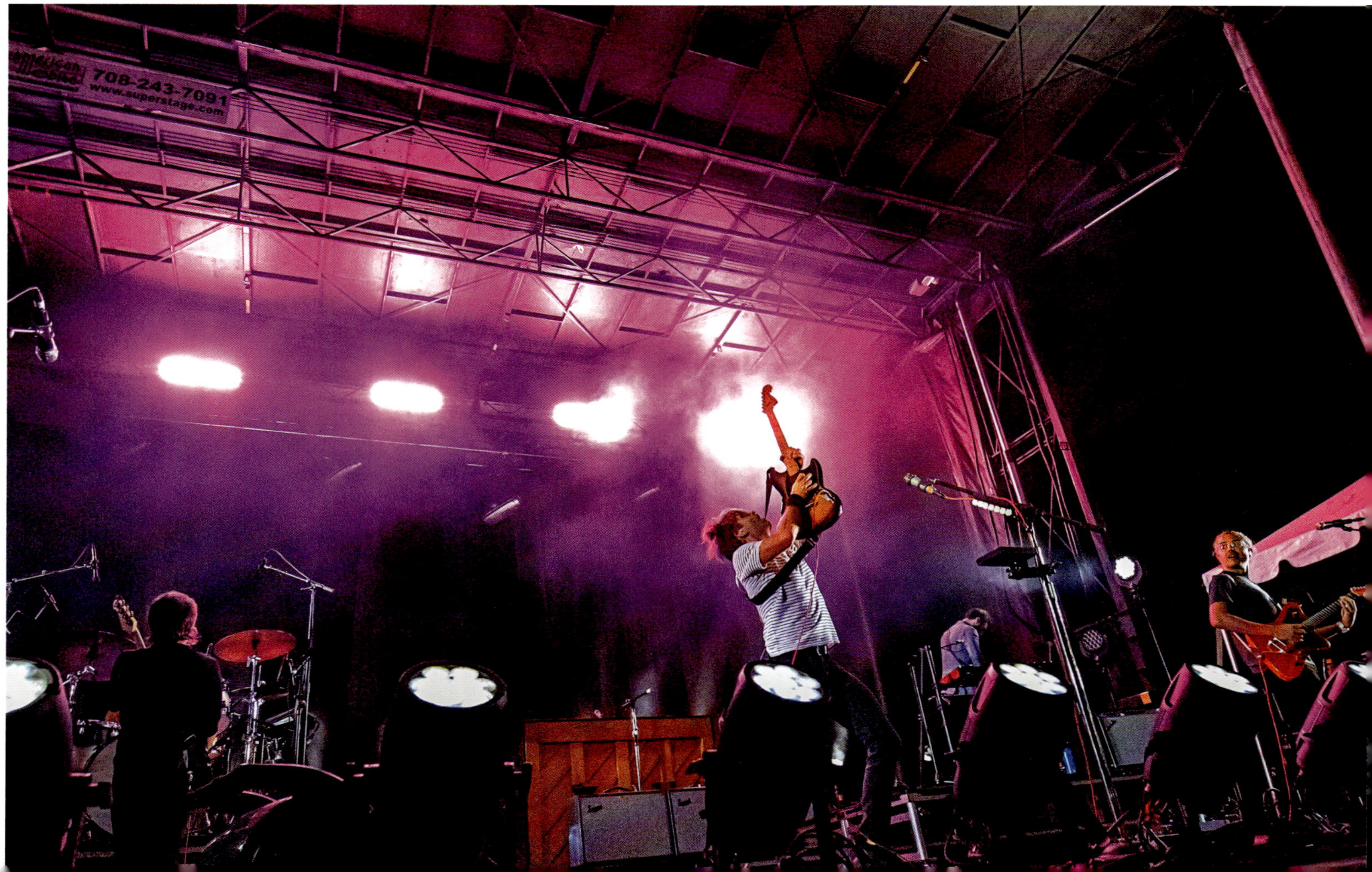
708-243-7091
www.superstage.com

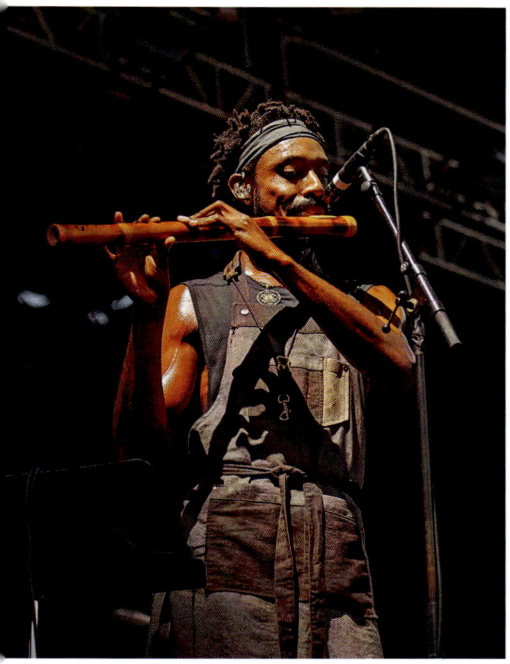

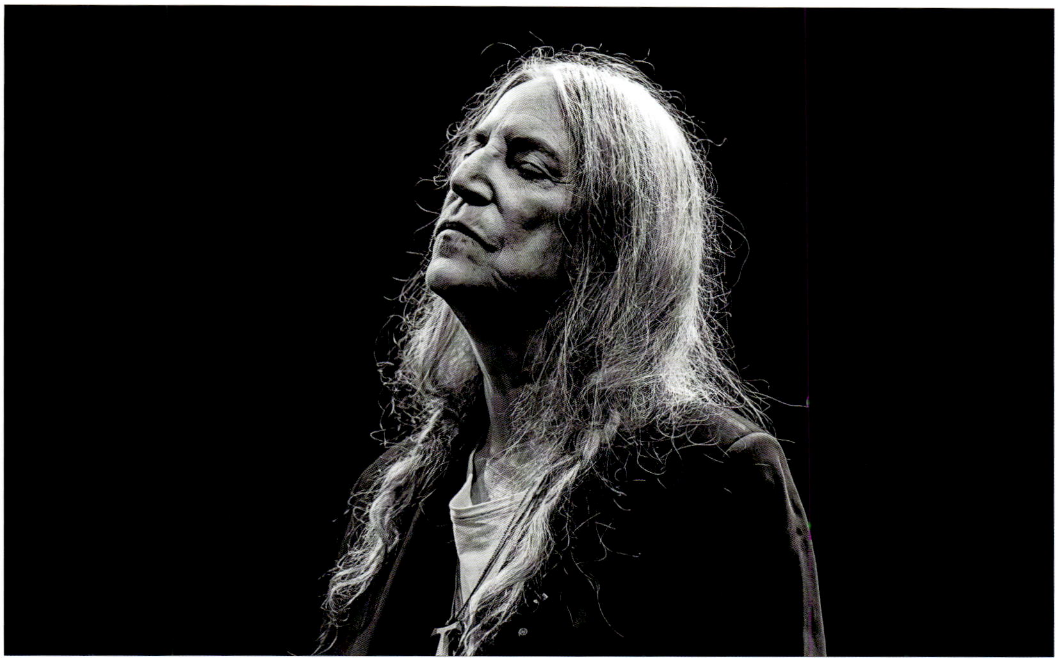

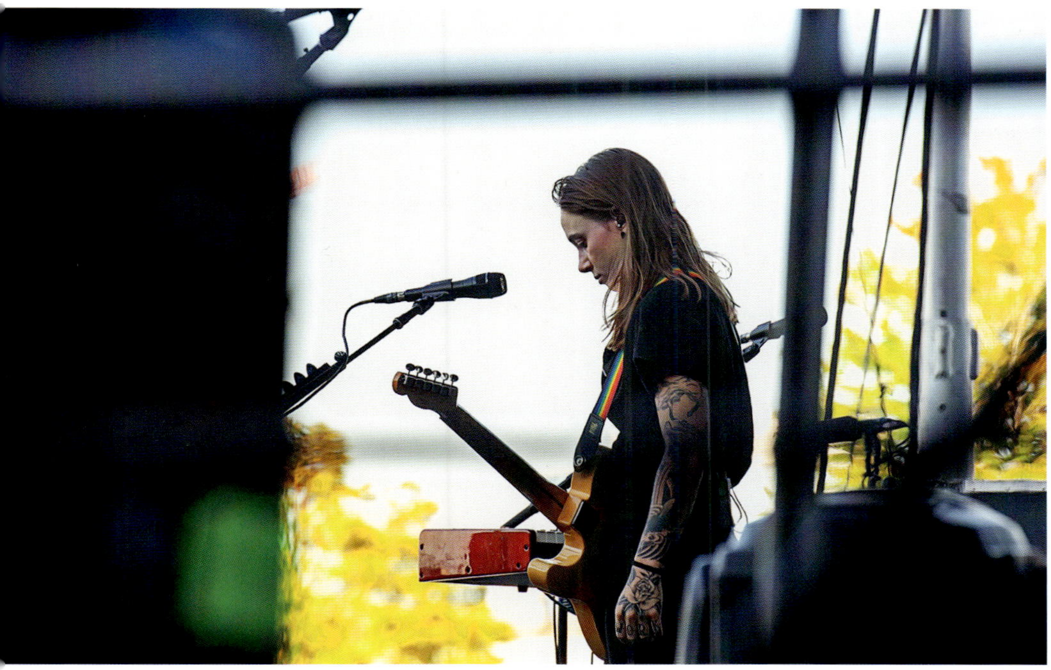

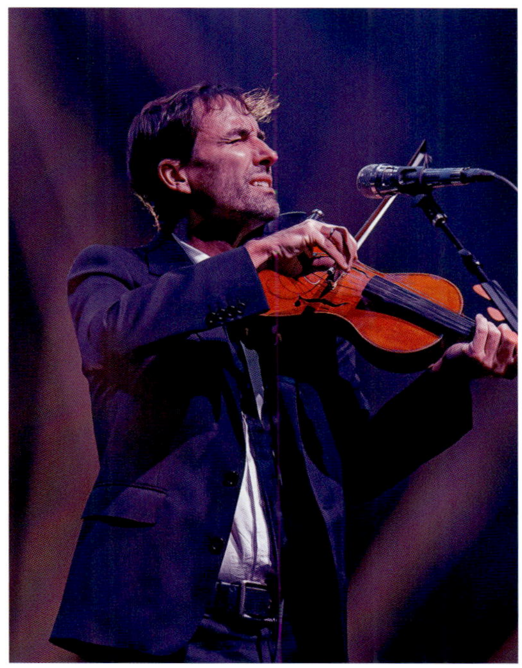

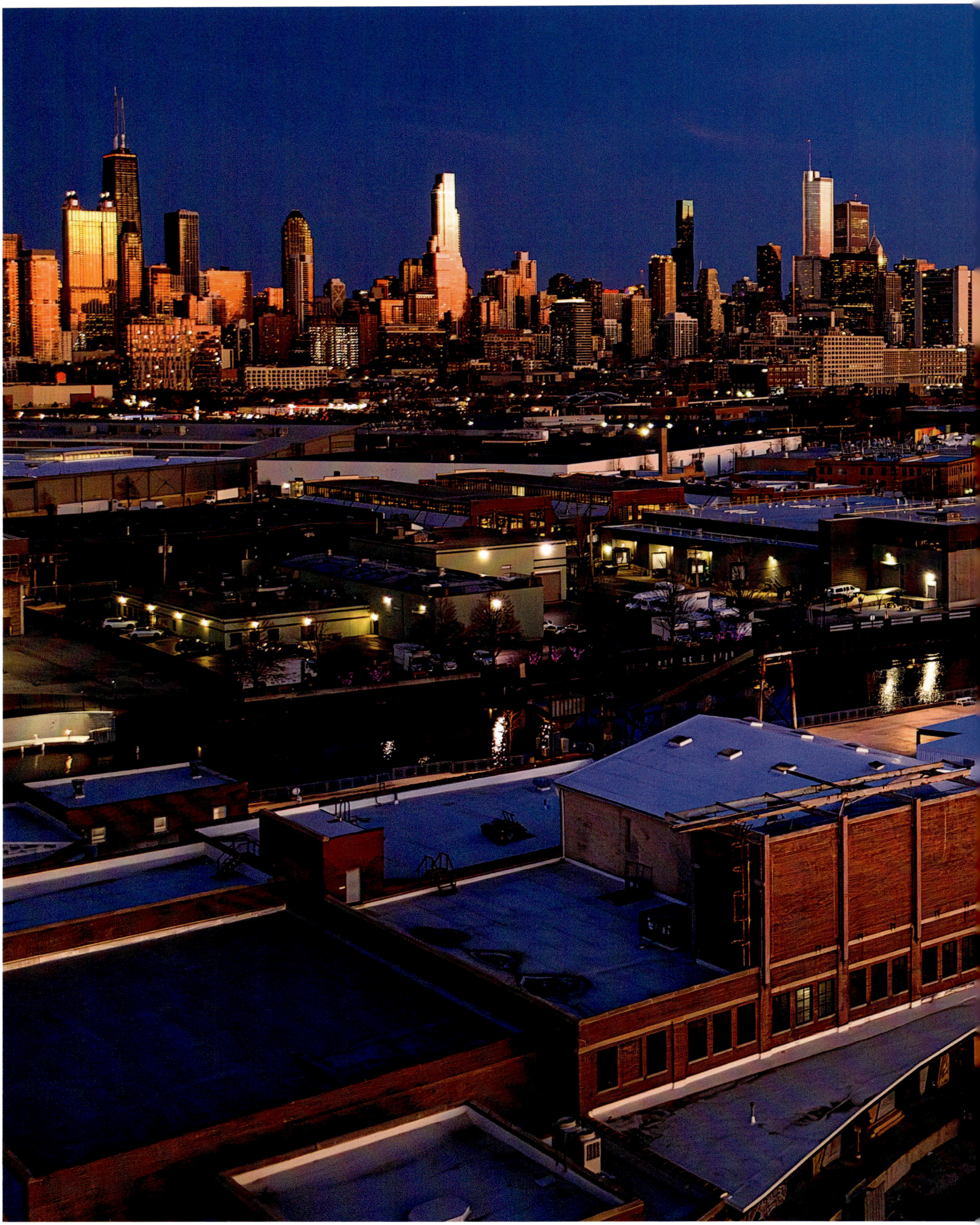

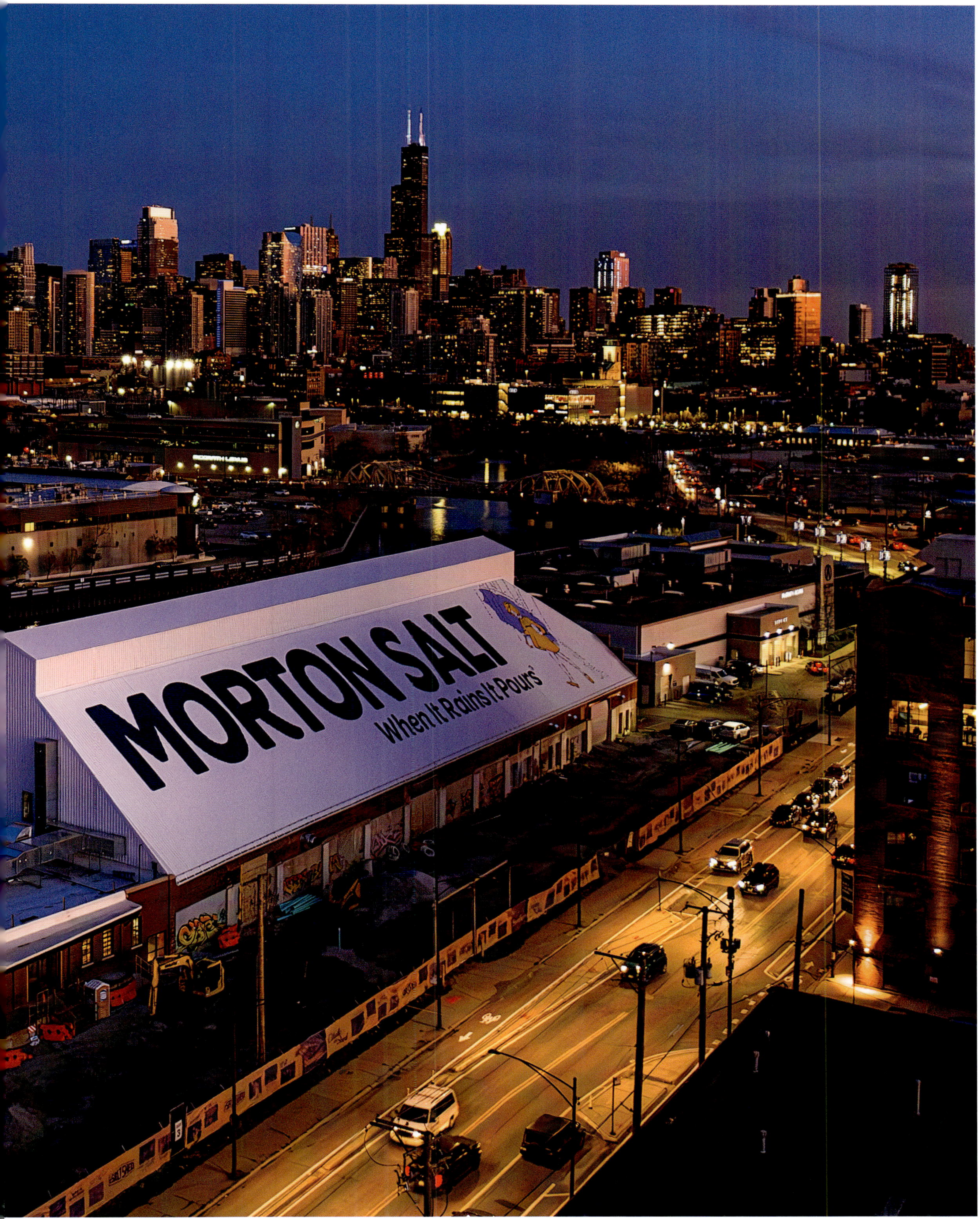
MORTON SALT
When It Rains It Pours

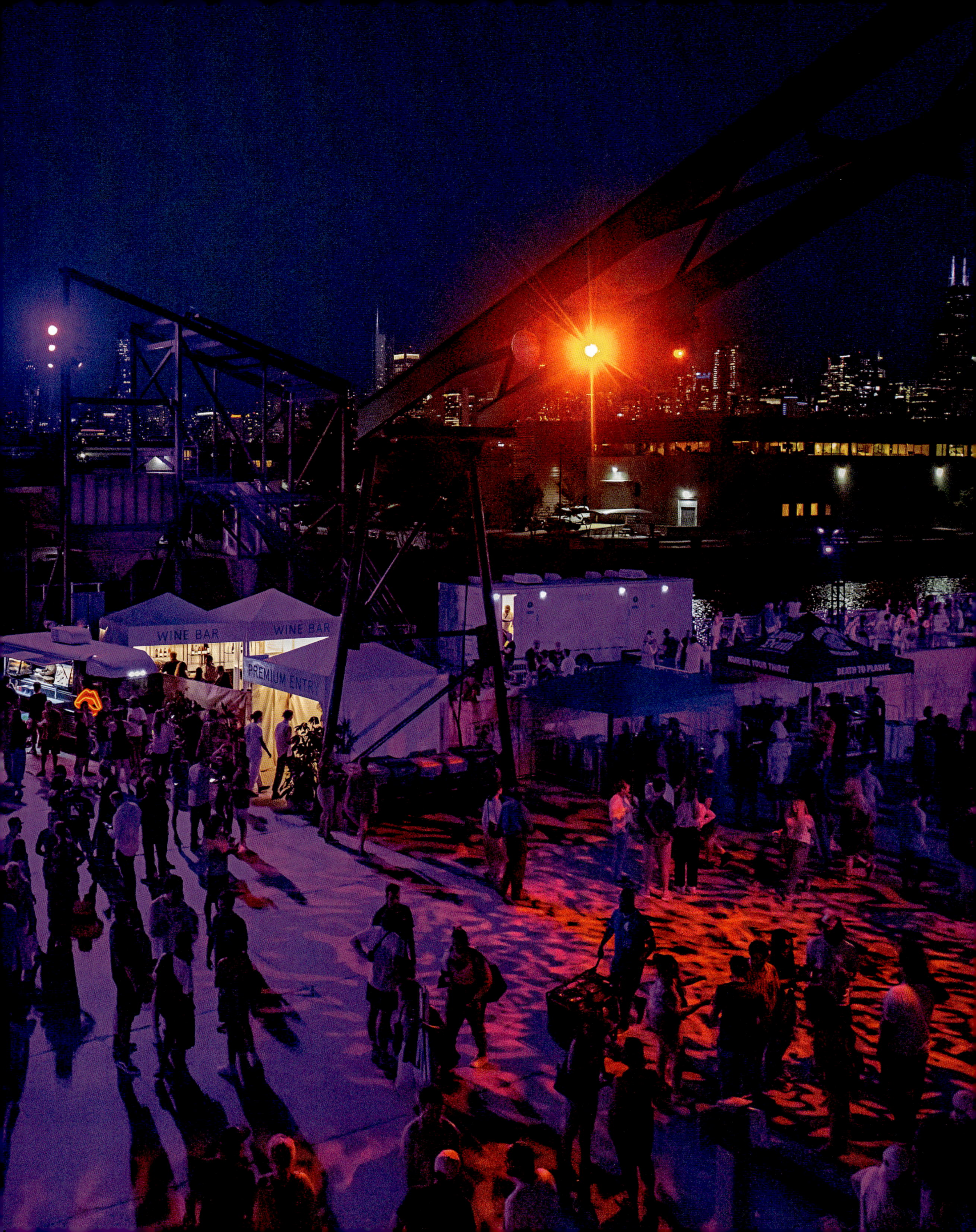
WINE BAR
WINE BAR
PREMIUM ENTRY

Afterword

Elston was always the locals' street to cut through the North Side of Chicago. As a teenager I would bike down its broad shoulders to get a glimpse of my city's grittier, more industrial side. The passing air full of the strange smell of the river and the stench of tanning leather. I'd weave under the viaducts that spill out toward the old steel factories and around the tiny beating heart of the Hideout, the old steelworkers haunt turned beloved music club. Towards the southern end of the ride, I would coast and lift my hands off the bars along the quiet expanse of the Morton Salt factory. Elston was where I first felt the spark of wonder at the meeting of industrial space and creative people—the feeling that you could make anything happen inside of these old, storied buildings.

When it comes to music, there is really no place in the world like Chicago. Musicians here are part of a fierce, extended family that has evolved through the legacies of blues, improvised, folk, soul, and avant-garde music. Our independent venues are our homes. Shows are our reunions. We know that genres don't define us, and our collaborators are not our competitors. We root for our brethren who fly off to the commercial wonderlands on the coasts, but we maintain our identity and our municipal pride for a reason: there's a rootedness and accessibility here that allows for constant creativity. And the architecture of our city—from the basements and alleyways to the old factory buildings and highway underpasses—all of it plays a role in what is possible here.

To build on existing foundations is a choice, and one that I believe is important to our world. Increasingly it seems like it's always an uphill battle to take the path that helps the planet, or that relies on humans over machines. Reusing something is a terrific exercise in creativity and a tribute to the laborers who made it in the first place. Our signature alleyways are really our bazaars, perhaps a lingering ghost of the markets that once filled up Maxwell Street—full of artifacts left from one era to be reborn in a new one. It's not news that vintage objects can make something beautiful, but what it does require is care, intention, and work. You need to feel a drive inside of you that makes you want to work with existing materials and try to reimagine them in a new light.

So much artistic spirit is passed down through spaces and the people who commune in them. The Salt Shed, in a way, feels like a cathedral for the modern era. Vast and

Afterword

formidable and yet full of emotional and human potential. It's the new big sibling to our small independent chapels of music worship. Repurposing the building was no small undertaking. I think about its bones and all the people who had to decide it was worth fighting for—salvaging every steel beam possible, warding off pressure to knock it down and start from scratch. But now, it is a structure that is part of the connective tissue between our city's industrial ethos and our cherished musical community. It's a demonstration of our choice to reuse and reimagine. A reminder of where we came from and that we care about holding on to, and improving, the things we hold closest to our heart. It is a space rich with memory for the people of Chicago—and beyond—to gather in and celebrate together.

Sima Cunningham

Chicago musician, producer, and presenter

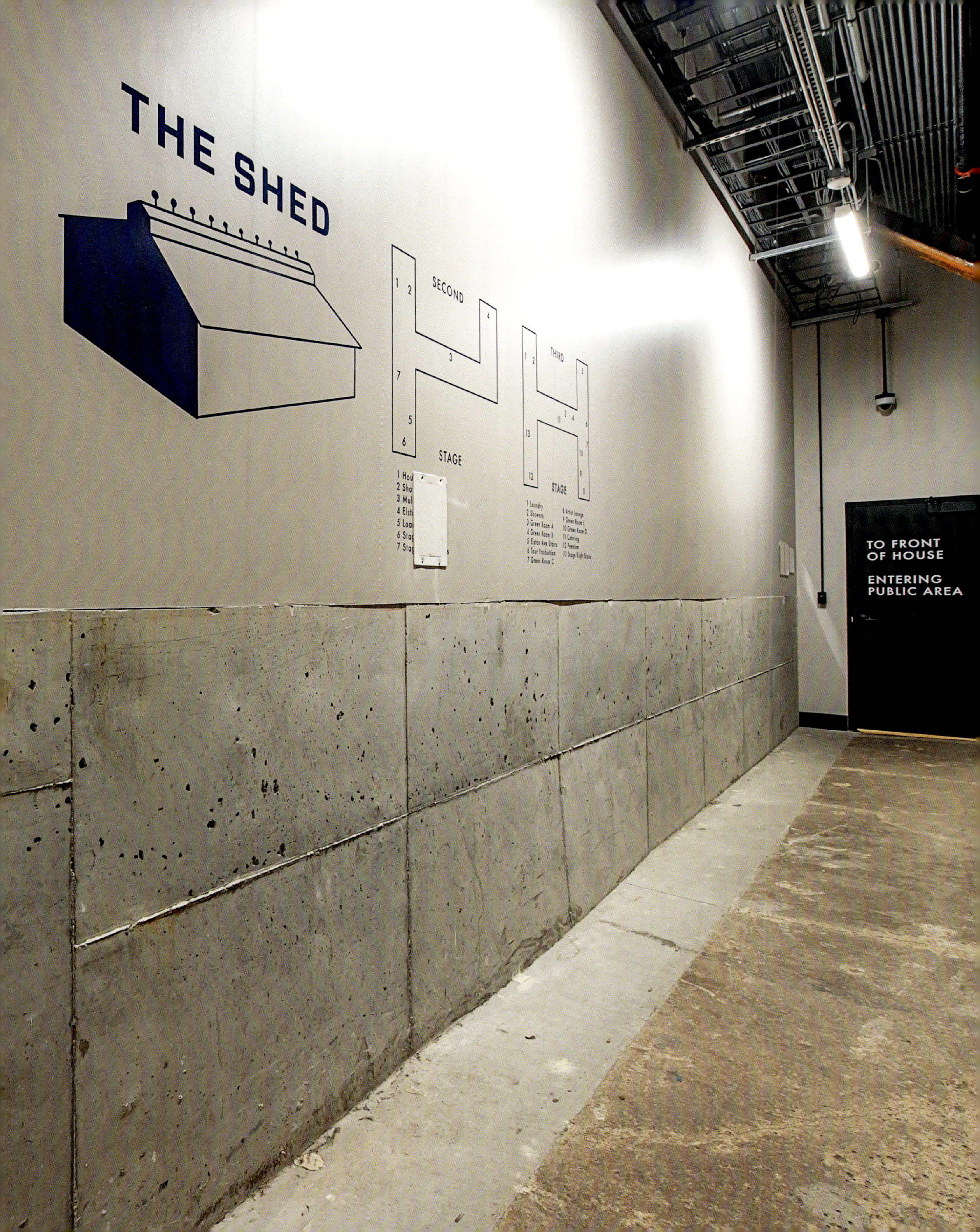
THE SHED
SECOND
STAGE
THIRD
STAGE
1 Laundry
2 Showers
3 Green Room A
4 Green Room B
5 Elston Ave Stairs
6 Tour Production
7 Green Room C
8 Artist Lounge
9 Green Room E
10 Green Room D
11 Catering
12 Premium
13 Stage Right Stairs
TO FRONT OF HOUSE
ENTERING PUBLIC AREA

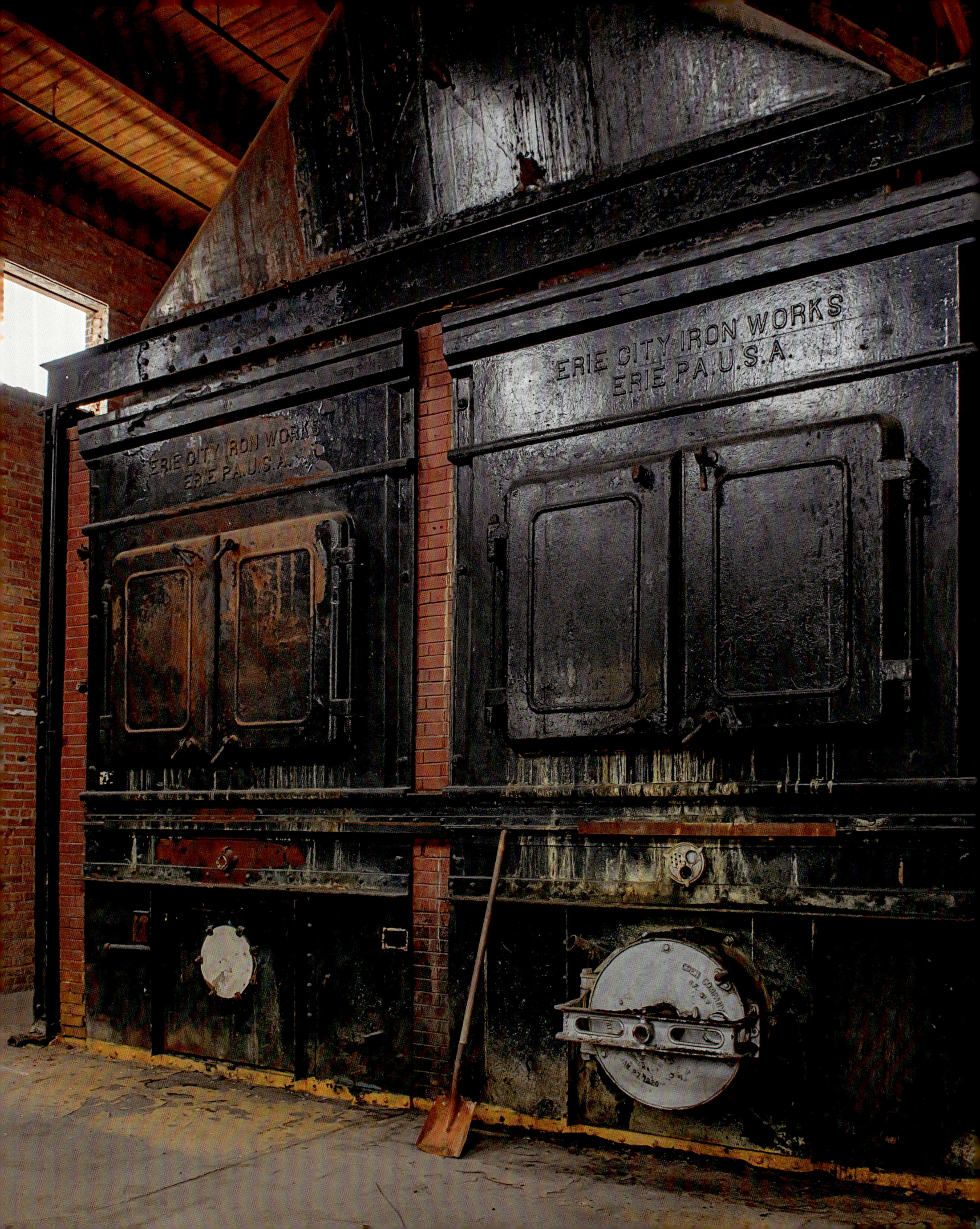
ERIE CITY IRON WORKS
ERIE PA. U.S.A.
ERIE CITY IRON WORKS
ERIE PA. U.S.A.

Acknowledgments

This project began as a solitary undertaking, but this book is the result of many wonderful collaborations, not least with Craig Golden, who said yes when I asked to photograph the old Morton Salt building. My heartfelt thanks go to Craig, who heads up Blue Star Properties, and to Bruce Finkelman, who leads 16″ on Center, the Salt Shed owners who dreamed up this venue. Later, I met two of their partners at R2 Companies, Matt Garrison, and Zack Cupkovic, who shared the complex story of what it took to buy the property. They couldn't have done it without investor Michael Polsky and family office, Skydeck.

Tiernan Martin, construction project manager, walked me around the property on my first morning and, thankfully, mentioned the upcoming removal of the historic sign. He and Lewis Schwenk, construction supervisor, kept me informed on the project's busy schedule and patiently answered my numerous questions. Eli Golden was always cheerful in the office.

All the crews were so agreeable; I'm grateful for the photos and for the many conversations. Daniel J. Majerowicz, plumbing foreman, shared his love of plumbing and gave me great insights. Mike Flade, electrical foreman, and Stephen Felty, ironworker foreman, regularly let me tag along with their crews. And I have much appreciation for the entire Salt Shed team and the breadth of what they do.

The Richard H. Driehaus Foundation provided financial support for this book. Morton Salt, Inc. contributed further funding via the recommendation of Amanda Mans and Brett Gregorka. Lynn Goldin and Henry Birnkrant were enthusiastic and gave additional sponsorship.

Richard Cahan looked at my photographs early on and encouraged me to continue with the series. He shared his knowledge of publishing and introduced me to Bernard Friedman and Mary Cullather of Snapshot Nation, fiscal sponsor for this book. Richard and his CityFiles Press partner, Michael Williams, helped me select a strong edit from hundreds of shots. Meg Handler, a talented photo editor, also assisted in shaping the photo story. To all those I interviewed for this project, I'm grateful for the insights you shared.

Our publisher, Sam Landers, of Trope Publishing Company, helped create a book that's true to what I experienced on the site. Michelle Fitzgerald, associate publisher,

Acknowledgments

talked me through the book's structure, writing and numerous details. Jack Van Boom and Hayle Silva worked on layout and design. And the importance of editors cannot be overstated. I appreciate you, Brad Wieners and Robert Loerzel. I'm grateful to my writing collaborators, Heidi Stevens, Paul Durica, and Sima Cunningham, too.

My dear friend, professor Patricia Stephens advised me about research, read my chapter introductions, and shared valuable feedback. Suellen Burns generously shared her ideas and resources and was a great help in moving this project forward.

Andy Zieba, assistant chief engineer at the building across from the Salt Shed on Elston Avenue, got me up on the rooftop numerous times. I had a perfect view. Maria Akbar kindly allowed me to photograph through their office windows. Amazingly, Lakes and Rivers Contracting took me out on a tugboat to photograph the Salt Shed from the Chicago River. It was an unseasonably warm November morning. What a superb day.

Thanks to the team that produced the City of Chicago Landmark Designation Report about the Morton Salt Company Warehouse Complex. It is a remarkable and detailed resource. I learned more from a *Curious City* radio piece produced by Paul Durica and Jason Marck for WBEZ. I spent a great afternoon at the Chicago History Museum's research center looking at the original 1929 architectural drawings by Graham, Anderson, Probst & White. If you get a chance you should go.

Over decades, Ron Gordon, a longtime friend, colleague, and mentor, helped shape my photography skills and work ethic. For many years, Tess Hartnack has lent her talent for design to my projects.

Scott Shigley and John Boehm generously assisted with drone photography and extra equipment.

Attorneys Robert L. Margolis and Steven L. Baron work with artists, among others. They make our lives a little easier. Thanks, you two.

Most of all, I'm grateful to my family and extended family, and to those who are no longer with us. I'm so appreciative to have a very loving circle of friends and neighbors, who listened, encouraged, and shared great ideas, insights, and walks. Your steady support helped keep me grounded.

My deepest love and appreciation are for my children who bring meaning and joy to my life.

About the Artist

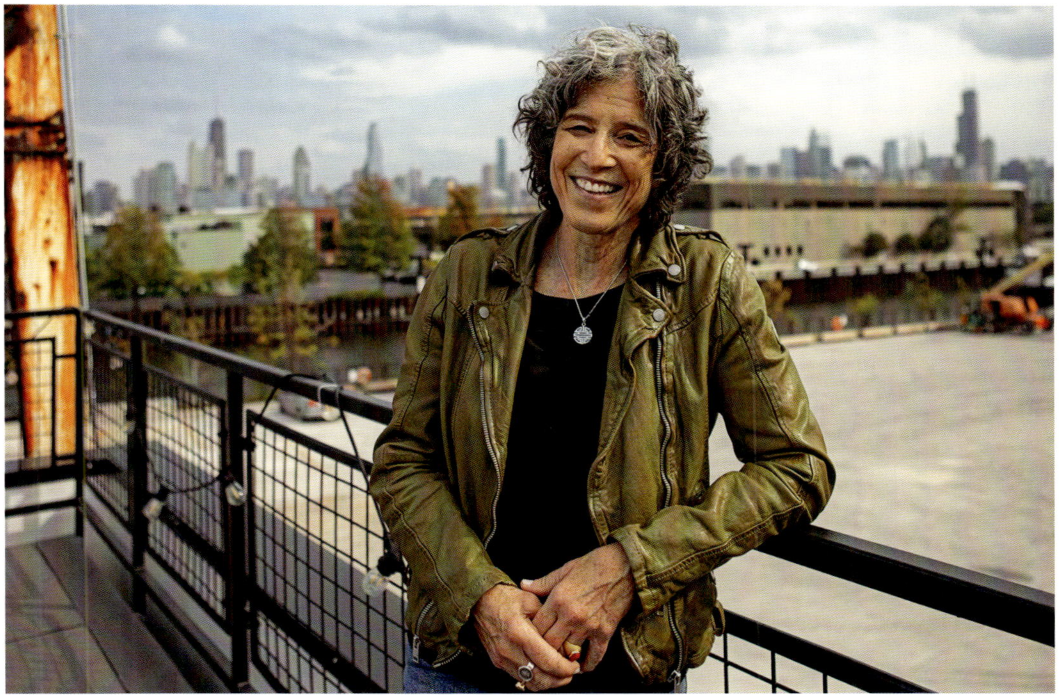

Sandra Steinbrecher is a Chicago documentary photographer working on long-term assignments about education, the arts, and community development. Her work supports and promotes those who are invested in transforming their communities and preserving history. Recently, she photographed the changing seasons at the historic Garden of the Phoenix in Chicago's Jackson Park, recorded the efforts to repurpose the former Anthony Overton School in Chicago's Bronzeville community, and collaborated with numerous artists, documenting their public art pieces around Chicago. Sandra was a silver gelatin master printer for over twenty years and, along with colleague Ron Gordon, made the exhibition prints from original negatives from a collection of Vivian Maier's acclaimed, historic images, seen around the world. Sandra's work was featured in the Smithsonian National Portrait Gallery's *The Outwin 2019, American Portraiture Today*, a highly competitive national exhibition. Her photographs have been on view at several galleries, including the Chicago Cultural Center and were featured in the CNN docuseries, *Chicagoland*. Her images have been seen in several publications including on Patagonia's blog *The Cleanest Line*, in *The New York Times*, *New City*, *Smithsonian Magazine* and *The Economist*.

LCCN: 2024935422
ISBN: 978-1-951963-25-5

Photographed, edited, and designed in Chicago
Printed and bound in China
First printing, 2024

Trope Publishing Co.

This publication is made possible through support from the Richard H. Driehaus Foundation.

DRIEHAUS
FOUNDATION

Additional financial support for this publication provided by Morton Salt, Inc.

The photographs from *The Salt Shed* are available for purchase. For inquiries, email the gallery at info@trope.com

+ INFORMATION:
For additional information on the Trope Edition Series, visit www.trope.com

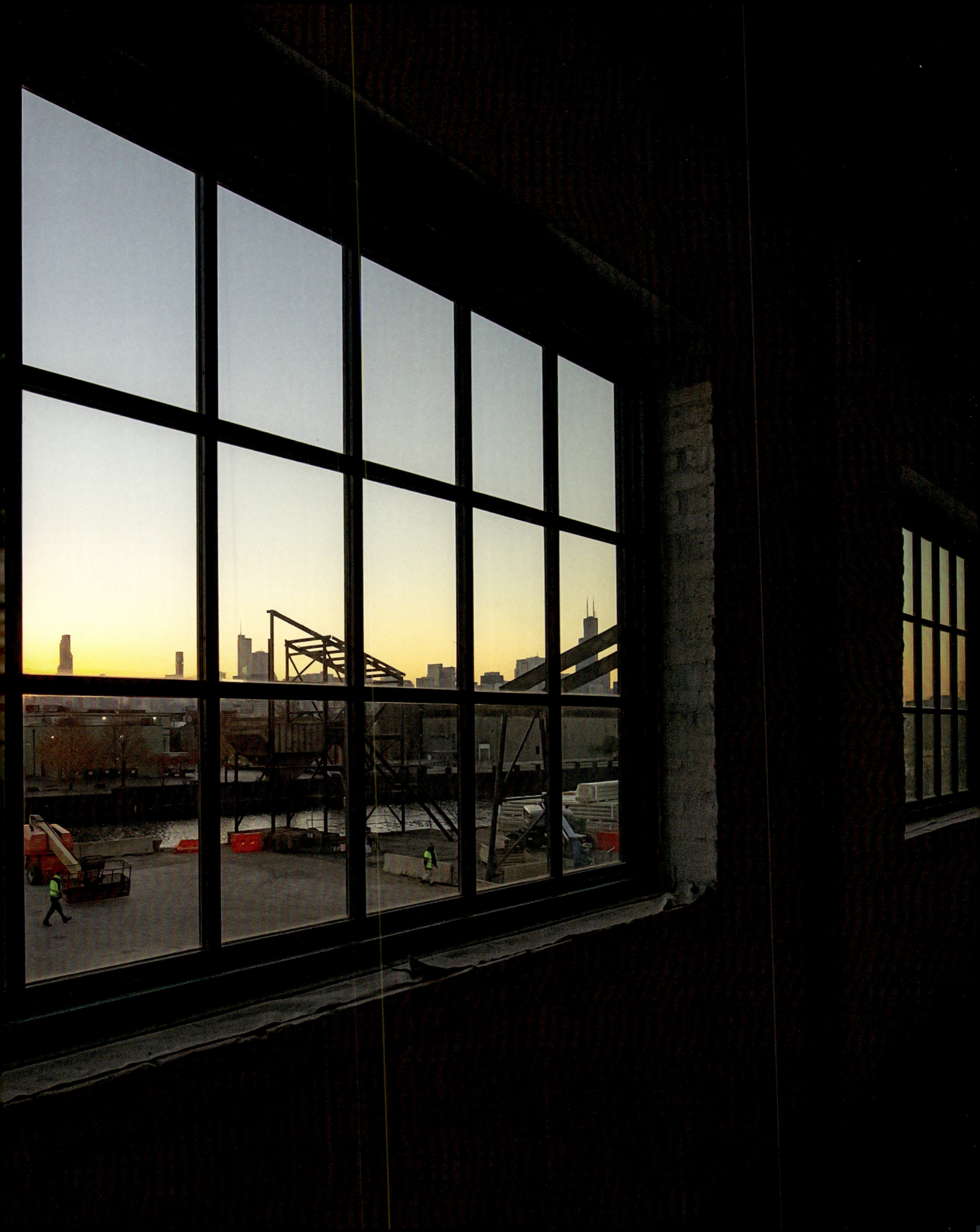

TROPE
PUBLISHING
Co.